WALL, WATCHTOWER, AND PENCIL STUB

WRITING DURING WORLD WAR II

JOHN R. CARPENTER

YUCCA
Publishing

Yucca Publishing books may be purchased in bulk at special discounts for sales promotion, corporate gifts, fund-raising, or educational purposes. Special editions can also be created to specifications. For details, contact the Special Sales Department, Yucca Publishing, 307 West 36th Street, 11th Floor, New York, NY 10018 or yucca@skyhorsepublishing.com.

Yucca Publishing® is an imprint of Skyhorse Publishing, Inc.®, a Delaware corporation.

Visit our website at www.yuccapub.com.

10 9 8 7 6 5 4 3 2 1

Library of Congress Cataloging-in-Publication Data is available on file.

Cover design by Yucca Publishing

ISBN: 978-1-63158-004-8
Ebook ISBN: 978-1-63158-037-6

Printed in the United States of America

Contents

Preamble v

Preface ix

I. "UNREAL WAR!"

1. Disbelief...3
2. The Curtain..16
3. Numbers...20

II. CARNIVALS

1. Black Magic..31
2. A "Stage-Prop World"...40
3. The Stage Moves Abroad...46
4. The Great Projective Screen: The Globe..............................51

III. THE FIRESTORM

1. "The Most Inhospitable Place on Earth"..............................59
2. The Field of Consciousness..66
3. The Mole's View and the Panorama.....................................76
4. Discovery: Eyes and "Tongues"...80

IV. A WORLD OF THINGS: OCCUPATION

1. Scraps of Paper, Plaster Walls...87
2. *In Medias Res*: People as Things.......................................95
3. "The New": The Shred of Platinum, the Explosion.............102
4. "Books, Toys, and Everything . . ."....................................107

V. ANIMALS

1. Flight 113
2. The Cracked Mirror 116
3. Animals, Angels, and History 124

VI. WALL, WATCHTOWER, CHIMNEY

1. Sending Messages 129
2. The USSR: Arrival 131
3. The USSR: June 22, 1941 135
4. Japan: "Prisoners of War," a Contradiction in Terms 142
5. Germany: Factories of Destruction 150
6. Communication across Time: The Boxes at 68 Nowolipka Street 157

VII. THE END OF TIME

1. The Riddle 167
2. Clocks 171
3. Narration 175
4. Calendars, Defeat, and the End of Time 180

VIII. DEFENSE

1. Armed Resistance 193
2. Ties that Bind: "City, City" 197
3. Ties that Bind: Farms and Fields 205
4. Which Past, Which Future? 211

IX. "WRITE AND RECORD!"

1. "Dear Reader . . ." 221
2. "Our Language Lacks Words . . ." 228

X. THE GREAT REVOLT

1. The Revolt against Rhetoric 235
2. Helen of Troy and the "Bloodthirsty Abstractions" 242
3. The Literary Movements 248
4. Which Tongue, Which Speech? 256

Notes 261

Preamble

For many decades, anniversaries of the Allied landings in Normandy were celebrated with pageantry and pomp. Presidents, prime ministers, kings, and queens made speeches, ships emerged from a hundred harbors up and down the English coast, met, and headed south across the Channel. Until the last years of the century, the end of the Second World War was reenacted regularly. In Paris the bells of churches and cathedrals pealed as the liberation of the city, by General LeClerc, was celebrated once again. Old Sherman tanks from the War Museum were cleaned, restored to running order, rolled noisily down the boulevards toward the Hotel de Ville where they were greeted by the mayor of Paris. Celebrations were held across much of the world, in London, Remagen, Torgau, Rheims, Warsaw, Vitebsk, Volgograd—formerly Stalingrad—Moscow, and even Berlin. Others were held at Iwo Jima and Okinawa. The end of the war with Japan was celebrated with a parade of ships and ceremonies at Punchbowl Cemetery in Hawaii.

Other anniversaries were more somber. Before 1990, reminders of the Yalta Conference, which redrew the map of Europe, were bitter. One of the most tragic anniversaries occurred in January 1995, marking the liberation of Auschwitz fifty years earlier.

The First World War was once called, "the Great War," but the phrase is obsolete. The Second World War was the most lethal war in recorded history. It was global, more than thirty countries participated in it. Many different wars were fought during the 1930s and 40s but for six years—between 1939 and 1945—they came together in a period of accelerating violence. The consensus figure of casualties is in excess of fifty million; for most people the figures are difficult to comprehend, and cannot even be imagined.

We describe writings that were made during the war itself. The writers were close to events, in extremely difficult conditions and under great pressure. The "pencil stub" in the title indicates the stress on writings during the years between 1939 and 1945. In response to the first invasions and occupations in 1939–1941, writers developed new ways to describe the experiences and events in which they participated. They developed entirely new forms and new themes. In the next four years these were to leave an indelible stamp on many countries, on their literature and culture.

English-speaking readers are familiar above all with the campaigns of the Allied armies. With the exception of the Battle of Britain, the war's many military fronts were far from home: in continental Europe, Africa, and Asia. Readers sometimes assume that "war literature" falls outside the boundaries of normal cultural history, or the history of literature. But the international nature of the war and occupation make it impossible to separate civilian from military issues. An accurate picture requires that we extend our frame to civilians, also to include writers who used languages other than English.

During the war years, all the literary traditions of the 1920s and 30s were put in doubt. Popular styles of expression and accepted ideas vanished. It was a new world. The new reality required new approaches, and a large number of writers became hostile to earlier conventions, mocking them and sometimes the very concept of "literature." But it was with words and verbal resources that they expressed their revolt; with the passage of time their own works would be considered "literature." Many of the themes and forms of the war years still cause surprise. A few are not discussed at all. Or they are completely avoided, even though they appear with extraordinary frequency in the writings from 1939 to 45.

Communication, in its many forms, acquired enormous importance. It was always accompanied by a sharp sense of urgency and the suspense that most writers thought was essential to experiences before 1945. Many of the most important international events and acts were kept in complete secrecy; a curtain of disguise hid much of the war. Knowledge of the war's outcome was not available. The presence of propaganda increased rather than decreased the need for accurate information. The effort to penetrate secrecy and disguise was difficult, often dangerous, and usually unsuccessful. The struggle to receive information—usually inadequate— the attempts to reach others or inform others using written or oral means, assumed overpowering importance.

Communication is the common thread unifying the themes we have selected. These are: disbelief and incredulity; territorial expansion; the firestorm and the front; the breakdown in the concept of what is human; the challenge of communicating from the war's camps; the elastic nature of time and narration; the power of defense; the encounter with the limits of language; the great revolt against earlier uses of language and literature.

Postwar readers often see the Second World War through the prism of national aspirations. Our approach is comparative, and in choosing multinational themes we risk going counter to some popular post-1945 conventions. However, the most pressing concerns of writers during the war itself were international, they were shared by others. When a broad spectrum of authors from different countries, in different languages, contributes to a theme—debating, questioning, and exploring it—the advantages of a comparative approach are great. The broader picture has a special kind of accuracy; it becomes possible to examine a theme within one time frame from several points of view, to observe its essential features and its full force.

We make use of translations available in English whenever possible, and if no published English version exists we have provided our own. Some of the material for this book first appeared in *Cross Currents: A Yearbook of Central European Culture,* and in *A Critical Guide to Fiction.*

Preface

"In time of war," historians have written, "the Muses are silent."[1] The belief that the arts—all the arts including literature—are silent in wartime is not hard to understand. From 1939 to 1945 casualties among writers were high. Many of the finest writers of the twentieth century were killed or wounded, and conditions for writing in occupied Europe were terrible. Government propaganda was shrill, and in every country censorship was enforced. In wartime, a writer has noted, everyone has to be biased. Time, supplies, books were lacking. In the Allied countries most writers, musicians, painters, philosophers, historians, and scientists were compelled to drop their work, and were able to describe wartime experiences only after hostilities had ended. We are sometimes reminded that many of the most famous works of world literature—*The Iliad*, *The Aeneid*, *The Song of Roland*, Shakespeare's *Henry the Fifth*—have taken war as their subject, but these were written long after the events described, when they had become legend and myth.

A partial list of manuscripts lost or destroyed during the war years makes grim reading. It quickly becomes long. Andre Malraux's *Walnut Trees of Altenbourg* was largely destroyed by the Gestapo in 1940; Alexander Tvardovsky's first version of *Vasili Tyorkin* was confiscated, and Alexander Solzhenitsyn's wartime diaries were destroyed. A multitude of manuscripts were burned in the incinerator of the Lubyanka Prison, Solzhenitsyn called them "a whole lost culture."[2] The countless manuscripts lost in concentration camps and ghettoes are a tragic chapter in the history of the camps. Anecdotes abound about individual manuscripts surviving against overwhelming odds. Curzio Malaparte, an Italian novelist and journalist for *Corriere della Sera*, hid a draft of his book *Kaputt* in the wall of a pigsty in the Ukraine in 1942. Miraculously he managed to retrieve it later. After he returned to Italy, he described an Allied bomb that struck the Bonpiani printing works on February 18, 1943, sending the edition of his book *The Volga Rises in Europe* up in smoke. The Russian writer and critic Mikhail Bakhtin was evacuated to Kazakhstan, and unable to find paper for rolling cigarettes so he used the manuscript of his work on Goethe for that purpose. Starting with the last page he methodically worked his way backward until the manuscript was consumed.[3]

But when the terrible writing conditions are taken into account, a different conclusion becomes clear. During the war years and immediately after, writing was empowered as rarely before. It was at a premium. Many writers and artists directly enlisted their activities in the struggle of the war. Dmitri Shostakovich wrote of his *Seventh Symphony* (1942): "Never have I worked with such a passion as at present. There is such a saying, 'when cannons roar, muses are silent.' . . . When our cannons roar, our muses raise their powerful voice. Never shall anyone knock the pen from our hands."[4]

Writers in English and in other languages raised their voices rather than lowered them during the war. Richard Hillary, Simone Weil, Yitzhak Katznelson, Wladyslaw Szlengel, and countless others worked with exceptional intensity. Writing became an important part of the war. In 1944, when they debated the issue of war crimes in the pages of *Le Figaro* and *Combat*, Francois Mauriac and Albert Camus were aware they were formulating national policy. Arthur Koestler boasted that the 1941 publication of his novel *Darkness at Noon* influenced the outcome of the French referendum on a new postwar constitution.[5]

Before 1946, very few people were in a position to reveal the content of the secret pacts of Hitler and Stalin, Molotov, Ribbentrop and Matsuoka with their numerous protocols. Many secret pacts had been made in the past. At the end of World War I an attempt was made to outlaw them, but it failed.[6] For the six years after 1938–39 the war was carried out under stringent disguise. The struggle with secrecy was tightly woven into the fabric of events.[7] As a result, communication in different forms, both written and oral, became one of the most valued and important activities of the war. It was the constant accompaniment of bitter conversations about disbelief in England, and in most other countries. Arguments about the nature and reality of the war would continue until the very end.

The struggle against secrecy and disguise was particularly urgent for decisions about armed defense. The discovery of the need for defense often came as a surprise, and had far-reaching implications. A new appreciation arose of the motivations for defense, and an awareness of their fragility; they could not be taken for granted. National attachment required immediate communication of what has been called the "ties that bind" or it failed. The breadth of this communication, and its amplification, were crucial. The power of the drive for defense, once awakened, could be great, and proved to be one of the strongest human motivations of all.

All of our chapters stress communication that took place during the war itself. Even on the fronts, protected by the strictest security, the dynamic struggle for good information was intense. The fronts were key places for collecting intelligence, they were also one of the greatest challenges for any participant to describe with words. Some remarkably talented writers were placed at the fronts.

Communication underwent a great trial in the context of the camps. The camps were one of the largest, most widespread institutions of the Second World War, and they were organized in a dismaying variety of forms. In the first two years—1939 to 1941—they were the receiving ground for deportations inside the USSR, and were central to that war. Throughout the years 1941–45 the camps continued to have a major role. They became essential to the German war against the Jews. The effort to maintain the secrecy of the camps—and the struggle against it—was one of the most intense "battlegrounds" of all. Every form and method of communication was tested; sometimes they succeeded, and more often they failed. But the successes were real and invaluable.[8]

The reader or historian who searches for policies based on "grand strategy" during the war is likely to fail.[9] If there were several "grand strategies" in place in 1939, all were changed, often radically, during the following years. When the secret Hitler-Stalin-Matsuoka pacts were overlaid by Operation Barbarossa, all conflicts were magnified, and actions became difficult to unravel.

One feature of World War II is that it was waged more against civilians than against armies. In many places, events went counter to all previous notions of strategy, self-interest, and concepts of human behavior. "War" frequently became a war against reality. The German war in the East, for example, went far beyond the aggression of armies bent only on territorial acquisition. The historian Michael Howard wrote, "On the Russian front Hitler was fighting a kind of war that had not been seen in Europe for around a thousand years; one not simply for the defeat, but for the virtual annihilation of his adversary."[10]

The physical landscape of Germans on the eve of the war was described by Norman Cohn as a product of "magical thinking . . . which had little to do with real conflicts of interest between living people." Extreme forms of the treatment of other human beings were not confined to Germany. On arriving in China, the Japanese General Yanagawa declared war "against every stream, tree, and blade of grass" in China. Events on the ground showed that this was not just hyperbole but extended to the Chinese population. "Nonhumans" were called *hinin*; the poet Ayukawa Nabuo described hair-raising scenes in which local Chinese, suspected of "having anti-Japanese thoughts," were dragged from their houses, taken into the country, bayoneted, killed, and kicked into mass graves. At the end of the battle of Okinawa, when Japanese civilians in hiding were persuaded to come out of their caves by Allied soldiers, they expected to see devils with horns and hoofs. Japanese women were told to stay away from Australian soldiers, if they came too close they were liable to give birth to kangaroos.[11]

When members of the Red Army invaded Estonia in 1940, some of them barefoot, they encountered prosperous, middle-class citizens of a democracy that had been independent for eighteen years. Yet soon, under Soviet occupation, having "anti-Soviet thoughts" became a punishable offense whether the "thinker" was Russian or non-Russian.[12] During the period 1939–41, the USSR sought to "decapitate" several neighboring nations. The term is Stalin's. It applied to the foreign country's leading professional classes, above all political and military, that were to be obliterated.

A few examples of the struggle against "reality" can be attributed to the desire to encourage troops, but often they were applied literally. During the war crimes tribunals in 1946, several judges objected to the term "military" used for wartime acts by defendants, categorizing them instead as "criminal." But the legal term brought new difficulties. Both secrecy and rhetoric were forcefully applied, they were inextricable parts of events. Reality was pliable. In the battle against reality, it was possible to win. With firepower, determination, and media control, a strong occupying army could enforce any claim. A defeated people, Simone Weil wrote, could be made to disappear: to become naught.[13]

It fell to individual writers to describe events, to interpret them, and find verbal forms for them. Probably the exercise of "power" can be seen best from the point of view of those on whom its effect was greatest—the civilians—not that of leadership or the dictators. Many who wrote in occupied countries observed a breakdown in the concept of the "human," and questioned the most basic human instincts, human psychology, and motivation.

They developed a variety of new "languages"—of metaphors, forms and concepts, observations, discoveries—that could account for what they observed in other people and also in themselves. These tested the extreme limits of words, and have altered profoundly our concept of the world. Many have extraordinary originality and power. It was the individual observer and writer who was called upon to explore the reality of this new world.

Experiences also called into question most of the older conceptions of time, of chronology, and sequence. This led to the rejection of many older concepts of history, its benchmarks and stereotypes. New attitudes to time led in turn to new approaches to narration and the way events are described with words. Narration—the description of a series of actions that have a clear temporal beginning, middle, and end—was often rejected. Many of the earliest writings stress the contradictions of time: its breadth, elasticity, and nonlinear sequence. Later, after 1945, written narration would be extended even further in new original directions.

Several active wars preceded the invasions in 1939. Andrei Sakharov recalled that in the Soviet Union, the 1930s were regularly referred to as a period of "war," while the word "peace" was used only for the period prior to World War I. Between 1939 and 1945 the USSR fought two very different wars. Also, the Nazi war against the Jews overlapped chronologically with the Second World War but was distinct from it.[14] For large numbers of people, occupation did not end in 1945 and continued in Eastern Europe until 1990.

Neither Britain nor the United States experienced the full brunt of the war in the form of enemy occupation or deportations. This gave a particular cast to the literature of both countries about the war. Peter Paret complained that British and especially American writers and historians have given far too much scope to "a popular, essentially romantic literature of war fought at a distance."[15] It often reduced the war to progress on military fronts; this left little place for the experience of millions of civilians under occupation or in the camps. One of many examples of the legacy can be seen in the career of Robert McNamara, who served with Charles Thornton and his "stat control" team during the Second World War. McNamara's conception of the events he observed was narrow, emphasizing air power and materiel. He entirely ignored the experiences of resistance and occupation. This was to undermine his approach to a later war, in Vietnam, as Secretary of Defense.[16]

It is tempting to deny a past as lethal as the Second World War, and to set it at a distance—even a very great distance—or reduce it to myths and patriotic aspirations. But the past is much closer to our present than we wish to acknowledge. When we look at forms that writers gave to their experiences during the Second World War, we can see that it is human nature they were describing; these are also our forms.

I
"Unreal War!"

1

Disbelief

In May 1940, near the port of Dunkirk on the English Channel, invading German armies trapped more than 350,000 British troops on three sides. Events were unfolding at break-neck speed. The German armies had penetrated deep inside France after a surprise attack through the Ardennes Mountains; the Maginot Line, supposedly impregnable, was lightly brushed aside. French armies were routed, their whereabouts unknown—it was the end of one of the most violent weeks of the war.

The German First and Tenth Panzer Divisions broke out across northern France. General Heinz Guderian ordered his tanks to continue advancing rapidly through France until the last drop of petrol in their tanks was used up. Guderian had praised the speed of tanks—their ability to achieve surprise and a breakthrough—in a 1937 best-seller in Germany, Achtung Panzer! *When the tanks appeared south of the Ardennes, the surprise, as he predicted, was complete. Rommel's Panzer Division was directed cross-country toward the Loire Valley, it avoided roads, traveling rapidly across fields.*

Further north, the Channel ports Boulogne and Dunkirk were under siege, the entire British Expeditionary Force was trapped against the sea. Defeat was inevitable. Thousands of soldiers on foot were streaming toward the port at Dunkirk, their fate uncertain. A desperate scramble to find boats, any kind of boat, was underway.

* * *

At the same moment, Herbert Read was composing a poem, "Ode, without Rhetoric, Written during the Battle of Dunkirk, May 1940." It reads in part:

> In the silence of the twilight
> I hear in the distance

the new guns.
As the evening deepens
searchlights begin to waver in the sky,
the airplanes throb invisibly above me

Unreal war! No single friend
links me with its immediacy.
It is a voice out of a cabinet,
a printed sheet, and these faint reverberations
selected in the silence
by my attentive ear.[1]

Read was listening to the impact of guns in the distance—"the new guns"—and the throbbing airplane engines overhead. He watched searchlights as they were moving. But the evidence of his senses lacked concrete reality, they lacked substance. The violent events were strangely muted. He was unable to grasp them.

A voice "out of a cabinet"?

"A printed sheet" about a distant meeting in the past, or the record of some unnamed conference?

The events he was witnessing "had no immediacy"? Read exclaimed, "Unreal war!"

As Read was writing, none of our contemporary, postwar information was available. War aims were not declared. It was a time when facts that became common knowledge after 1945 were unknown. Read was confessing to a difficulty shared by countless others at the beginning of the Second World War, it was true of ordinary citizens and leaders alike. It was true not only in England but in other countries already attacked, or soon to be attacked. Disbelief and incredulity were almost universal. They were responsible for some of the worst miscalculations during the early years of the war 1939–41, and later, all the way until 1945. Many witnesses came to think that disbelief—the refusal to admit the presence of danger despite all concrete evidence to the contrary—was the most important theme of the entire war. It was the most likely to cause death or eventual submission, in this sense the most lethal. At the same time it was a widespread human weakness, and not easy to explain. One observer predicted that future historians would marvel at one thing during this period more than any other—the refusal of the Western democracies to take seriously the mortal threat to their existence.[2]

Disbelief often seemed harmless. But it was closely tied to defense, the decision to take up arms or not take up arms in self-defense. It arose initially as a response to secrecy, to disguise, disinformation, and the confusion that veiled events. Often it would lead to defeat in its many forms of captivity, occupation, or deportation. The use of disguise and surprise continued throughout the period 1939–45. One of the war's most important features was that the outcome could not be known until the very end. In a sense it should not be called the "Second World War" but perhaps something else, until the surrenders in 1945 when it acquired its name. There were constant changes, surprises, sudden reversals, and defeats. And the refusal to believe the extent of danger, despite contrary evidence, also continued to the end.

During the war years disbelief was considered by many to be important, urgent, and very dangerous. Writers attempted to counter it as forms of communication, both written and oral, acquired enormous value and importance. The "pencil stub" in our title refers to this ongoing effort, and the extremely difficult writing conditions during the period.

As Read's title indicates, he deliberately avoids any "rhetoric." The title is significant, the poem might be considered low-keyed or muted; it is also remarkably straight-forward. It is a reminder that Read felt the need to communicate with others as directly as possible. He sought to avoid the wishful thinking and complacency of the "phoney war" period. It was now a time when rhetoric must be abandoned. In his modest way Read was declaring that the defeat at Dunkirk—later some would claim it was a "victory"—was a watershed event. War had arrived and had to be faced, the evidence accepted. Illusions should be discarded.

Read's modest poem expresses no panic and is certainly not heroic. He captured a state of mind that was almost universal as he evokes the widespread disbelief and incredulity between 1937 and 1940. Countless arguments about the possibility of war—whether it would take place or not, which events were bluff and which were not—are caught in an ambivalent balance. Read captured the plight of the individual civilian at a moment when he was most vulnerable, on a path that stretched toward the future: a path that was new, opaque, without markers. An admirable feature of the poem is that Read is able to isolate the theme of disbelief: he pinpoints and addresses it.

A noteworthy admission of Read's poem is that he sees the disbelief in himself. The poem is a confession, he stresses the inadequacy of his own reactions. The exclamation point after "Unreal war!" admits the failure and stresses it.

Soon after Read wrote his poem, the war came to Britain itself. Daily bombings by the Luftwaffe, what is called "The Battle of Britain," lasted from July through October 1940. But the inability to appreciate danger continued as before. George Orwell, a talented writer, described the first aerial attacks on England in an essay, *The Lion and the Unicorn*. At this point his reaction to the attacks on British cities probably strikes most postwar readers as unusual:

> As I write, highly civilized human beings are flying overhead, trying to kill me. They do not feel any enmity against me as an individual, nor I against them. They are only "doing their duty," as the saying goes. Most of them, I have no doubt, are kind-hearted, law-abiding men who would never dream of committing murder in private life.[3]

The collection of Orwell's writings during the first years of the war, titled "My Country Right or Left," is a curious work that displays the widespread complacency and disbelief of the time. He is unwilling at this point to call the German planes "the enemy," and with an open-minded attitude he attempts to humanize the Luftwaffe pilots. War—the first bombardments of British cities—was a silly misunderstanding, the soldiers of both sides simply following orders from above. They had no lethal intentions. For Orwell at this time, class allegiance was more important than nation. He had no wish to defend the "capitalist" classes.

But it was no longer the beginning of the war. Orwell was writing after the defeat of most of the British Army. More than seven countries in Europe had already been violently invaded and occupied. More startling, Orwell penned these lines after reading and reviewing Hitler's *Mein Kampf* for the *New English Weekly*. But for many people the act of reading was not enough to dispel disbelief. Hitler's book made only a dim impression on Orwell. He admitted in his review, "I have never been able to dislike Herr Hitler"—a remark he was soon to regret.

For Orwell and most English men of letters, Fascism and Nazism were vague concepts. Orwell's prose works remind us that before 1939, British writers had only marginal knowledge of Germany and its political system. Convincing portraits of Nazi Party adherents were rare in English and American literature.[4] In 1940, how could Orwell or any other British writer have known that in a memorandum written earlier the same year, General Jodl explicitly ordered "attacks against the British homeland," and "terror attacks against the English centers of population"? Or that the German Wehrmacht already had a blueprint named "Operation Sealion" to invade England after the conquest of France? In the event of a successful landing in England, Germany had a plan to deport the entire British male population between the ages of sixteen and forty-five to the Continent and Germany itself. The official title of the plan, published in the London *Times* in 1945 in its entirety, was: "Orders and Instructions for the Establishment of a Military Government in England after the Projected Invasion in 1940."[5] But this was hidden by secrecy. If the plan had been successful, the fate of the nation would have been unspeakably tragic.

A widespread and complacent culture of disbelief grew during the early war years. At first it was the period of the so-called "phoney war," in France the *drole de guerre*. "Munich"—written often in quotes because the city's name indicated an optimistic attitude—had made war unlikely. People were convinced "war" was nothing but a bluff. Jokes about the "phoney war" became popular. The word *"Sitzkrieg"* was coined, a pun on the word *blitzkrieg* or "lightning war," implying everyone was sitting down rather than fighting. Humorists spoke of "the Bore War," a pun on the earlier "Boer War" in Africa. In France, Louis Aragon spoke of "the time of crossword puzzles," *le temps des mots croises*. In Parisian cabarets they sang mockingly, *"les canons font boum boum."* The self-confident literature of the "phoney war" made fun of the sheer possibility of war.

In Anthony Powell's novel about this period *The Kindly Ones*, a typical passage occurs: "'News doesn't look very good.' I said. 'Do you think the Germans are going into Poland?' There seemed no particular object in avoiding banality from the start, as the evening showed every sign of developing into a banal one."

The experiences of other countries offered much information about a war that had become increasingly international, but the delusion was widespread that events a hundred miles away could not happen at home. Throughout history the use of verbal reports to compare attacks in nearby countries has been precious communication, hindered often by difference in language.[6]

The philosopher Bertrand Russell argued that if the Nazis invaded Britain, they should be treated as friends, coerced if necessary by civil disobedience. He argued that they would be too embarrassed to retaliate. It is difficult to imagine a more complete misunderstanding of reality. If such a belief were taken seriously the country would be stripped of effective defense, conquest by Germany would be made without a battle.

Disbelief and incredulity were among the most contentious topics in the first years of the war. Was talk of war a bluff? How great was the danger? If other countries were attacked, could one's own country somehow escape? The arguments and discussions were accompanied by anxiety, frustration, and suspense.

The postwar reader is often unaware of these writings in the first years of the war, and the many heated disputes that accompanied them. The history of the war with its ending in 1945 has been written many times over. The outcome is no longer in doubt, the names of the victors and defeated are well-known. The suspense is lost, the reader usually thinks he knows better. The infusion of postwar information into most narratives about the Second World War has been almost universal, especially in popular media and film.

The postwar writer attempting to reconstruct events is often at a disadvantage, his postwar perspective a liability. A historian, H. Stuart Hughes, observed that "second-hand parties and historians cannot give the full sense of events as reality in the process of becoming—*because they know the outcome.*"[7] Revisions and corrections of history regularly use hindsight. Raymond Aron criticized our popular acceptance of what he calls "retrospective illusion," and the tendency to project the present, with its updated perspective, onto the past. In his study of narration J. P. Stern observed, "All historical knowledge goes against the grain." In an earlier century, Voltaire called these "tricks we play on the dead."[8]

The writings by English authors during the early years of the war are highlighted here because they offer a remarkably broad range of attitudes. Ordinary citizens and writers had time—precious time—to confront major problems, to discuss, debate them, write about them. The curtain of occupation did not fall over the country, extinguishing dialogue and exchange of views. The literature of the time contains both expressions of extreme illusion and, simultaneously, an awareness of danger. As the violence of bombing continued, there was still no consensus. British writings during the early war years highlight the crucial nature of both oral and written communication, and the lively exchange of information. Read's description of the war's "unreality" was repeated by other authors in different ways.

For example, Stephen Spender wrote that he and Louis MacNeice doubted the war "was for a purified cause." They turned inward toward personal subject-matter, avoiding the world of outer events. The spectrum of British attitudes in 1940 was wide: it included a powerful pacifist movement; complacency; still vivid memories of World War I; belief that rearmament increased the chances of war; "placatory appeasement" (Winston Churchill's phrase); conservatives intent on maintaining privileges and the empire; a political left that believed capitalism was a larger problem than war or invasion by Germany. A historian observed that "the idea of maintaining peace through strength was not in fashion." Noel Annan noted in his "group-portrait" of the period *Our Age*, "Hitler did not weaken the peace movement. On the contrary, the smell of danger strengthened it."[9] Kingsley Martin, editor of the *New Statesman*, wrote that "if only Hitler spoke, all would be well." Views were often combined with a self-righteous religiosity that believed sin and evil could be overcome successfully by the example of unilateral virtue, trust and good will."[10]

Major British writers took part in discussions of conflicting views. As bombing of cities and airfields continued, uncertainty became intense: would the nation survive? No one knew what the outcome would be. It was impossible even to guess. The diplomat and writer Harold Nicolson kept one of the finest journals of the wartime period, and wrote in 1940: "In ordinary times one seldom thinks how odd it is to have no knowledge of what may happen even within the next hour, but now the consciousness of this ignorance becomes acute. I see the future only in terms of color: scarlet and black."[11]

What stands out is the extreme range of opinions expressed, often contradictory, and the intensity of the debates. If disbelief was rampant so was the need felt by many to combat it, to struggle against it. The contemporary discussions are reflected in most serious nonfictional and fictional works of the period. Their sheer number is overpowering. The result was a matter of suspense, of high drama.

The arguments were significant, their outcomes important, because they influenced the decision to take up arms in self-defense, and—ultimately—determined the country's survival as an independent sovereign state. Everything hung on the discussions and communication in its broadest sense. Other countries had similar debates that were tragically cut short by events. Britain was relatively unprepared, but with swift change, and luck, the country managed to mount a vigorous self-defense, barely avoiding defeat. The margin of "victory" was razor-thin.[12] If Germany had continued its attacks on the southern airfields for two more weeks, if it was not diverted by London as a target in revenge for the bombing of Berlin, it would probably have prevailed.

The conflicts of the time were especially well suited to the novelist and short story writer. They were not obliged to create a linear narrative, with knowledge of the outcome; they were free to render the unpredictability of the time with all its psychological conflicts. Novels, autobiographies, memoirs, nonfiction and fiction, all evoke the disparate points of view and individual differences.

Writers used many of the novelist's devices, especially psychological highlighting, to illustrate and dramatize conflicts. One passage in Richard Hillary's novel *The Enemy Within* leads to a dramatic confrontation, a climactic conversation between two friends:

> Yet I wanted to hear his arguments. I had an idea that the issue for him was an apprehension of something related to faith and not to any intellectual concept. My chance came when we were sent down from Montrose to Edinburgh by train to fly up a couple of new Spitfires. We had the compartment to ourselves. I didn't temporize but asked him straight out his reasons for fighting the war. He gave me that slow smile of his. "Well, Richard," he said, "you've got me at last, haven't you?"[13]

The discussion that follows plumbs the depths of two different, even contradictory motivations and attitudes toward the war. They were both fighter pilots. One is motivated by a strong religious faith that he believes requires active military defense. The other—Hillary at this stage in his life—has a secular, questioning attitude.

Heated discussions mark most works of the time. Opposed beliefs and opinions divided friends, family members, and colleagues. In this atmosphere the "war" was not a clear struggle between one country and another but among Englishmen and women, a battle among themselves. After 1945, a deliberate effort was made to play down these great divergences of opinion during the early stages of the war. Generosity toward those who opposed the war—or were lukewarm—was recommended. Unity was stressed. But we should make no mistake about the intensity of the "debates" and conflicts, and how much was at stake. The best writers such as William Sansom and Richard Hillary, when they evoke 1940–41, show that everything was at stake. It could have ended entirely different.

The "Battle of Britain" was probably observed by more civilians than any other battle in the Second World War. It took place in the open air, above major metropolitan centers and in clear view from the ground. Civilians outdoors could pause and follow the maneuvers of airplanes overhead. Scrambled Spitfires and Hurricanes fought in close airplane-to-airplane combat with German Dorniers, Stukas, and Messerschmitts at altitudes ranging from 1,500 to 20,000 feet.

What was the attitude of the large audiences for these noisy "shows" taking place in the sky? For some, they were unwanted distractions from recreation or the enjoyment of gardens. A young pilot, Kenneth Lee, wrote a vivid description of a close encounter with tragedy; his Spitfire was shot down over rolling countryside, he was wounded.

> I was taken to a local golf club, just inland from Whitstable, to await an ambulance. I was in shirtsleeves, slightly bloodstained. But I couldn't help hearing members at the last hole complaining that the distraction of the Battle in the air was disturbing their putting, while once inside a voice demanded, "Who's that scruffy-looking chap at the bar? I don't think he's a member."[14]

Lee's irony was sharp. He points out an uncomfortable fact that a significant part of the population chose to take lightly or ignore crucial, dramatic engagements of the war. Club members refused to interrupt leisure activities and entertainment, in this case putting on greens. They were unable or unwilling to make the connection between a bleeding man, taken for treatment to the clubhouse bar, with airplanes fighting in the sky overhead.

Another pilot, Peter Simpson, was shot down by a low-flying German Dornier, crash-landing on another golf course. His reception was more hostile than Lee's; enraged golfers brandished their clubs menacingly, and threatened him. Farmers, too, were upset when an airplane, shot down by the enemy, intruded on their fields. Douglas Turley-George remembered a crash he barely survived, his Spitfire cutting a deep swathe through a cornfield: "The furious farmer wanted to know 'Why the bloody hell couldn't you have landed in the next field?'"[15]

The violence of bombing by the Luftwaffe continued to mount. Disbelief was often accompanied by shock, which made it enter another psychological dimension. Some sought refuge in unreality. In a short story *The Mysterious Kor*, Elizabeth Bowen described a soldier and his small sister in a park at night, watching huge opaque balloons in the sky above them. The girl imagines they are in a legendary city she calls "Mysterious Kor, recently discovered by anthropologists."[16] Bowen explained in a "Postscript" that during the Blitz many people had strange, deep, intense dreams. The stupefying events were impossible to understand. The girl's fantasy was actually an attempt to make sense of what she was observing. For the child, everything was riding on the fate of the city. She imagined all was lost, even the name "London," which became an archeologist's "Kor." In her novel *The Dressmaker,* the author Beryl Bainbridge also described unusual dreams. In a sociological study *Living through the Blitz*, Tom Harrisson noted long-lasting effects of traumas from bombardments in a chapter, "Psychiatric and Shock Impacts."[17] Bowen and Bainbridge used the short story and novel to render these "shock impacts."

In the summer of 1940, attitudes slowly shifted. William Sansom worked as a fireman in London, and had ample opportunity to observe ordinary people in their bombed homes. He noted in his collection of stories *The Wall* (1941) that as the Blitz continued, an awareness gradually arose in each individual that the attack was not directed against an abstract government or army, or navy, it was a war against *him*, an average citizen, living in a residential neighborhood.

At first, it caused surprise. The experience had to be repeated for him to accept it. Sansom made this surprise one of his main subjects. He emphasized the vulnerability of ordinary people:

It was like a sandpapered ramrod down your throat, and your lungs puffing out like a pouter pigeon. Then dead, dead silence. Then, as though some time afterwards, a slow shower of bricks from everywhere . . .

A man was buried up to his shoulders. His steel hat was blown right away. Fire broke out in the debris all around him. He would have been burnt, buried there with his head sticking from the hot ground, if others had not struggled over and dragged him out. He had his pipe in his mouth all the time. Later they put forty stitches in his scalp . . . And only that morning, on such a fine April day, he remembered taking a turn in the park opposite the Kingston House Depot and strolling, at peace, by the new spring flowers.[18]

Extreme effects are contrasted with a moment of peace. The sense of violence is achieved by combining closely observed details with speed. The contrast at the end with the spring morning acts as counterpoint or foil.

Though it was a time of maximum violence, Sansom admitted it was difficult to put that violence into words: "The violence and its reflections may be written down—but never the core of the violent act itself. In the first place, language fails."

Sansom often used architecture—buildings, destroyed walls and ceilings, fragmentary rooms—to give structure to events and the lives of people who were inside. In *Westminster at War,* Sansom recounted how a man arrived home late during a night of bombardment. It was dark, and hard to see. The man did not realize the house where he lived had been sliced in two. He returned by his habitual path, extremely tired, and made his way up the well-known stairs. As luck had it, he went to bed in the half of the bedroom that was still standing. In the morning, when he woke in broad daylight, he was so frightened by what he saw he was unable to move. He had to be brought down with a ladder.

Richard Hillary carried the surprise stressed by Sansom a step further. The focus of *The Enemy Within* (1943) is denial and disbelief—not only in others but in the author himself. Hillary was a pilot, in the first chapters of the book he presents himself as arrogant and immature. His Spitfire was shot down but he continued to see the war in what he called "aesthetic" terms. Like many others he was unable to conceive the serious stakes of the war, or to imagine a real German invasion.

Gradually, after many discussions with friends, a pacifist prominent among them, after crash-landings and brushes with death, lengthy hospitalization, and excruciating plastic surgery, Hillary had a realization: "With awful clarity I saw myself suddenly as I was. Great God that I could have been so arrogant!" The structure of the novel is a gradual curve that leads to an overpowering epiphany.

It is followed by two resolutions: to fight, and to write his book. The anger and fury he felt during a German bombardment of London are particularly convincing because Hillary rages against himself as well as the Germans—against his own earlier stupidity. The main part of the blame falls not on "others" but on Hillary himself. The "enemy within" of the title is his own worst instincts, his comfortable denial of the magnitude of the enemy threat.

Hillary presented disbelief as part of a process, a first step that led to the realization of a new reality. He succeeded in describing the unwillingness of an average individual to realize, truly to see, the destruction around him. It was not obvious. He dramatically evoked the sense of unreality of the times in order to stress the next step, what he called the need "to wake up." Hillary did not survive the war—he died in January 1943—but he was unequivocal, his whole act of writing and his book were an act of communication with his readers: a call to end delusions.

Perceptive observers noted that highly placed leaders and ordinary people alike failed to assess danger. The difficulty was found at every level of society. Writers sought explanations, new concepts or metaphors to account for the failure. Denial and delusion were not harmless but part of a deeply self-destructive process. Some wrote it was a kind of "suicide." Others spoke of arrogance, stupidity, the mind "breaking down," paralysis, self-deception, insanity. Winston Churchill wrote intemperately of "the acme of gullibility." It seemed that the provisional social consensus before the summer of 1940 was based on pure fantasy.[19]

Many non-British writers lost their sense of surprise well before their British counterparts. The Czech writer Jiri Mucha left Prague after the capitulation in 1938, fought the Germans with the Czech Fourth Legion in France, and made his way to England. He complained about his new English hosts:

> Himmler, Heydrich, the Gestapo: the caveman has a free hand for the duration. The human louse sits in a gaol, dangles from the gallows, passes out in torture chambers, and the chaps in black don't even realize that they have done harm. That's just what people can't understand in England, where the cave man's soul has almost disappeared. Let them ask you. Evil? What evil?[20]

The passage drips with sarcasm, and is not quite fair. But it evokes the exasperation of a talented writer who had already fought the Germans earlier in continental Europe.

The difficulty in assessing danger was international. No country could claim greater foresight than others. In *The Gathering Storm*, Churchill complained that during the Blitz the United States stood idly by and simply "gaped," offering no help. When it was the turn of the United States to be subject to an attack—at Pearl Harbor in December 1941—the surprise and chaos were total.[21]

Poland, France, Holland, Belgium, Norway, Denmark, and Britain were all victims of a military doctrine—the blitzkrieg or "lightning-fast war"—that deliberately exploited surprise. Psychological disbelief in the hostile intentions of others was not a peripheral concept: it was built into the core structure of military strategy. With troop movements concealed, an overwhelming initial attack was intended to create panic and paralysis. Surprise would forestall assessment of danger and social debate, or the decision to take up armed defense. The doctrine confirmed that effective defense required time.[22] The attacks by the Soviet Union beginning on September 17, 1939 partly built on the attacks by Germany seventeen days earlier; deception was more elaborate and thorough than the preparations for the German invasions.[23]

A historian has written that democratic societies had an additional handicap. They "are incapable of understanding political regimes of a different character . . . They are accustomed to think in liberal, pragmatic categories. Conflicts are believed to be based on misunderstandings . . . extremism is a temporary aberration, so is irrational behavior, intolerance, cruelty."[24] Disbelief could be stubborn, realization of danger was often slow following a halting, unfolding arc of events.

Writers in all the invaded countries explored the experiences of disbelief and surprise. They gave them a variety of forms, ranging from French novels describing the *exode* or exodus—when millions of civilians took to the roads in panic—to the novels of the German anti-Nazi writer Theodor Plievier, and a Holocaust novel such as Elie Wiesel's *Night* ("It was neither German nor Jew who ruled the ghetto—it was illusion"). But most of these works had to wait until after the war before they could be published.

In many countries, uncensored literature was completely shut out. In June 1940, Harold Nicolson saw the future in terms of colors: scarlet and black. In continental Europe it was black. A curtain fell.

2

The Curtain

In April 1945, a U.S. Army unit, the Ninth Division, advanced into the Harz Mountains in Germany. The war almost over, the soldiers were far from large cities. A landscape of hills led to low mountains. The soldiers reached a small village named Degenershausen. The village was inconspicuous, without importance, and three ancient castles stood in the village. Inside one of them the soldiers found a room and, neatly stacked and tied in bundles inside, were all of the old letters, proposals, and counterproposals exchanged between the German and Soviet governments during the period from April to September 1939. Other documents up to 1941 were included. Most important was a signed copy of the Hitler-Stalin Pact, rumored to exist but never seen or confirmed until that moment.[25]

The Nazi government in Berlin had ordered these documents to be destroyed, but a meticulous, historically minded archivist in the German Foreign Office refused to carry out the order. The documents he saved were written by diplomats representing Hitler (Ribbentrop, Weizsaecker, Schulenburg, Schnurre), diplomats representing Stalin (Molotov, Merekalov, Astakhov), and Hirohito (Matsuoka). The main theme of the documents was the expansion of the three states in all four directions of the compass. Expansion was to take place not only in Europe but in Africa, the Near East, and Asia.

The neatly bundled documents included the first and most famous secret protocol to the Hitler-Stalin Pact, signed by Molotov and Ribbentrop. It divided up Eastern Europe between Germany and Russia. Five different secret Protocols were added to the Pact, effectively terminating the independence of twelve countries. A provision was also made for a German bombing attack on London.

Soviet officials denied the existence of the Pact, and after 1945 continued to assert they found no evidence of it in their archives. In 1948, the U.S. Government Printing Office published all the documents found at Degenershausen in their entirety. For the next forty-five years, the

USSR continued to denounce the documents as forgeries. It was only in 1991 that the new Confederation of Russian States—or "Russia"—publicly displayed their authentic second copy of the secret Pact, with Stalin's clear signature. It was exhibited to the public in the Tretyakov Gallery in Moscow.[26]

Other secret documents that influenced and determined events in the war were found in the quaint village in the Harz Mountains. Until then much that happened during the six years 1939–45 had been inexplicable. Major events, their causes and motivations, seemed impossible to understand. One historian compared them to men lurching and groping inside a dark room.

Documents showed that the talks leading to the Hitler-Stalin Pact had been initiated by the Soviet Union, and Ambassador Merekalov. Matsuoka, the Japanese foreign minister, signed the Pact in Berlin in April 1941. The "Serov Plan," for the invasion and occupation of the Baltic states in 1939–40 by the Soviet Union, also came into the possession of the Allies. Germans captured the documents when they attacked the USSR in 1941 and these, in turn, fell into the hands of the Allies in 1945; this trove of secret papers was known as the "Riga Archive." Documents for the Wannsee Conference in 1940, when the first plans were made for the destruction of the Jews, disappeared, but minutes of the conference were eventually found.

The Hitler-Stalin Pact included a map that carved Eastern Europe into Soviet and German "spheres of influence." The euphemism opened the way to multiple invasions, and became a blueprint for armed occupation. It redrew many of the borders in Europe, and created artificial entities such as the "Generalgouvernement," a hybrid term incorporating part of Poland into a new area intended for ethnic cleansing. It was ironically referred to during the war years as "the G.G." The secret Protocols ended the sovereignty of eleven states: the three Baltic states, Finland, Poland, Slovakia, Hungary, Rumania, Bessarabia, Bulgaria, and Yugoslavia.

During the twenty-two months from September 1939 to June 1941, some 60 million civilians were caught within the far-flung boundaries of the Hitler-Stalin Pact. With the inclusion of Imperial Japan in early 1941, the total of civilians would exceed 100 million.[27] These numbers are high and difficult to imagine, the number of casualties during the war years is also extremely hard to imagine. A historian wrote, "One might think that the historians could have arrived at a consensus. In reality, no such consensus exists. Certainly 48 million died and maybe as many as 60 million, depending on when and where you begin the count, and whose figures you believe."[28]

For the civilians on whom the pact was to have the most direct effect, the plans were unknown. Words such as "occupation," "annexation," and "maintaining peace" were intended to mislead. "Deportation," itself a euphemism, became "mobilization of labor." One of the most cynical euphemisms was the "*Aktion AB*" ("General Pacification Action") by the SS.[29] The populations were of different nationalities and ethnic groups, speaking a variety of languages. One writer called them a "kaleidoscope" of nationalities. Czeslaw Milosz, winner of the Nobel Prize for Literature in 1980, referred to the secret Hitler-Stalin-Matsuoka Pact as a great "Pandora's box." He wrote: "In the trade of territories between the Soviet Union and Germany in August 1939, whole countries were reduced to the role of objects."[30] This was true in an unexpected literal sense: the exploration of relations between humans and things—or material objects—was to become a major theme in twentieth-century literature.

As borders were redrawn, as towns were emptied and the deportations of whole villages carried out, new groups of camps and satellite camps were created for the deported civilians. Two of the largest camp systems in the world grew even larger.

The most rudimentary information was lacking. Hastily scrawled notes and written communications rarely reached their intended destinations. An exchange of messages was more likely to be in this form:

> As the iron doors of a train clanged shut a little cloud of paper messages was dislodged, and they drifted to the ground. The clang of these iron doors coming together was a sound impossible to forget. From the gratings fluttered down showers of white scraps, atoms of paper on which were written names and addresses, last messages begging not to be forgotten, broken sentences and prayers.[31]

The anonymous author of *The Far Side of the Moon*—a collection of many of these writings—notes that no one was able to pick up the scraps of paper from the ground. But it was from these chaotic beginnings that the sending of messages became a widespread activity. Reception of messages usually failed, but the desire to reach a recipient—any recipient—was great, the number of attempts enormous. A few messages, aided by luck, succeeded in having great influence. Some, as we shall see, were to change the course of the war.

The messages were rarely written with concern for literary qualities. But the author of the passage above has given it some of the features of form. In her description the messages on scraps of paper take on a life of their own, they float in the air. They might be unread, lost, or destroyed, largely futile efforts and the senders unknown, but they continue to be animated—they drift, independent of any reader, almost without volition of their own, like thoughts. They are not forgotten.

These written communications were to continue to the very end in 1945. Many postwar writers of narratives highlighted them, developing them—their intent, writing, and transmission—into longer works. Often they considered them to be important benchmarks as they built on them and extended them into finished, published works. Gradually, ordinary people as well as writers found new, original ways to give meaning and shape to their experiences.

3

Numbers

The secrecy hiding much of the war was a major stumbling block for all participants whether military or civilian. It was difficult enough to be aware of the fate of members of one's own extended family, local group, or home town.[32] Most people were reduced to uncertainty and a state of waiting. One of the greatest needs was for communication and the transmission of basic, seemingly simple information.

The war years were a time of great movement of peoples, a time when many different wars unexpectedly came together in what we call the "Second World War," but knowledge of most of the important events and collective numbers was lacking. The greatest possible challenge was to find words, concepts, or forms, for what was largely unknown. Some of the finest writers wrote eloquently about the difficulty of finding ways to describe what was unknown or hidden. Others narrowed their frame of reference to what they knew with certainty: individual people, things, what was specific, concrete, close at hand.

Numbers took on entirely new dimensions. It turned out that they were extremely hard to grasp. Numbers gave rise to insoluble problems of communication. Arthur Koestler complained about numbers in an essay he wrote in 1943. In vivid language he wrote, "Statistics don't bleed; it is the detail which counts. We are unable to embrace the total process with our awareness; we can only focus on little lumps of reality."[33]

Koestler believed it was a problem of human psychology, similar to denial. He described it with other examples:

Distance in space and time degrades intensity of awareness. So does magnitude. Seventeen is a figure which I know intimately like a friend; fifty billions is just a sound . . . Thus we all live in a state of split consciousness. People go to cinemas, they see films of Nazi tortures, of mass shootings, of underground conspiracy and self-sacrifice. They sigh, they shake their heads, some have a good cry.

But they do not connect it with the realities of their normal plane of existence. It is Romance, it is Art, it is Those Higher Things, it is Church Latin. It does not click with reality. We live in a society of the Jekyll and Hyde pattern, magnified into gigantic proportions.

Koestler wrote "On Disbelieving Atrocities" in 1943. He had escaped from occupied France by way of Spain to London. He gave lectures, and tried to describe to English audiences what was taking place in Continental Europe. He believed he failed completely. The reason seemed to be that the human imagination cannot take in the substance of large statistics, or give them reality. It can relate only to the most immediate surroundings, "little lumps of reality." The imagination was pitifully limited when confronted with complex and invisible international events, it could take in only very small items or "lumps." At a certain point—as an involuntary reaction—the mind turned away. The problem was inherent in the ordinary average human.

Koestler wrote that as he lectured, he often felt he was battling a strange entity: a "transparent screen . . . a dream barrier which stifles all sound." He struggled unsuccessfully with this barrier. "You can convince them for an hour, then they shake themselves, their mental self-defense begins to work, and in a week the shrug of incredulity has returned like a reflex temporarily weakened by a shock." The listeners have good will, but still the struggle ends with a shrug.

The description recalls the complaint by the Czech writer Jiri Mucha; other writers observed similar "mental self-defense mechanisms" both in England and European countries. They "could not get through" to people around them. Some were "contra-suggestible."[34]

Even when true versions of events were available, they were avoided or shunned in favor of other alternatives. It was not just a matter of lack of information; it was a distinct preference for falsehoods. It seemed to indicate a widespread psychological mechanism, anyone was capable of it. If it was universal, it could be exploited easily in all parts of the world.

A similar psychological mechanism seemed to hold sway in large groups. For example, it was observed inside the large German concentration camp at Sachsenhausen, near the city of Muenster in northern Germany. Sachsenhausen was also a training center for the SS. A perceptive description of the difficulty in grasping numbers as they are orally communicated was written in Odd Nansen's journal, *From Day to Day*.[35]

This was one of the most remarkable documents to emerge from the war: detailed, meticulously objective in a concrete setting and, what was more, written on the spot. Nansen's journal was kept hidden in a breadboard, a small compartment hollowed out inside with precision craftsmanship in a woodshop.

Nansen was an architect and skilled drawer, son of the polar explorer Fritjof Nansen. He wrote most of his journal at Sachsenhausen. Nansen described the spread of incredulity in this way:

> Figures for the dead, killed, and "transported" buzz around us. One has heard this, another that. It's all as certain as amen in church, they've been talking to so-and-so who saw it themselves, or have a friend who saw it. It's practically hopeless to keep any sort of reliable journal on what goes on here . . . I have always tried to trace the source and get as near to it as possible before writing down the story. And while thus employed I have often found that stories which have gone through many retellings, and been distorted, have by no means always grown worse than the reality.
>
> The reason is obvious. Figures can easily be exaggerated, hundreds becoming thousands and thousands ten thousands; but the essential thing, the devilry itself, that they were killed, that they were struck and kicked, racked and tortured, they went about half naked, that they ate out of the dustbins, that they died out on the parade ground or at the gate of the *Revier*, or were clubbed to death by the *Blockaelteste* and kicked into the privy . . . that some of the "corpses" in the pile of corpses were still living and that they went into the furnace just the same and were burned alive . . . this and much more can simply not be exaggerated. The plain fact is that reality is stronger, more dramatic, and far more gruesome than one can grasp on hearing it recapitulated. Normal human imagination falls short, therefore a secondhand account is always paler and more "plausible."[36]

The "normal human imagination falls short": and so does the human ability to understand. The author presents a mixed, multinational collection of prisoners, not a single national group. He describes a dynamic process among people who could all be considered eyewitnesses. He echoes the famous description of eyewitnesses by Thucydides in his history of the Peloponnesian War: that what "witnesses" tell one another quickly becomes distorted, changing the real features and nature of the event described.[37] In Nansen's version, the closest, or first, witness was not the one others were inclined to believe. The process was collective. Retellings, paradoxically, made events appear less bad than they actually were, less lethal in their implications, but the figures were inflated to be more "dramatic."

In Albert Camus' novel *The Plague*, numbers became the most important theme of the book. Written after the war the novel's concentrated focus is on behavior during the war itself. Camus describes a largely fictional city called "Oran," an allegorical setting that resembles occupied France before 1945. By extension it is the greater war.

The inhabitants of Oran, it turned out, were unable to accept events that took place under their very eyes. Camus was interested in the reactions of ordinary citizens; their psychology was normal yet peculiar at the same time. The magnitude of events escaped them. "The reaction of the public," the narrator observes, "was slower than might have been expected. Thus the bare statement that three hundred and two deaths had taken place in the third week of plague failed to strike their imagination. The public lacked, in short, standards of comparison." The numbers of the sick or victims of the "plague"—like those of the Second World War— were met with apathy. A meaningful benchmark was lacking, some kind of concrete comparison that could be easily grasped or visualized.

The narrator of the novel, Doctor Rieux, reflects on other "plagues," that is, other wars, that took place in the course of history. He returns to the theme of numbers:

> "Figures floated across his memory . . . But what are a hundred million deaths? When one has served in a war, one hardly knows what a dead man is, after a while. And since a dead man has no substance unless one has actually seen him dead, 100,000,000 corpses strewn across history can be no more than a foggy notion . . . Ten thousand dead is equivalent to five times the capacity of a large movie house.
>
> So, to see things clearly, this is what should be done: get the audiences from five movie theaters to assemble at the entrances, take them to one of the city squares and kill them on the spot. At least one could then see familiar faces in that anonymous heap.[38]

As the narrator struggles to explain the public's apathy, his irony is biting. It is harsh Swiftian satire. It is also ethical satire that criticizes indifference. Camus' sympathies are clearly with life, with the living, but he is exasperated by the ease with which the townspeople write off large numbers of human beings, at least in their minds.

If accurate statistics fail to excite the imagination, what was to be done? It was only too easy to become callous about others beyond a narrow circle of friends, family, and acquaintances. This explains why Camus dramatized the scene of the death of a child in *The Plague;* it became central to the structure of the novel, providing what he called a "standard of comparison." This, he wrote, is what each unit of "statistics" really refers to, what people listened to with such apathy: living and breathing human beings, in his book a young child.

The observations by Camus and Koestler about numbers were echoed by other writers: "Big figures become statistics, and statistics have no psychological impact."[39] As the war continued, many writers felt obliged to reevaluate the workings of the "normal" human imagination. Even at Birkenau, incredulity was rampant. "Pinch me!" a friend asked Krystyna Zywulska in her narrative, "maybe I'm dreaming." A hundred miles further to the east, in a Soviet labor camp, the same phrase was used by Margarethe Buber: "Pinch me!"[40]

If self-deception took many shapes, disguise itself—or deliberate disguise—often took countless shapes and forms. It was not only used as tactics at the front. Constraint, media falsehood, and the manipulation of numbers underlay the entire conception of the war, its inception and execution. They inevitably became major themes of the writings about the war. They were only too effective as the war accelerated with increasing violence and more countries took part. The geographical spread of events was too wide for any single onlooker to follow the divergent strands, or see where they led.

Emanuel Ringelblum wrote that new arrivals from Western Europe at the Warsaw ghetto had no idea what to expect. (Its population was 450,000 at its peak.) He wrote that deceptive reports were published by the German-controlled media. Rumors swirling inside the ghetto were planted by the Germans themselves.[41] In *The Drowned City,* Michael Mazor described a history professor who tried to persuade the inhabitants of the Warsaw ghetto that they were in no danger at all.

With blazing evasive eyes he tried to persuade us that we were all under the influence of a pessimistic psychosis that was distorting our sense of reality. He countered all our objections concerning the confirmed, incontestable facts with countless examples from different historical periods in which people succumbed to a collective psychosis of anxiety before a nonexistent danger . . . He spoke garrulously, nervously, as if he wished above all to persuade himself . . . Alas! Reality defeated him.[42]

Mazor described how, a day later, the "professor" was arrested in a roundup, and never seen again.

The presence of deception and disguise was woven into most narratives about the war. It was a great stumbling block and a challenge for writers. Only in January 1945, the German armies and SS were interrupted in their effort to hide all traces of their camps. What Generals Guderian and Jodl called after the war at Nuremberg "a masterpiece of concealment" was interrupted before it could be completed.[43]

In the USSR, secrecy continued to the end of the war and long afterward. As a victorious power they were able to maintain control over most official documents. But a major breach in the secrecy of the Soviet camps, with their huge numbers of prisoners, occurred in July 1941, when Stalin signed what is known as the Sikorski Pact. The pact was signed, under duress, shortly after Germany's invasion of the USSR. It permitted Poland to recruit an army of Polish soldiers inside the Soviet camps, then to leave the country via Iran and join Allied armies fighting in the West. This opened the way for a wave of new writings about the Soviet camp system.[44] Freed soldiers brought with them harrowing stories, and many were excellent writers. Most of them were convinced that the Soviet camps, with their huge numbers of prisoners, were an important variable in the conduct of the war. They were not just a political topic, or peripheral to the fighting of the Second World War; but made a major contribution to the war and its outcome. Stalin told Milovan Djilas, the Yugoslav writer and politician, "We opened up our penitentiaries and stuck everybody into the army. The Red Army is not ideal. The important thing is that it fights Germans . . . while the rest doesn't matter."[45] "Penitentiaries" here meant camps above all, and prisons.

In a short story set in Siberia, near the gold mining camp of Kolyma, the Russian writer Varlam Shalamov used a mountain, a bulldozer, and a ravine to tell a powerful story about deception and numbers. Shalamov was one of the finest Russian writers of the wartime period. Alexander Solzhenitsyn—who won the Nobel Prize for Literature in 1970—had great respect for him, and proposed that they collaborate in writing *The Gulag Archipelago* together. Shalamov declined because of ill health.

In Shalamov's story, a new American bulldozer, received under Roosevelt's Lend-Lease aid program, is used to explore a path on a forested mountain slope. Begun in 1941, the program sent trucks, machines, and American technology to the USSR. The prisoners decided to try out the American bulldozer with its gleaming new blade. They then make a discovery. A mountain had been laid bare and transformed into "a gigantic stage for a camp mystery play."

A grave, a mass prisoner grave, a stone pit stuffed full with unde-caying corpses was sliding down the side of the hill, revealing the secrets of Kolyma.

In Kolyma, bodies are not given over to earth, but to stone. Stone keeps secrets and reveals them. The permafrost keeps and reveals secrets. All of our loved ones who died in Kolyma, all those who were shot, beaten to death, sucked dry by starvation, can still be recognized even after tens of years. There were no gas furnaces in Kolyma. The corpses wait in stone, in the permafrost.

With my exhausted, tormented mind I tried to understand: How did there come to be such an enormous grave in this area? I am an old resident of Kolyma, and there hadn't been any gold mine here as far as I knew. But then I realized that I knew only a fragment of that world surrounded by a barbed-wire zone and guard towers that reminded one of the pages of tent-like Moscow architecture. Moscow's taller buildings are guard towers keeping watch over the city's prisoners. That's what those "buildings look like. And what served as models for Moscow architecture—the watchful towers of the Moscow Kremlin or the guard towers of the camps? . . . I realized that I knew only a small bit of that world, a pitifully small part. Much can be hidden in the folds of the mountain."[46]

Shalamov realizes that he doesn't know, and can't know, who is in this huge grave retained by permafrost. Who were they? How many? What numbers were involved? How did they die? The title "Lend-Lease" provides a clue. The American aid program to Russia began in 1941; the prisoners had not worked in the gold mines, they were probably transported to Kolyma during the 1942–45 war, but they might equally well be from the 1939–41 war, or from Stalin's repressions, the great purges and trials of the years 1937 and 1938. These possibilities merge together in the phrase "tens of years." Can they be kept separate? It is an open question. It strongly suggests we will never know the real demographics of the war.[47]

The narrator realizes he can grasp "only a pitifully small fragment" of this "mystery play." The small fragment is in stark contrast to the huge scale of the mountain, its ravines and forests. Gradually, the magnitude of what is hidden is revealed.[48]

Shalamov makes a point similar to that of Camus and Koestler: an individual can take in only the tiniest bits of reality. And he reinforces this with a powerful use of contrasts that evoke history, religion, mystery, geography, and the most basic elements of nature.

II
Carnivals

1

Black Magic

*I*t was a world of magic, of lights, performances, and music. There were crowds, and spoken words, and always magic: carnivals, flags, and pleasure. For many there were excursions in the countryside, familiar songs around a campfire, and adventure. Friendly groups and flirting. Hardship had been conquered, good times were ahead.

For others it was black magic. People disappeared. Relatives and friends vanished into thin air. A person, suspecting nothing, might be suddenly transported hundreds of miles to a distant city. Borders and frontiers lost their importance, lost their significance and slowly disappeared. There were many casualties but it was peace. Everywhere was good feeling, friendship among peoples and among nations. It was as simple as "getting on a bus." And there was the attraction to a force, a powerful, irresistible force, as if to a great magnet. Abroad, rewards were waiting, high positions, estates and fortunes ready for the taking. No, this was not war at all, it was magic, it was pleasure.

One would have to be a block of wood to remain unmoved. These were the carnivals, they were for everyone. Lights and music, drums, parades, and always flags, thousands of flags. The carnivals favor the night. They are opaque. These words are empty, hollow slogans . . . No, they are moving, and they inspire. They are a disguise, a frontal offensive. Words with one purpose, to hide. This is magic. This is the curtain.

* * *

A traveling "Variety Theater" arrives in Moscow at an unspecified time. An advertisement announces its arrival:

TODAY AND EVERY DAY
AT THE VARIETY THEATER
EXTRA ATTRACTION

IN ADDITION TO REGULAR PROGRAM
PROFESSOR WOLAND
AND HIS BLACK MAGIC ACT
ACCOMPANIED BY A FULL EXPOSE

The members of the theater troupe find lodgings in the city. Soon it succumbs to what is called "mass hypnosis." Unexplained events occur, accidents, and widespread hallucinations. There are strange cases of levitation. People are suddenly transported involuntarily over hundreds of miles of space, and can't explain how it happened. The leader of the Variety Theater, Woland, is a combination of magician, illusionist, and hypnotist.

The events described in the remarkable novel *The Master and Margarita* are all fictitious, yet it captured the atmosphere of magic in the USSR on the eve of the Second World War. The "first" Soviet war of 1939, when the USSR was allied with Germany, would soon begin. Mikhail Bulgakov's novel evoked the period with all its mystery and sinister threat.[1] *The Master and Margarita* was written over several years, when the cult of Stalin was at its height. The novel was never published during the author's lifetime; it appeared in print only in 1966, twenty-six years after the author's death in 1940. It was, however, one of the finest literary works written in Russian before war broke out in 1939.

A member of the traveling Variety Theater is named Behemoth. He is part human and part cat:

Ivan gasped, looked up and saw the hateful stranger in the distance. There was a third member of this company, who had appeared from heaven knows where: a tom cat, huge as a hog, black as pitch or a crow, and with a huge mustache, for all the world like a rakish cavalryman's. The trio marched off, the tom cat walking on his hind legs.

This description alone was probably enough to prevent publication of the novel. Stalin had a large mustache. Alexander Solzhenitsyn was arrested in 1945 for writing a phrase in a private letter, "the man with the mustache." The cat walks on his hind legs, like a human; Stalin was sometimes compared to a cat, for example in Bulat Okudzhava's song "Black Cat," written after Stalin's death.

The capital finds itself in the grip of "black magic" and collective psychosis. People are transformed into demons. Victims turn into tom cats. An investigation is called for. Events gripping the city become known as "The Woland Affair." The official press writes about "this strange case, which smacks of diabolic powers with an admixture of hypnotic tricks and obvious criminal elements . . ."

The novel is filled with unbelievable, violent events disguised as "magic." They can be explained only as a new kind of reality. There are countless disappearances. People are turned into demons and cats. Many simply vanish—no one knows where. Documents are forged. There is much madness. Some of the characters are put in "a famous psychiatric clinic." One chapter is titled ironically "Schizophrenia, as Said Before." People are run over by streetcars, not once but many times. A severed head bounces on the pavement. People die, others who don't die wonder why they are still alive. It is a time of numerous obituaries but the journalists who write them don't know what to say.

A recurrent motif in the novel is the loss of one's head. During a performance inside the Variety Theater, Woland says:

"This character bores me. What shall we do with him?" "Off with his head," someone said sternly in the gallery . . . "Off with his head. That's an idea! Behemoth!" he cried to the tom. "Action! Ein, zwei, drei!" And an unheard-of thing came to pass. The tom's black fur bristled and he gave off a soul-rending miaow. Then he gathered himself into a ball and, like a panther, sprang right up into his chest and thence upon his head. Growling, the tom sunk his plump paws into the thin, brushed-up hair of the master of ceremonies and, with a wild howl, twisted the head around twice and tore it off the heavy neck.

Two and a half thousand persons in the theater screamed in unison. Blood spurted in fountains from the torn arteries and flooded the shirt front and the dress coat. The headless body padded absurdly with its feet and sat down on the floor.

The tom cat gave the head to a helper, who raised it by the hair and showed it to the public. Then the tom commanded that the head be "put back on." This was done flawlessly. The traces of blood disappeared, the man was given a package of bank notes, and told to leave.

The graphic scene is cruel and brutal. It is treated in an ingenuous way, not exactly humorously but at the same time the pain is never stressed. Many people have their heads taken from them: "The guest returned, and reported that Room 120 had a new tenant. They had brought someone who kept asking that his head be given back to him." In one episode, a severed head bounces on the city's pavement. There is a serious discussion of the "theory" that when a head is severed, man's life ceases. Or is it only an illusion, a magic trick?

Bulgakov uses several devices that make the Variety Theater appear to merge with the greater city that surrounds it. The audience participates in the performances, shouts, shrieks, expresses approval and disapproval. When it is dissatisfied with a speech, or impatient, a man may shout from the gallery, "Off with his head." By extension the stage inside the theater becomes the "stage" of the city. For example, an ambulance is called to take away "the unfortunate master of ceremonies" who has lost his head, then had it reattached. "Incidentally, it was either then or a few moments earlier that the magician, together with his faded armchair, vanished from the stage. And we must add that the audience never noticed it, so absorbed it was in the extraordinary things on the stage."

Near the end of another spectacle: "The point is that a veritable babel broke loose in the Variety Theater after the final scene. Militiamen ran toward Sempleyarov's loge, the curious clambered up the barriers, there were infernal bursts of roaring laughter and wild shouts, drowned out by the golden jingling of the cymbals in the band.

"And the stage was suddenly empty. The swindler Fagot, along with the brazen tom Behemoth dissolved into thin air, vanished as utterly as the magician had vanished earlier, together with his faded armchair."

By vanishing and disappearing, by merging with the excited audience, the Variety Theater becomes the greater city. It becomes the capital, Moscow.

What is the meaning of the loss of heads? It is a motif that constantly recurs in the novel. Although it is treated with humor, without question it is a stylized depiction of terror under Stalin. The novel evokes the atmosphere of unexplained events and fictions of a society in the grip of "supernatural" forces, violent acts disguised as magic or "witchcraft." They are so widespread and numerous they can be explained only as a "new kind of reality." Several historians, Roy Medvedev and others, have insisted that Stalin never relied on force or fear alone, he preserved the trust of a large portion of the Soviet people. This was based on a high degree of manipulation, complete control of the media, and the frenzied transfer of officials from one place to another. It was impossible to know who was merely transferred, who was arrested, transported to a camp, or executed. The policy was deliberate, attested by countless memoirs about the period. People were unable to keep track—keep count—of family and friends.[2]

The tricks and sleights-of-hand that went into this "trust" of Stalin were endless. One startled British observer in Moscow happened to see Stalin emerge from a little side-door in the Kremlin wall, and ascend Lenin's mausoleum. No crowd was gathered. As disciplined troops thundered past, loudspeakers relayed amplified cheering to compensate for the complete absence of spectators.[3]

Andrei Sinyavski, the critic and essayist, wrote that "the main thing in *The Master and Margarita* is not these indirect or direct references to Stalin and to contemporary reality, rather it is the novel's atmosphere, shot through with Stalin's somber currents. It is the mass psychosis that has locked society in a vicious circle of denunciations, where the secret police, the prison, and the interrogations are presented as a sort of theater in imitation of Stalin's own theater of denunciations and repressions."[4]

According to Sinyavsky, Bulgakov was the one artist capable of depicting Stalin's "nocturnal" spirit, and who succeeded in creating a lasting monument to what was a unique epoch. Schematically, Stalin is described as Woland. His magic has two faces, light and dark. One half of his personality belongs to the bright light of day, when people rejoice, when buildings are built and parades take place. The principal business, however, is done at night. Stalin was always known for his late hours, and the meetings in his dacha that began only after midnight. Arrests, executions, political intrigues, and governmental sessions all took place mostly at night. In the person of Woland, Stalin appears as a unique artist in his "profession," and as an astounding conjuror. He is the one who orchestrates executions and show trials, a perfidious wizard towering over everyone in his eerie solitude of omnipotent, evil spirit.

The novel has episodes of fantasy that charm the reader. For example, a broom knocks on the door of Margarita, the novel's heroine and female protagonist. It dances on the floor, "with its bristles up. It beats a tattoo on the floor, kicked and pulled toward the window. Margarita squealed with joy and jumped astride it." The next chapter, "Flight," describes

Margarita's journey on the broom high over Moscow, at night, accompanied by birds. They fly over the countryside, on to "Satan's Grand Ball."

What is the relevance of *The Master and Margarita* to the Second World War? It must be remembered that it looks toward the first multiple invasion by the USSR against its neighbors in 1939–40, not the second Soviet war or the so-called "Great Patriotic War" that started only on June 22, 1941. The novel was written in the last years of the 1930s, and describes a society gripped by manipulation, unexplained events, fictions, rumors, and gossip. In 1939 the very real invasions were also disguised by secret provisions of the Hitler-Stalin Pact, cloaked in disguise and euphemisms. "War" was officially denied. In terms developed by Bulgakov, the events were a potent combination of magic and theater. Countries were not "conquered" or "invaded" but bloodlessly "annexed" without need of military invasion, as if by supernatural power.

The late 1930s in the USSR were a time of what has been called "High Stalinism." "In the minds of millions," Ilya Ehrenburg wrote, "Stalin was transformed into a mythical demigod; everyone trembled as they said his name." The phrase "mythical demigod" was only partly rhetorical. Medvedev and others wrote of the "deification" of Stalin:

> The social consciousness of the people took on elements of religious psychology: illusions, autosuggestion, the inability to think critically, intolerance toward dissidents, and fanaticism . . . Not conscious discipline but blind faith in Stalin was required. Like every cult, this one tended to transform the Communist party into an ecclesiastical organization, with a sharp distinction between ordinary people and leader-priests headed by their infallible pope.[5]

It took the form of gigantism. A single man became associated with the landscape of Russia, its mountains and terrain. Thousands of factories and firms were named for Stalin, and cities: Stalinsk, Stalino, Stalinir, Stalingrad, Stalinbad, Stalinkan, Stalinovarosh—the variants are countless.

The style of most writings contemporary with *The Master and Margarita* was panegyrical. For example:

> On his affectionate face something else could be read:
> "We are as strong as a rock, as a cliff,
> We are an unshakable force,

We are the embodiment of liberty, humanism, beauty."[6]

Or:

Everybody knows his name
Even the wind whispers it,
Light reflects from it—
Stalin.[7]

Almost all the literary works reflecting the cult of Stalin are crude flattery. They have little literary interest and are usually pompous, over-decorated, cold. This is why Bulgakov's *Master and Margarita* stands out. There is awe for Woland, and Bulgakov successfully captures it in his novel. It is the whispered awe for a powerful magician whose tricks work and cannot be understood. The novel skillfully mixes both parody and realism: parody in the two personages of Behemoth and Woland—who had models in contemporary life—realism in the loss of heads and descriptions of contemporary life.

On the eve of the multiple invasions in 1939, the atmosphere in Moscow was a combination of fear and mobilization. For eight years there had been a "Socialist Offensive" within the country with rules of "military" operations and declared "battlefronts." A network of camps, penal colonies, and special settlements called *spetsposeleniia* enmeshed the country. Roy Medvedev observed that expansion was presented in political and social, or class, terminology, and expansion abroad was based on methods already well developed inside the country.

On the day of the first Soviet invasion, September 17, 1939, some two hundred Russian writers attended a meeting of the Moscow chapter of the Union of Soviet writers. The meeting was described the next day in *Pravda,* which can still be read. Writers congratulated the Red Army on their annihilation of the Polish state—that is, the half that remained after the Nazi invasion of the Western half two weeks earlier. The same issue of *Pravda* contained a poem by Nikolai Aseev, "Fully Erect,"[8] which boasted that now "Only crumbs remained of Poland." In *Pravda* two days later, Margarita Aliger—subsequently known for poems about the defense of Leningrad—published a passionate poem titled "September 17, 1939" expressing her deeply held conviction that Poland should perish.

The September 19 issue of *Pravda* contained as many as thirtynine articles, poems, stories, and testimonials praising the Soviet invasions. A massive, ongoing literary campaign was launched to justify them. Probably it was the most "literary" act of war of the entire period 1939–45. The same writers who were enlisted to denounce Poland in September 1939, wrote comparable stories and poems a few months later denouncing Finland and the three Baltic countries. They all approved of the Hitler-Stalin Pact, without mentioning the secret protocols. The list of writers who eulogized the multiple invasions reads like a Who's Who of the Soviet literary establishment: Alexander Tvardovsky, Margarita Aliger, Valentin Kataev ("Travel Notes"), Samuil Marshak, Viktor Gusev, Yevgeni Dolmatovsky, Mikhail Zhivov, Maksim Rylskii, V. Pertsov, Vasili LebedevKumach, K. Potapov, Aleksander Prokofiev, Nikolai Tikhonov, Ilya Selvinsky, Wanda Wasilewska, Aseev, Kirsanov, and Mikhail Isakovsky.

In this outpouring of literary or quasi-literary works, a number of poems evoked "holy hatred" of small neighboring countries, described with scorn and spite. "Holy hatred" had been used before, in campaigns to justify xenophobia.[9]

The mobilization seemed complete. The country was flooded with works of assent. If there was a common theme, it was that there was no "war," the action was "friendship," a neighbor's "invitation," "liberation," anything but war or hostile invasion.

Other metaphors were evoked to explain these multiple "annexations." One was magnetic attraction:

The land calls to itself,
    attracting the hearts of people.
The land of work,
    the country-magnet.
And three countries have
    come close
to the magnet of the world—
    To Stalin.

—Semen Kirsanov[10]

There is no trace here of the humor, parody, or critical spirit of *The Master and Margarita*. But the aura of hyperbole and magic continued.

Later events in this first "war" were tricks worthy of Woland's Variety Theater. Synchronized elections in the three Baltic countries resulted in 92.8 percent, 97.8 percent, and 99.19 percent communist majorities. As the newly appointed legislatures met, armed NKVD guards ringed parliament buildings and lined the inside corridors. The next official act of signing was not an act of surrender but of "Friendship." An Estonian writer—a Surrealist named Semper—was present as a newly elected member of parliament, and sarcastically called it "the finest piece of fiction ever written by the Estonian people."[11]

After 1945, Soviet censors tried to obliterate references to these invasions, and remove them from memory. Books were altered or destroyed. Attention was focused instead on a second war that began on June 22, 1941, the so-called "Great Patriotic War." Soviet literature about the early war years was so heavily censored that the writings must be considered a product of compulsion, a broken genre. The attempt to disguise and draw a curtain over the invasions was so complete that they almost disappeared from the written record. One work stands out, however, that miraculously skirted the razor-edge of parody and truthfulness to the time. It succeeded in combining magic with mystery, tricks and disappearances with invisible threat: *The Master and Margarita*.

2

A "Stage-Prop World"

Territorial expansion was one of the great forces let loose during the Second World War. Programs for expansion began well before 1939, and were immensely popular. They were often celebrated in a carnival-like atmosphere. Spectacles and light shows drew enormous crowds.

The end of the war brought an abrupt about-face. After 1945, territorial expansion was discredited both as an aspiration and as a literary theme. A poet wrote after the war:

> a murderous power is held by the Zeitgeist
> that is the devil of fashion the devil of passing time
> the epoch's clock stops—the gods go down to the bottom[12]

But before 1939, expansion was one of the great popular enthusiasms. Almost all European countries had dreams of expansion, and they exerted great patriotic appeal. Few leaders or political parties could afford to ignore them. The depth of their appeal at the time posed a dilemma for writers. In most countries they lent their talents to the campaigns of national expansion.

One of the earliest countries to stage mass spectacles with an expansionist theme was the Italy of Mussolini. A writer noted that Italian fascism was the first movement to create a military liturgy, a folklore, and even a style of dress.[13] In Mussolini's Italy the ancient Roman Empire was revived, called *romanita*; not only in Italy but throughout Europe students in schools were taught to admire the empire of ancient Rome. It became a historical benchmark for the successful state. With its praise for the expansion of empire under Augustus, Virgil's *Aeneid* was held up as a model. The Roman example gave prestige to most contemporary notions of empire.

In Italy, empire was celebrated above all as carnival. Ceremonies lasted the entire day. Businesses were closed, Mussolini reviewed youth and athletic groups, and at night Rome was transformed: "Ruins of the past were floodlighted to enclose a modern fantasy of white pillars and gilded symbols of fascism . . . There were illuminated fountains, huge pylons spouting flames and everywhere flags without end and banners." Martial arias were played from operas by Bellini and Verdi. A favorite was Rossini's rousing "William Tell Overture."[14] Mussolini gave speeches from the balcony of the Palazzo Venezia that schoolchildren were required to learn by heart. When the Italian Army conquered Ethiopia in 1936, Mussolini spoke to a huge crowd from his balcony and "declared" the new fascist empire. He shouted to them, "Are you worthy of it?" The crowd roared back, "Yes!" The king, Victor Emmanuel III, assumed the title emperor of Ethiopia. But no one missed the point that Mussolini was playing the role of a new Augustus.[15]

The center of Rome was demolished to make way for parades. Whole historic neighborhoods, with narrow streets and old buildings, were gutted in the space of a year to make a wide thoroughfare. This was the new "Master Plan" to make Rome the essence of "the Modern."[16] Crowds numbering more than 100,000 could walk the three miles through the center of the city, from the Colosseum past the Via dell'Impero to Piazza Venezia. Many new buildings appeared with Latin plaques boasting of "the new Fascist Empire." Fascist monuments and architecture celebrating Mussolini's empire can still be seen throughout Italy. Hitler visited Rome in 1936, Mussolini visited Berlin in 1937; both visits were accompanied by massive crowds and fanfare. When Mussolini returned to Italy, he introduced the "goose step" march.

The writer Umberto Eco has argued that Italian Fascism was basically hollow. It was a collage, a tangle of contradictions. What it had to offer was rhetoric, rhetoric that excited the populace, shows that pleased, entertained, and provided employment. The impact of Italian Fascism never went beyond its borders except for Ethiopia and, briefly, Greece. Its greatest contribution was the success of its carnivals, rituals, and ceremonies.[17]

In Germany, similar "rallies" and carnivals mobilized even larger crowds, literally transforming them. They succeeded in turning civilians, workers, and soldiers into a lethal force that could be sent far beyond the country's borders. What was the meaning of the rallies in Nuremberg? Those who participated were often unable to answer the question, at a loss for words. Descriptions invariably returned to the need to be there— to experience the rallies at first hand—in order to say what they were about. Above all they were a shared experience, a powerful instrument for mobilizing society.

Many German writers and artists left Germany during the early years of the Nazi regime and lived abroad. Klaus Mann, older son of Thomas Mann, left for exile in southern France, and wrote a sharply critical letter to the well-known poet Gottfried Benn, an early supporter of the Nazi regime. Benn was a respected older writer and physician who fought in World War I, and remained in Germany. Benn replied to Klaus Mann with an open letter, "Answer to the Literary Emigrants"[18], asserting that the exiles had no right to criticize the regime because they did not have the "dynamic experience" of the rallies. Benn's letter was widely circulated and reprinted.

For Benn, it was not ideas or even ideology that compelled assent, but the experience of rallies and parades: their magic, lights, and darkness, taking part in the spectacles and merging with the huge crowds. "Lost is the individual," he wrote. "Down with the ego."

Hostile to much modern art, nevertheless the Nazis were innovators: music, lights, architectural setting or stage, choreographed movement, all came together, divisions between the artistic genres disappeared. It seemed to be the synthesis of art forms advocated earlier by Wagner in his tract "The Art Work of the Future," the "total work" to encompass all arts called the *Gesamtkunstwerk*. The massive rallies left a deep imprint on everyone present.

The historian Joachim Fest noted that they had "a special intimate character. Their striking symbol was the dome of lights: walls of magic and light against the dark, threatening outside world."[19] Even foreign visitors were impressed. Sir Neville Henderson described the effect of massed searchlight beams as "a cathedral of ice." One hundred and thirty sharply defined searchlights were placed at intervals of forty feet, visible to a height of twenty to twenty-five thousand feet, then merging in a general glow. "The feeling was of a vast room, with the beams serving as mighty pillars of infinitely high outer walls."

The French writers Robert Brasillach and Drieu la Rochelle traveled to Germany to take part in the rallies, and recorded their vivid impressions. The right-wing French writer Alphonse de Chateaubriant was dazzled.[20] A young Swedish exchange student, guest of a German Lutheran pastor, attended a rally, and wrote later "I had never seen anything like this eruption of immense energy"—this was sixteen-year-old Ingmar Bergman who later became the famous filmmaker and director. "For many years," he wrote, "I was on Hitler's side, delighted by his successes and saddened by his defeats." After 1945, when he learned about Hitler's camps, he changed his mind.[21]

William Shirer, American correspondent for the Columbia Broadcasting System, described a rally in Nuremberg: "I'm beginning to comprehend, I think, some of the reasons for Hitler's astounding success. Borrowing a chapter from the Roman church, he is restoring pageantry and color and mysticism to the drab lives of twentiethcentury Germans. This morning's opening meeting in the Luitpold Hall on the outskirts of Nuremberg was more than a gorgeous show; it also had something of the mysticism and religious fervor of an Easter or Christmas Mass in a great Gothic cathedral. The hall was a sea of brightly colored flags. Even Hitler's arrival was made dramatic. The band stopped playing. There was a hush over the thirty thousand people packed in the hall. Then the band struck up the *Badenweiler March,* a very catchy tune . . ."[22]

Shirer went on to describe how the critical faculty was swept away at such moments. Every lie was "accepted as high truth itself." It was a crucial point. In the conflict taking place between mass communication and disguise, between propaganda and secrecy, the rallies were intended to sweep away skepticism or criticism and create a new reality.

The rallies became immensely popular among ordinary German citizens. Holidays were declared, participants were caught up in the organized events. Whole families journeyed for miles to attend them. Festive parades with marching bands were staged in Nuremberg, Munich, Weimar, and other German cities. Young people were organized to take part in outdoor excursions, hiked together, and sang songs—the *Wandervogel Lieder*—around campfires.[23] A large number of German memoirs looked back on the years of the 1930s as the happiest of their lives, especially if they were years of childhood and youth. Much pleasure was to be had, carnivals, ceremonies, and outdoor activities masking much of the police brutality of the times, and the use of camps for political opponents.

Leni Riefenstahl's film *The Triumph of the Will* provides a vivid introduction to the rallies in Nuremberg, especially their sinister side. It has been called one of the most powerful and most repulsive films ever made. The techniques used in the film and the rallies were similar. Comparable devices can be found in literature and the other arts. The film demonstrates how the rallies were not neutral entertainments in time of peace—unlike the Italian parades—but created an omnipresent enemy. They glorified expansion in space, colonization, and power.

One episode in Riefenstahl's film resembles a religious litany. Some two hundred thousand participants are massed together, and a clear voice rings out:

"Comrade, where do you come from?"

The German word for "to come from" had the literal meaning "to stem from," as if from the soil.[24]

At a distance another voice rings out: "From Silesia." The same sequence is repeated with variations:

"Comrade, where do you come from?"
"From the Danube."
"And you, comrade, where do you come from?"
"From the Black Forest."
"Comrade, where do you come from?"
"From Koenigsberg."
"And you, comrade, where do you come from?"
"From Pomerania."

The German verb is repeated, bringing with it associations of origin, birth, and soil. By means of voices originating in different positions in space a large portion of Europe is brought within the compass of the stadium and rally area. In the sequence of place names there is a clear progression toward the East.

A symbol, and object, reinforcing the soil metaphor was the spade. Groups of men in formation carried not rifles but spades, responding to commands of "Shoulder spade!" and "Down spade!" With the command, Reifenstahl's lens zoomed onto the spade, magnifying it where it was sunk in the earth between the leather boots of the man holding it, the shaft resembling a tree trunk. These were symbols of territory and colonization, the soil metaphor effectively obliterating frontiers on a map.

In the course of the rally, darkness fell. Vivid effects were created by the movement of searchlights, flags—some twenty-one thousand of them— and other illuminated symbols. The rally then became a tour de force of contrasting light and darkness. Searchlights poked holes in the night, playing at length on standards and insignia. There was much shaking of hands, saluting, pledges of loyalty, ceremonial transfer of insignia ("I am handing you the new insignia"), consecration of flags by burying a hand in the cloth and swearing an oath.

The rallies were repeated in other German cities, and continued their powerful effect on participants. All this took place at "home" during peace, but through evocative symbols they were associated with expansion. Many German writers, philosophers, even art critics stressed an act of contemplation that contained seeds of violence. Today these writings seem to be forms of kitsch, but combined with the "magic" of the rallies they exerted a powerful appeal. Writing about landscape, for example, Ludwig Clauss claimed that "The Nordic soul has an innate urge to push on into the distance." In "What is German in the German Arts," Kurt Karl Eberlein wrote: "German art is homeland and homesickness . . . It is the language of the homeland even in an alien atmosphere." Eberlein described the typical room of a German house, and childhood, in these terms: "Anyone who knows this German room image knows what I mean. The soldier—not just the painter or tourist—carries images of his childhood and what is familiar to him into the trenches and onto foreign territory."[25]

Despite the simplicity of these notions they referred to the same drive toward expansion vividly evoked in the Nuremburg rallies. Erik Erikson thought that "*Lebensraum* had an essentially magic meaning." Hugh Trevor-Roper wrote that expansion and colonization in the East "was the real message of Nazism. It is the burden of *Mein Kampf*."[26] Frontiers were superficial, they could be easily conjured away as if by magic. The notion of "Greater Germany" (*Grossdeutschland)* could be expanded like an accordion.

3

The Stage Moves Abroad

Thomas Mann warned his compatriots that the earlier German Romanticism had a sinister side. With great prescience he warned that it led to self-absorption, the cult of subjective feeling or *Sehnsucht*, and xenophobia. These were accompanied by an apocalyptic strain, self-pity, and the abdication of a sense of responsibility.[27]

The projection of emotions against a landscape and the world of nature was a regular feature of European Romanticism. It was a common device and stockintrade, sometimes called "the pathetic fallacy." For example the German Romantic writer Ludwig Tieck (1773–1853) anticipated by many years the subjective use of landscape by the National Socialists in his novel *Franz Sternbald's Wanderings*. A young man passes through a dense forest, "All the trees seem to call after him, and apparitions to emerge from behind every bush, seeking to detain him . . . He reels from one memory to another and loses himself in a labyrinth of strange feelings . . . Am I mad, or what is happening to this foolish heart? What invisible hand plucks all the strings of my being?"[28]

Nature seems to echo human emotions. In an early form we find the fusion between the individual and surrounding space that characterized the Nuremburg rallies. It was carried further and new elements were added, self-absorption, and indoctrination. Projection against surroundings became the wholesale denial of those surroundings; a gap of willed ignorance opened between a person and the outer world.[29]

Official directives in 1939 granted impunity to all Germans living in the East. In a speech by Hitler on August 22, 1939, his military commanders were told to "close their hearts to pity and act brutally, with the greatest harshness." Another of the war's secrets, revealed only after 1945, was Hitler's order (*Fuehrerbefehl*) to Heydrich in 1939 on "social policy." Civilians under martial law were considered subhuman, and under deliberate attack. Shootings began immediately, and what has been called "the culture of massacre."[30]

Many of the writings by Germans who took part in the invasions are purple prose. The authors often lack a sense of where they are, even in what country. Everything is seen through a subjective prism.

In one example it is Russia, but it could be Germany or almost anywhere else:

Our uniforms grew darker as the earth darkened, almost as if by magic, and our footsteps seemed to be setting the rhythm of the whole mysterious universe. The blackness of night was spreading behind us, and we fell silent, hushed by the respect which immensity imposes on simple men. Our group of soldiers, members of an army hated throughout the world, was seized by an indefinable emotion . . . The favorite song of the SS rose up like a hymn to the earth, offered to men:

So wide the brown heath goes,
All that there is belongs to us . . .
Then darkness engulfed us, a darkness that seemed made for nothing more than watching over us.[31]

The passage expresses pleasure and even relish in the hatred of others. The writer projects his feelings outward, nonsubjective reality dissolving and disappearing. The point of view is highly sentimentalized. It is a type of rhetorical kitsch, nonetheless it has some power.[32]

At the age of fifty-five the writer and physician Gottfried Benn was called up for the invasion of Poland. He saw the invasion in terms of the Nuremberg rallies: the progression from the one to the other was almost seamless. At this point in his life, however, he was older than most soldiers, and more critical. For him the invasion was not serious enough: "Here, too, universal unreality, a sense of two-dimensionality, a stage-prop world . . . All this creates a spacefilling impression of individual expansion . . . What prevailed here was spaceshamming: pontoon bridge crossings, blasts about to go off."[33] Benn was struck by the subjectivity and irrationality in the German military effort. It was "magic" and like a fairy tale. Yet it was war. "Here, too," Benn wrote of his barracks, "sheer dross in concept and form; primary rain magic, celebrating nocturnal torch fumes."

As he walked around the garrison blocks he detected the presence of too many dreams and illusions. He observed the younger lieutenants, products of the Hitler Youth Movement; he was astonished at their limited mental baggage. "They have received an education whose essence was the systematic uprooting of any mental and moral content of life from books and actions, and the substitution of Ostrogothic princes, daggers, and hay-mows to spend the night in after a forced march." As fighting soldiers, however, they were well trained.

Everywhere Benn saw gullibility: "The masses go on believing their leaders' twaddle . . . High and low, general and soldier on K.P. make a mystical totality of fools, a prelogical collective of gullibles. Something doubtlessly very Germanic and centrally explicable only in this ethnologic sense." Gottfried Benn's later writing rises above the effusions and "twaddle" of other authors as well as his own earlier misplaced enthusiasm. He retained a critical sense; satire is present in his tone, and the selection of metaphors.

Satire was perhaps the only genre that produced good writing about the German invasions. Another older writer, Ernst Juenger, traveled in the wake of the invading Panzer army in Lorraine in 1940, and left vivid descriptions of the German staff feasting in French chateaux as they made their way toward Paris. The chateau of the LaRochefoucaulds was in their path. Juenger and other German officers dined outdoors by candlelight, with a full complement of the oldest wines from the LaRochefoucaulds' cellars. They organized a tasting session.

Juenger noticed the litter of empty wine bottles on the road, one bottle for each step. He remarked, "This *debauche* is doubtless part of our tradition of campaigns in France. All the invasions by Germanic armies were accompanied by raids like those of the gods in the *Edda*."[34] This was soft, or very ambivalent, satire. The comparison with Scandinavian gods was sentimental, and wishful self-glorification.

Hans Habe wrote more pointed descriptions in *A Thousand Shall Fall* (1942). A Swiss writer, Habe fought to defend France with an international regiment of volunteers. He was taken prisoner and worked as interpreter for the German Army occupying Lorraine. His satirical descriptions of looting are real acts of literature. All the shops selling luxury goods in Nancy were stripped of their contents. The wives of German officers were particularly rapacious, and after several weeks a declaration from Berlin ordered all officers' wives to stay behind in Germany.

Habe's description of the struggles inside a store selling silks is excellent as red-faced German officers come to blows with each other over the merchandise.[35] Similar scenes of the passionate pursuit of plunder are described with a sharp eye and the satirist's use of telling detail. The objects of pursuit were perfume, leather goods, soaps, luxury clothing, ladies' wristwatches, chocolate in all forms, and prostitutes, long lines of waiting German soldiers forming on the sidewalks. It was a war for booty and wealth—war as a type of utopia.

In the spring and summer of 1942, Panzer armies of Operation Blue went east toward Stalingrad. With the spring weather and new equipment, morale had improved. They bypassed Stalingrad, advancing south toward Rostov and the Caucasus. Just beyond the horizon—they were certain—was oil. The literature describing this campaign is euphoric, intoxicated, the advance seemed limitless. "As far as the eye can see," wrote Clemens Podewils, war correspondent attached to the Sixth German Army, "armored vehicles and half-tracks are rolling over the steppe, pennants float in the shimmering afternoon air." General Paulus was ordered to send motorized groups down the Volga to the Caspian Sea. Field Marshal List was to seize the whole eastern border of the Black Sea and the rest of the Caucasus. Writers who went on these campaigns used purple prose, drenched in enthusiasm and sentiment.[36]

One writer who looked critically at the eastern campaigns was Theodor Plievier. Hostile to the Nazis, skilled at characterization, he had a talent for describing panoramic scenes that combined horror with mordant parody. Like Benn he stressed the unreality in the minds of the characters he describes. In his novel *Moscow,* he satirizes a fictional "General Bomelburg" who gives an impassioned speech to his German troops deep inside Russia, at the outskirts of Moscow. They are fighting, he tells them, "for Greater Germany . . . Our own towns and villages are at stake."

In Plievier's novel *Stalingrad* he explored further the theme of subjective space, And the "defense" of a "Greater Germany" that was far—very far—from Germany. A soldier asks a general: "Must we defend the fatherland on the Oskol, on the Don, on the Volga?" Another soldier reflects: "They had intended to go much farther, to the Ganges, on forever."[37]

In a visionary passage of his novel Plievier writes:

The express train races along without ties or rails, and you, general, and I, also a general—both of us are nothing but connecting rods, universal joints, crankshafts, part and parcel of the screeching steel . . . And the vehicle is thundering along at full speed—past trees, telegraph poles, butts of houses, bleeding torsos, men with bandaged heads, suicides, women with hands clapped over tear-stained faces . . . and we ride and do not know where we are riding, what we are riding over, what is shrieking so loudly under the rims of our wheels. The Fuehrer sits in the cab and cannot see, for the windshield has been made opaque by snow, dirt, bones, and the coagulated blood of the columns that gave one shriek of horror before they were run down. The Fuehrer drives and you, general, and I, a general, know nothing, we see nothing, we are only rolling wheels crushing men and horses and steel beneath us.

This is no nightmare. It is reality.

According to Plievier the war was a form of "self-induced madness, a mass psychosis unique in history." The magic and propaganda that accompanied the German Army was a theatrical "show," "an extravagance and a Herculean jest, a procession with fireworks, hunts, and human sacrifices, a gory sightseeing tour through many countries, a Ship of Fools setting out for the unknown under an imbecile captain."

The ultimate German stage set was the East.

4

The Great Projective Screen: The Globe

Territorial expansion was one of the most uncontrolled forces of the Second World War. The number of works that praised national expansion was great, and the magic of populist appeals, of self-flattery, produced widespread assent. Their effects were overpowering; few writers were able to resist the appeal during the war itself.

Expansion was a major motive behind the protocols of the Hitler-Stalin Pact that redrew maps of Europe, the Near East, Asia, and Africa. The Soviet invasions of 1939–40 were clearly expansionist, praised by the more than two hundred Russian writers who gave enthusiastic support in 1939.[38]

But the Allied countries, too, had aspirations toward expansion. Each had a presence abroad, and historical precedents to follow. It is well known that Churchill and Roosevelt had very different views about the future of the British empire. On the other hand Germany, Japan, and Italy all believed that the British Empire was old-fashioned, weak, a product of another century and no longer viable; as it crumbled, parts of it were destined to fall into their hands.

A country did not need to be large in order to have aspirations to expansion. Many had potent myths about places with roots deep in history, or the sense of a broad landscape with space woven into its culture. In the eyes of ordinary, peace-loving people steeped in these myths, they appeared natural and unquestioned. Some form of territorial expansion was viewed as a birthright. For example, in the 1930s, the Polish slogan "from sea to sea"—*od morza do morza,* from the Baltic to the Black Sea—was invoked by nationalists. One of the smallest countries of all, Albania, seized on the outbreak of war as a pretext for expansion, and attempted to reclaim what once belonged to the Ottoman Empire. A writer observed an armed Albanian band crossing a frontier in 1939 intending "to fix old border lines between Crna Gora and Sultan Hamid's territory of old."[13] Space was intimately tied to history and religion—to language, culture, ethnicity—and had multiple identities. One town often had several names in different languages. The borders existing in men's minds often contradicted those drawn on maps.

Writers who tried to resist the prevailing current of enthusiasm for territorial expansion had a thankless task. They could be attacked easily for lack of patriotism—or worse. Public sentiment put great pressure on writers. Rules governing what journalists could write were rigorously enforced, although readers were usually unaware of them. The war years were littered with confiscated manuscripts; sometimes of high quality, for one reason or another they went against the grain.

Parody or humor remained the writer's best weapon but it required a delicate balancing act. *The Master and Margarita* is a case in point, it was only published in Russian in 1966–67 well after the author's death. It would seem that the Italian writer Curzio Malaparte had a real possibility of publishing his parody *Kaputt* during the war itself. The book was completed by 1943, he was accredited with the newspaper *Corriere della Sera,* and was once friendly with Mussolini. But his manuscript was seized by the Gestapo, he was thrown in jail. Theodore Plievier's novels *Moscow* and *Stalingrad* were not published in Nazi Germany. He was an exile, and at the time of the battle of Stalingrad was in Alma Ata in the USSR.

Two novels in English show the difficulties in writing about the theme of expansion. Pearl Buck, winner of the Nobel Prize for Literature in 1938, criticized British imperial expansion in her novel *The Promise* (1942). She described a British officer who loses his platoon in the Burmese jungle and encounters a young Chinese nurse. They are able to converse in English. Their discussion is an exploration of conflicts and misunderstandings:

> She heard him say, "We have a responsibility to this country." When he said the word "responsibility," he lifted his head and looked over the greenness of Burma, through which the road cleft like a silver sword.

> "Why," she asked, "why do you feel responsible for this country?"

> "Because," he said soberly, "it is part of the Empire."

"But why the Empire?" she persisted. "Why not let these people have their own country to hold and to rule?"

"One cannot simply throw down a responsibility," he said gravely.

"One has to fulfill it."[41]

The British soldier argues earnestly and the discussion becomes a study in incomprehension. Each of the two young people represents a defeated army, each tries to extract a meaning for the future. For this critical book, Pearl Buck received many vitriolic letters from her English readers.

A large portion of Norman Mailer's novel *The Naked and the Dead*, before its conclusion, is devoted to an American Army unit crossing a fictitious snowcapped mountain, Mount Anaka. [42] It overlooks the Pacific, lacks specific, concrete features and is allegorical. Two of the novel's main characters, Cummings and Croft, become obsessed by the mountain. The American unit covers endless terrain trying to cross it. In an interview about his book, Mailer explained that this expedition expressed his criticism of a war he thought was going on and on needlessly, one conquest leading to another.[43] Very few readers understood Mailer's intentions or applauded them.

All agreed that the forces for expansion had extraordinary power. At a time when balance was needed, or criticism, it was usually prohibited. Some of the most original works used parody or satire, but as long as dreams of empire captured popular sentiment, especially during the war itself, parody met an uncertain welcome.

Of all the countries taking part in the Second World War, it was probably Japan that had the most potent mythology justifying expansion. Large outdoor ceremonies dramatized the emperor's mythical genealogy. His divine ancestor was the sun goddess. By a powerful metaphor the emperor's genealogy was projected outward onto much of the world. The phrase *Hakko ichiu* meant literally "eight corners of the world, one roof" or "everyone under one roof." The emperor was at the apex of the roof. According to the mythological worldview, the Japanese empire would create a new world order with "the entire world under one roof." The world was a single "family," the emperor its patriarch. The "blood of the Yamato race" was to be "planted in the soil" of most of East Asia.[44] As Japanese Imperial armies advanced, they were accompanied by this mythology; portable shrines were carried just behind the front, and set up for daily ceremonies.

A talented writer, Hanama Tasaki, described one of the most impressive Japanese ceremonies in his novel *Long the Imperial Way.* The ceremony, called "Rededication," celebrated the emperor's birthday. The sun was the emperor. As it slowly rose above the horizon at dawn, the ceremony became a moving celebration of space. Tasaki presented this ceremony in all its solemnity. Soldiers—spotlessly dressed—were massed in formation on the deck of an aircraft carrier in the South China Sea. Filled with tense anticipation, they expected to witness a divine event.

The first tinge of gold was showing in the eastern sky, and in the patch of light which slowly materialized on the ocean's surface, the men could now see the motion of the unending rollers . . . "Fix bayonets!" the Battalion Commander ordered in a low voice, and the soldiers removed the shining bayonets from the sheaths hanging from their hips, and attached them to the tips of their rifles. The major and the other officers drew their long swords from their scabbards and held them against their shoulders . . . The upper rim of the rising sun was now fully visible, and the gold which shone seemed to be living and vibrant with the excitement of the moment.

"Present arms!" the Battalion Commander called in a voice in a voice which sounded tense and suffocating, like the ultimate and total voice of the living. The soldiers raised their bayoneted rifles and guns in precise unison, and the officers lowered their swords with a flourish to their sides. The eastern horizon was now in its full glory as the sun stood poised and almost unmoving on the horizon's rim for one moment, as if in answer to the troops' salute. Then with a last flourish of its mighty, golden rays, which reached out in answer across the ocean surface to the saluting men, it disengaged itself from the horizon and started on its inevitable journey across the sky.[45]

The emotions of the men watching the spectacle were profound awe and humility. Their "very being seemed to have melted into the powerfully embracing radiance of their surroundings." Moving speeches were made, the soldiers shouted in unison *"Tenno Heika Banzai!"* and rifles, decorated with the imperial chrysanthemum, were raised in the air.

The scene is described with much lyricism and solemnity, almost too much. Indeed it is deliberately inflated by the novelist. They are in the South China Sea, and Tokyo is a thousand miles away in a straight line to the north. Yet they are worshipping the emperor not in the north but in the east.

An element of doubt is introduced. A recruit asks, "Honorable Squad Leader, why is it that when worshiping the Emperor's Palace, we always face eastward no matter where we are, not northward?" Simple uneducated soldiers had noticed the contradiction, they were saluting the emperor in the wrong part of the world. The discussion that follows is skillful parody and undercuts the grandiose emotions of the rising sun ceremony. The questioning of divine mythology by corporals and privates becomes humorous, then hilarious. What were they doing there? No one could explain. For a brief moment on the South China Sea the imperial mythology collapsed.[46]

* * *

When encountering these works, the postwar reader confronts a perennial problem. An older generation passionately held beliefs that a succeeding generation rejects with equal passion. When the reader encounters lavish ceremonies glorifying expansion, and the euphoria accompanying them, they seem like science fiction, or they might be episodes from Charles MacKay's popular nineteenthcentury classic *History of Popular Delusions and the Madness of Crowds.*[47]

Such delusions appear unreal, but they exerted passionate allegiance. Many people believed during the early war years that they were not at "war" in a pejorative sense at all. They were embarked toward a new and better epoch. They had received invitations to utopia; vaguely imagined areas of the map, and distant parts of the world, were theirs for the taking. They were launched on an enterprise of magic and carnivals, of pleasure and intoxication, of euphoria, exaltation, and awe.

III
The Firestorm

1

"The Most Inhospitable Place on Earth"

The firestorm at the front was intended to destroy an enemy armed force, and to put a sudden stop to all human activity, all communication. A successful front created a place of destruction where no life was possible, no perception, no observation. To stop the firestorm and bring the front to a halt was of overwhelming importance but often it was impossible.

Massed cannons were placed so closely to one another that they almost touched, and they could lay down a field of fire in which no one could possibly survive. The firestorm was also intended to create fear and panic. Dive-bombing Stukas with high-pitched sirens were calculated to create fear, and the horses often near the front would stampede wildly.

Even when soldiers were not physically present the front could create collective panic. German soldiers coined the term "Panzerschreck" for the fear in Allied armies caused by their Panzer tanks. After interviewing Allied prisoners of war in Africa, Rommel bragged he had won a "moral victory" even before a battle began because of the Allies' fear of his Panzer tanks.

The front was a site for the constant fabrication of myths. The military created their own myths in the attempt to influence motivation and morale. The civilian media followed the front at a distance, filtering it through censorship and accounts by the correspondents who created myths in turn. Many fictions about the firestorm lingered long after the conclusion of the war: about the superiority of some advanced weapons, about morale, about training, and the fighting qualities of armies, about strategies.

Some of the long-lasting myths continue to be repeated into the twenty-first century, and one among many was that the front was a place of "blind force." Yet the quest for information, and the need for intelligence at the front, were always crucial, and never ceased. The great need was for eyes, ears, "tongues," precise observations communicated with words or any means available: by accurate coordinates, aerial photography, radio, or code. The front was not a place of blind force but of both hiding and discovery: to see over it, past it, or behind it, from above or from below— the front was one of the most important "battles" of all. The firestorm was a duel, and the array of weapons for fighting it was countless.

* * *

"Take cover in the houses! . . ." No one knew who had cried out. We obeyed mechanically. I slipped under a gate at the corner of the square and the rue Margraine. At the same moment the German tanks turned into the narrow street. They didn't seem to be moving down the street, the whole street seemed to be moving—moving with the armored cars. They filled the street. They took it with them. The red maws of the tanks drilled their flaming tongues into the walls of the houses. It looked as though each tank peeled a piece off the crust of the earth. But for this very reason we were not frightened. The whole thing seemed unreal. It was more like a bad movie of the future, with warriors from Mars and synthetic men popping out of bottles. Everything moved as on a screen. We felt that it couldn't go on much longer.[1]

The firestorm—the concentrated front—was not supposed to be described with words. It was intended to produce shock, death, and complete destruction. It did not allow time to think or consider alternatives, to take stock, or write words. Except for the most highly trained soldiers the violence of the event had no counterpart in previous experience.

The author described an early front in northern France, German Panzer tanks entering a small town in Lorraine in 1940. The passage has several of the main features found in most descriptions of the front. The writer questions the reality of the entire experience, "The whole thing seemed unreal." The concept of what "reality" is has suddenly been put in doubt. Second, the author resorts to metaphors as he attempts to describe the experience, but these are rejected almost as soon as evoked. They are unsatisfactory. The firing guns are "tongues," "drills," but the metaphors are not repeated. Traditional images are not adequate. The whole street moves, it is subjected to a new, overpowering force. The crust of the earth is being peeled away. The word "hallucination" is never mentioned, as if everything else was a hallucination except the reality of the tanks. Reality is inverted.

Other features found in descriptions of the front are expressed in abbreviated form. There is great speed. The front moves so fast the observer cannot get his bearings. It is another world. The traditional links of cause and effect no longer seem to apply. Strangest of all, fear also disappears. As the observers watch they are "not frightened." The sense of a new reality has obliterated normal, pedestrian fear, but this suggests only a deeper fear. The statement should probably be taken with a grain of salt; fear is clearly present but requires a new word, the author has lost the reactions he had in the past. It might be good to be unhampered by fear but it is also dangerous. Perhaps, he thinks, some mistake is being made. The event must be temporary, "We felt that it couldn't go on much longer."

There is art and inventiveness in this description, and the author expresses a sense of mental division as if only a part of himself was present. The metaphors are not pretty. He almost gives up his attempt to describe the event, and disowns his experience. He resorts instead to popular culture and film—"a bad movie" with Martians—as he searches for counterparts in normal experience.

This encounter with the Panzers turns out to be central to the narrative. All the other events flow from it. Defeat in many tragic forms, French regiments of mobilized criminals dissolving, units of African soldiers (*joyeux*) and Legionnaires wandering about aimlessly, Germans not bothering to round them up. Inexplicable changes of collective mood take place. There are drunken orgies, and hopeless efforts to resist the powerful current of retreating French soldiers. Huge herds of horses panic because of strafing Stukas with sirens. Despite the confusion and the kaleidoscope of scenes, the encounter with the tanks stands out: the "firestorm." All secondary episodes follow this lethal event.

As the Second World War continued, the concentrated firestorm repeatedly determined the success or failure of whole armies. It determined also the fates of whole societies. Movement on the front was followed by conquest, and the subjugation of immense numbers of civilians. However, the engagements with Panzer tanks tended to be brief. One French prisoner was asked how long the "war" had lasted for him. "Ten minutes," he replied.[2]

The front was one of the most frequently written-about features of the war. The sheer number of works highlighting the fronts is striking; as the war accelerated literally thousands of correspondents accompanied the different armies. After 1940, the fronts moved far from the English-speaking countries, and were spread over much of the world. Journalists bridged the gap between battles at the front and civilians at home; they communicated between the soldier's world abroad—in Tunisia, Egypt, Crete, Syria, India, Burma, the Pacific Islands—and the home countries. Families could follow the progress of the war in distant countries by reading newspapers and looking at maps. These provided superficial benchmarks, and progress could be measured by the positions of the fronts.

For those at home the front was usually the one described by war correspondents. They provided a context, or veil of interpretation. They also determined how the public viewed the front-line battles: what images or words would be used, how much or how little accuracy was required. Some of the correspondents enjoyed enormous prestige and even acquired heroic status. Their names became household words, and famous writers took part: Ernest Hemingway, John Steinbeck, John Dos Passos among others.

But it was unusual that a correspondent captured the reactions of a soldier subjected to the firestorm. The front was a place intended to cause destruction and fear that were contagious and disabling. Fright and intimidation were as important as producing casualties, but the Correspondents almost never described it realistically.

There was not one type of front but many. In the course of the war they changed: and they could change rapidly. The front was a merciless school for those who did not learn quickly, adapt, or improve. A military historian observed that the English-speaking Allies had to learn how to fight "from scratch" in North Africa. Another made a similar observation about the steep "learning curve" of the Red Army.

Three examples highlight the front at different stages of the war. The first passage describes the anticipation of a soldier dug into a defensive position, waiting for a German tank attack he believes will come in his direction. It shows the difficulty in observing or distinguishing the "front" at all. He can see almost nothing, yet he feels—by the greater reverberations in the earth under his feet—that an attack is coming:

> "Are they really so close? Why are they so close? And what is making this noise?" The roar now seemed to be ramming itself into the space between earth and sky. It no longer resembled a rumbling iron ball; it came out of the distance, now in great avalanches of thunder, now in powerful reverberations that echoed in the deep channel of the river, steadily approaching with a remorseless and frightening

persistence. The earth began to shake like a living body. And still the red and blue flares continued to soar in a semi-circle over the village, as though sending out guiding signals to the oncoming roar.

"What is it? Tanks or aircraft? Is it just about to begin? Or has it already begun? Someone must order . . . I must do something!"[3]

The writer was a young soldier in the path of General Manstein's *Panzertruppe* speeding to assist the German Sixth Army, surrounded inside the city of Stalingrad. Yuri Bondarev wrote the novel *The Hot Snow* about his experiences in the winter of 1942–43.

Characteristically he asks questions. No answers are forthcoming. The violence is largely expressed through the descriptions of sounds. Images and metaphors are unexpected, outside normal categories of human activity: an iron ball, an avalanche. The inert earth is suddenly activated and becomes a living body. The whole surface of the earth is put into motion, recalling the description of Panzers in northern France. The writer is ignorant of causes, and can only perceive effects he is unable to identify. He does not even know if an approaching attack is with tanks or airplanes, nor does he know if it has begun or not. He understands almost nothing about what is happening. The passage ends with an expression of complete helplessness.

When, afterwards, he discovers that Manstein's army has passed on top of him, and he is finally able to stand up, it defies belief.

Many writers described the extended experience of the front not as an encounter with unreality but with a dangerous form of insanity. A fine example is found in *The Trap* (1950), a novel by Dan Billany, a British writer who did not survive the war. Billany took part in the fighting in the North African desert; he presents events from the point of view of a participant and officer who was responsible for the lives of others. He had to think quickly and clearly. His unit came under the sustained shelling of an aimed barrage:

It shook our nerves, made our hearts thump, and gave us no rest. Right and left, before and behind, the air was incessantly split by explosions. The screaming, cracking and rending of projectiles made one unbroken roar.

A colossal *"crack!"* seemed to lift the earth itself. Metal whistled into our pit, biting into the earth. Phillimore prodded with his boot a piece of hot shrapnel as big as his hand, and shook his head . . .

I was in some physical terror myself, but it had only infected one side of my personality: because at heart I did not entirely believe in the reality of what was happening. Other things that had happened even years earlier in my life were real: I believed them, they fitted me and shaped me. For instance, the fear, when I was very small, that my father would beat me for running behind a motor-lorry and stealing a ride . . . All these things happened to a real me in a real world which I didn't make and was more of my choosing.

And this battering of explosives in the desert was so improbable and unlikely that I (that personality which had known reality and remembered it) simply did not believe. It couldn't be so, it was preposterous, reality was not like this. You couldn't take it seriously. It was outrageous, romantic, illusory. It was an illusion.[4]

The field of vision was bounded by danger from the air—the Stukas were "great birds pecking at them"—and German guns that had taken their range. An additional reason to be afraid was the silence of British artillery. Only later he learned they had retreated, leaving him cut off.

Most important, he was not in control of his own mind. The rational side was possessed by fear, even panic, while the irrational side refused to give credence, denied reality, and neutralized the fear. Each moment he was afraid a shell "will lift the tank in a fountain of blood," but he was saved, he wrote, by "the imbecile certainty that it couldn't happen. Thank God the Unconscious is stronger than logic: its fictions are the only facts we really believe . . . My reasonable terror couldn't get down to the foundations of my being."

Rarely has the conflict between different kinds of reality within the mind been described so convincingly. Billany shows how the mind throws up lifesaving illusions, products probably of the instinct for self-preservation. Was the panic neutralized at the expense of denying a greater danger? He was not insane, but close to it. At the same time, he was remarkably clear in analyzing his own divided reactions.

Like other writers who described the front, Billany focused on the limitations of the single, inadequate point of view. His sensory field was excruciatingly narrow. The dangers were at the periphery, invisible.

Billany survived the tank combats in the North African desert. In 1944 he was killed in Italy, probably by an Italian civilian. The manuscript of his novel was found and published after the war.

Other writers described the reactions of prolonged shock at the front, and instances of insanity. The word is perhaps a misnomer because the condition was thoroughly grounded in real, concrete events. James Jones explained the title he gave to his book *The Thin Red Line*: there is "an old saying" that a "thin red line"—a very fragile line—"divides the sane human being from madness." Dan Billany described how madness assumed different guises of unreality, hallucinations, and "fictions"; another writer, William Manchester, speculated that for much of the time soldiers in close combat were insane.[5]

All firestorms at the front had several common features: a maximum concentration of force, shock and speed, as well as the sustained attempt to create a zone where no life was possible. In the following example it was the turn of a German regiment to be subjected to concentrated attack. In 1944, in Normandy, a Panzer division was shelled in a lengthy artillery attack followed by "carpet bombing." The airplanes were Flying Fortresses, twelve thousand feet overhead. From the ground they were both invisible and inaudible:

> Back and forth the bomb carpets were laid, artillery positions were wiped out, tanks overturned and buried, infantry positions flattened and all roads and tracks destroyed. By midday the entire area resembled a moon landscape, with the bomb craters touching rim to rim . . . All signal communications had been cut and no command was possible. The shock effect on the troops was indescribable. Several of my men went mad, and rushed round in the open until they were cut down by splinters. Simultaneously with the storm from the air, innumerable guns of the American artillery poured drumfire into our field positions."[6]

Such was the front under what came to be called "carpet bombing." The source of the bombs could not be located with the physical senses. Shock, accompanied by madness, is vividly presented, yet the effect was ultimately "indescribable" and could not be rendered by words. The author was a disciplined professional soldier, a general, who tried to maintain objective distance during the event. Very few of his men survived. That he remained alive was probably a matter of chance.

2

The Field of Consciousness

The description of the front was one of the greatest challenges for a writer who was also a soldier. The point of view was narrow, limited, the senses of a single person always inadequate. The front was opaque. It moved far too fast. What was available was a small field of consciousness and perceptions. Antoine de St.-Exupery wrote: "the field of consciousness is tiny. It accepts only one problem at a time."[7] This "field" was invariably different from that of the historian and most postwar writers. It was also very different from that of the war correspondent. A problematical feature of the front was this very small field of consciousness of the individual. It resisted most of the traditional, popular kinds of narration. New techniques had to be developed to describe an event and, at the same time, remain faithful to participation in it.

Most narrations of events, any events, establish a perspective with a "point of view." Even in different types and genres of literature a consistent point of observation is necessary to describe a series of events, to give them coherence. The point of view could be that of the author, or an observer; or it could be a group of different people, or a fictitious character. An author's choice of a point of view is one of his most important decisions. It relates the characters to each other, and provides a temporal sequence. The people described should be able to communicate with one another, and the writer must communicate with the reader. They must be able to meet in a consciousness or a language that is shared. Sometimes this compromise has been called "the middle distance"; it goes back to the eighteenth and nineteenth centuries, and earlier still. "Realism" depends on it. A literary historian has written, "each age has its agreed-upon middle ground."[8]

The front, however, had little or no "middle ground" available. No person—no soldier or civilian—had the privilege of occupying the safety of a middle distance. In literary criticism, point of view is usually treated as a technical matter of style, but in works describing the front and especially the firestorm the point of view was qualitatively different. The lack of a middle ground distinguishes most narratives about the front from narratives about events during times of peace.

One American writer described a typical episode, a minor encounter in fighting on the Italian peninsula:

Over their heads and before their eyes the machine-gun sent its bullets in their vicious arc. It was death, alive and spitting. For all Tyne knew, some of the men had been hit already. There was no way of knowing. No way at all. Pictures flashed across his mind and were gone before he could grasp them. Everything speeded up; the world was moving at a dizzy pace. He could not keep up with it. It was going around faster and faster. In a minute it would fly away.

A dull explosion came from behind the farm. Then another and another. The bridge. Ward.

And then everything that had been moving so fast stopped dead. The world stopped. Time stopped. The war stopped. What had spun so fast, what had nearly hurled Tyne among the stars was stopped dead, with such violence as to shake his body the way a woman shakes a mop from a window.[9]

The writer describes an encounter with an enemy machine gun. The passage is composed of unanswered questions. Effects, once again, are registered without the causes clearly identified. The writer was thrown upon his own resources, in this case metaphor and rhythm; at the end he compares himself to a mop. He was challenged to match language and choice of words to the field of vision. He also writes with a jagged sense of speed. Time abruptly accelerates. Then it stops. The style of narration had to be adapted to the speed and violence of the front, otherwise it would falsify them.

Experiences at the front did not necessarily pass into words at all. Many noticed that the opposite occurred. When the novelist John Steinbeck was in Italy in 1943, serving as military correspondent for *The New York Herald Tribune*, he tried to account for his observation that normally talkative, articulate men avoided speaking about combat: "They would talk about their experiences right up to the time of battle, and then suddenly they wouldn't talk any more."[10] He speculated that in prolonged battle the nerves became numbed as if "packed in cotton." Afterward, a defense mechanism prevented the mind from remembering the harsh experience.

Some writers made the difficulty of consecutive narration a deliberate feature of style. They might stress the opacity of the front, or the narrowness of the individual's point of view, or the difficulty of identifying causes or effects. In the following passage an officer observes fragmentary actions:

Something flashed—dark and sudden, causing a wind. The plaster started to fall from the wall. The netting shook as though it had been struck hard . . . And suddenly the yard was completely full of people, running, shouting, green, black, and striped. The one in the vest was already in the hut. He vanished into the doorway. The Germans were firing wildly. Then they stopped. You could see them running. It was easy to tell them by their full, unbelted greatcoats.

All this happened so quickly that I had no time to think. There was nothing at all around us. Valega and I. And someone's cap on the gray asphalt."[11]

Something flashed—what was it? Probably a shell but the identification is not made. Visible signs and sense data are registered but they are effects of other events. Rapid actions and impressions are noted, causal connections left out. These are the connections usually supplied only afterward by the reflecting mind when a series of events has run its course. Here their absence is an important part of the experience itself. The sequence is fairly clear: an initial shelling, then an advance on foot over a sixty-meter yard at night in house-to-house fighting. The novel was Viktor Nekrasov's *In the Trenches of Stalingrad*, one of the best works about Stalingrad in 1942.

Nekrasov's fidelity to actual events sometimes produces puzzling discontinuities. His paragraphs have different kinds of action, and different kinds of time or rhythm. Some are rapid, some slow. These correspond to lulls in action, followed by an abrupt series of events occurring in a burst: "They are running at us and also shouting. The black ribbons disappeared. In their place was a gray greatcoat and an open mouth. It also disappeared. A thumping started in my temples. My jaws ached for some reason. The Germans were no more to be seen."

The texture of events has not been reshuffled to form a retrospective after-the-event perspective. Omniscience with its knowledge is avoided. The experience is given in the original context as it was unfolding. A reader might wonder, what was the greatcoat? Why was it noticed at all? And the open mouth? Was it alive, standing, or dead? How did it disappear? In Nekrasov's novel, unexplained concrete images often beg for answers but do not receive them.

In a different part of the world, a talented novelist made the opacity of the front a central feature of his style. James Jones' *Thin Red Line* described the death of an American officer, Second Lieutenant Blane, on the island of Guadalcanal. His unit was unable to see a Japanese machine gun that was dug in to a hillside above them. They could hear only a "clatterbanging" sound but could not pinpoint it:

> It took several seconds for the still hidden Japanese gunners to raise their fire, and 2nd platoon was ten yards down the gentle little slope before it was unleashed against them. Nine men fell at once. Two died and one of them was Blane. Not touched by a machine gun, he unluckily was chosen as a target by three separate riflemen, none of whom knew about the others or that he was an officer, and all of whom connected . . . He lay on his back and, dreamily and quite dumb, stared at the high, beautiful, pure white cumuli which sailed like stately ships across the sunny, cool blue tropic sky. It hurt him a little when he breathed. He was dimly aware that he might possibly die as he became unconscious."[12]

The physical senses in this passage do not lie. They convey precise, vivid impressions. But they have little use, they do not provide the most important information. None of the men in this scene understands the exact nature of the events in which they participate. The Japanese soldiers have little more awareness than Blane. They do not know that three bullets have hit Blane simultaneously or that he is an officer. The passage builds up what might be called *multiple ignorance*.

Blane does not know he is dying as he loses consciousness, and he dies unaware of his own death. He thinks the only bullets that might strike him will come from the machine gun, and he is wrong. Blane's sensations,

the beauty of the clouds, the smallness of the pain he feels, are all deceptive. The senses of each person are alert but the most important events are
hidden, inaccessible. The construction of the narrative, with its several
points of view, is original. The perspective of the officer is radically narrowed, and is inadequate for comprehending events. But the same is true
for all the other participants.

The journalist Ernie Pyle, transferred to the Pacific Theater after several years in Europe, noted that the fighting in the Pacific had a unique
ferocity and cruelty.[13] No prisoners were taken. Captured Allied soldiers
were often beheaded or badly mutilated.[14] Collective hatred was close to
the surface, there was much taunting of the enemy, shouts, provocation,
and exchanged insults. This was a deliberate and important feature of the
Pacific front. At one point James Jones encountered an American soldier
who had been beheaded, hands tied behind his back, his head sitting on
the chest, the genitals severed and stuffed into the mouth of the severed
head. The men who came upon the scene were very badly shaken. Jones
described their different reactions.

Fronts were often sanitized by the newspaper correspondents, and
seemed to resemble each other. But this impression is false; they were almost
always dynamic, changing, and made use of deception. They were fought in
vastly different kinds of terrain. Fighting often took place at night in Europe,
on the Eastern front in Russia, and above all in the Pacific Theater. The
Japanese Army favored nighttime offensives; especially after 1942, many
Japanese attacks were at night because of increasing Allied air dominance.
This was the most hidden, blind front of all, and the most disorienting:

> It was so quiet you could hear the men breathing. Everybody was
> alert. We saw small lights flickering in the jungle at the bottom
> of the ridge. During the day we had strung wire on the ridge and
> fixed empty cans with cartridges in them to make noise. Everyone
> was straining to see and hear but there was nothing to see. We
> heard soft mutterings down in the jungle. I thought I saw a shadow
> approach our position. The tin cans rattled, someone shrieked. We
> threw grenades over the ridge and Japanese rifle and machine-gun
> fire opened up on us.

> The first Japanese wave swarmed into our position. It was a con-
> fusing struggle lit up by flashes from machine-gun fire, grenades

and mortars. Dark shapes crawled across the ground. Men fought on the ground with bayonets and swords, shouting curses . . . In the flickering light I saw three Japanese charge our number-two gun. I shot two of them but the third ran through one of my gunners with a bayonet, which I warded off with my hand. Someone had shot him that instant and he dropped at my feet, dead. About seventy-five of them broke through our position and moved down the other side. The others vanished, melted away down the slope."[15]

It was a landscape of darkness, "everyone was straining to see and hear." The field of consciousness was completely opaque, informed more by sounds than images. To describe such combat required unusual skill.

An important dimension of all fronts without exception was the air. Air support and dominance was crucial to the front on the ground. Many insisted—Montgomery with particular emphasis[16]—that the two could not be separated. Air superiority was essential for intelligence and for discovery. Aerial photography accompanied the fronts most of the time, locating coordinates to aid artillery on the ground. Tactical air support was requested by radio, also from the ground. Germany took an early lead in the use of aerial photography for battlefield intelligence but the Allies soon followed. It was in constant use by all sides.

In North Africa, ongoing photography accompanied every move. An attack by Generals Horrocks and de Guingand in the North African desert involved these preparations:

We worked out in detail the number and position of all vehicles and guns which would be required for the assault. These were concentrated in their proper places behind 30 Corps front very early on; but they were not the real operational vehicles. They were spares and, above all, dummies. Though the German aircraft photographed these concentrations constantly, they always remained the same, and there was no sudden increase just before the battle. As the assaulting divisions moved into position, their operational vehicles merely replaced the dummies, the change-over taking place, of course, at night. In my sector dummy dumps and workshops began to spring up like mushrooms.[17]

71

This was not the front that newspaper correspondents were permitted to describe. It shows how a constant rivalry or duel for intelligence took place at the front. Only rarely was it static, what was occasionally described as a "slugging match"—it was dynamic and changing. Intelligence and deception, discovery or the lack of it, were always crucial.

If speed was an outstanding feature of the blitzkrieg front on the ground, it was especially true of the air. For the writer in the air, accurate use of language to match rapid actions was a supreme challenge. Speed for a pilot required a new set of reactions and adjustments, swift and precise at the same time,

If he was a writer, it required entirely new rhythms. A number of pilots were outstanding writers. Richard Hillary described shooting down his first German airplane:

We ran into them at 18,000 feet, twenty yellow-nosed Messerschmitt 109's, about five hundred feet above us . . . Brian Carberry dropped the nose of his machine, and I could almost feel the leading Nazi pilot push forward on his stick to bring his guns to bear. At the same moment Brian hauled hard back on his own control stick and led us over them in a steep climbing turn to the left. In two vital seconds they lost their advantage. I saw Brian let go a burst of fire at the leading plane, saw the pilot put his machine into a half roll, and knew that he was mine . . .[18]

"Two vital seconds," then a single frozen second. The outcome was determined in these brief spans of time. Hillary's style is alert and deft. The language reflects speed, the active verbs coming one after the other; the movements—his own and his opponent's—are both registered, he even notes involuntary movements of the German pilot inside his cockpit.

Perhaps more than any other writer, Pierre Clostermann developed a language adapted to speed. Clostermann was an Alsatian, a member of the "Alsace" squadron in the RAF These pilots, representing Free France, came to England after the French defeat in 1940.

Clostermann disclaimed any literary pretensions. He wrote in the preface to his book *The Big Show*, "I ask the reader not to expect a work of literature." But his work was widely praised by writers and figures as different as William Faulkner and General Charles De Gaulle. After the end of the war, *The Big Show* was reissued eight times.

Clostermann could make the simple act of flying a vivid encounter. Later he flew a Tempest, a powerful airplane difficult to handle—he called it a "brute," a *fauve*—and was engaging German jet aircraft at speeds of more than five hundred miles per hour. An attack on the German airfield and naval base at Grossenbode displays Clostermann's writing skills in the last year of the war. More than one hundred German fighters were in the air at higher altitudes, there were twenty-four British Tempests:

> I released my auxiliary tanks and went into a vertical dive, passing like a thunderbolt at 600 m.p.h. through a formation of Focke-Wulfs which scattered about the sky like a flock of swallows. I straightened out gradually, closing the throttle and following a trajectory designed to bring me over the airfield at ground level.

> All hell was let loose as we arrived. I was doing more than 500 m.p.h. by the clock when I reached the edge of the field. I was 60 feet from the ground and opened fire at once. The mottled surface of the anchorage was covered with moored Dornier 24's and 18's. Three lines of white foam marked the wake of three planes which had just taken off. A row of Blohm und Voss's in wheeled cradles was lined up on the launching ramps. I concentrated my fire on a Bv 138. The moorings of the cradle snapped and I passed over the enormous smoking mass as it tipped up on the slope, fell into the sea and began to sink.

> The flak redoubled in fury. A flash on my right, and a disabled Tempest crashed into the sea in a shower of spray. Jesus! The boats anchored off shore were armed, and one of them, a large torpedo boat, was blazing away . . . I instinctively withdrew my head into my shoulders and, still flying very low, veered slightly to the left, so fast that I couldn't fire at the Dorniers, then quickly swung to the right behind an enormous Ju 252 which had just taken off and was already getting alarmingly big in my gunsight. I fired one long continuous burst at him and broke away just before we collided. I turned round to see the Ju 252, with two engines ablaze and the tailplane sheared off by my shells, bounce on the sea and explode.

> My speed had swept me far on—straight on to the torpedo boat which was spitting away with all her guns. I passed within ten

yards of her narrow bows, just above the water and the thousand spouts raised by the flak. I caught a glimpse of white shapes rushing about on deck and tongues of fire from her guns. The entire camouflaged superstructure seemed to be alive with them. Tracer shells ricocheted on the water and exploded all round over a radius of 500 yards. Some shrapnel mowed down a flock of seagulls which fell in the sea on all sides, panic-stricken and bleeding. Phew! Out of range at last.

I was sweating all over, my throat so constricted that I couldn't articulate one word over the radio. Without realizing it I had held my breath through the whole attack and my heart was thumping fit to burst.[19]

Even the release of tension at the end—and the held breath—is expressed by the rhythms of the sentences. It is a tour de force of mimesis, words and observations mimicking actions as they unfold at great speed. If he used metaphor it was invariably precise. His narrative reflects the manner in which it was written: all his texts were composed within the day in which the action occurred, shortly after landing.

A reader of Clostermann's narrative might be tempted to ask: Why was he there at all? What led him to run such risks, on an almost daily basis? The question could be asked of almost all those who fought at the front. The death rate for the pilots was exceptionally high. Didn't personal survival turn them away from the front?

In Clostermann's writings it is fascinating for the reader to observe the weave of both strong motivation and fear: of aggression and compassion, anger and recoil. He knew the enemy that had overrun his native Alsace, incorporating it into the German Reich. He never hesitated in his decision to join the RAF He deeply felt the need for armed defense, like some of the other writers to be considered later; he was convinced he must take the war to the enemy. This motivation is found in small details of the passage above: in his anger, in the surge of excitement at the "concentrated fire," in satisfaction at the surprise and panic he has caused, and the destruction to the naval base.

Fear is present in the passage from beginning to end. His own fear is grudgingly accepted. His survival depended on it, and on an awareness of actions coming from all directions at once. Sources of danger are, literally, everywhere. Throughout much of the flight he is in enemy range, and that awareness is present in the smallest details, in the tension of his head and shoulders. The entire passage, from beginning to end, mimics his held breath.

Later, German radar-assisted flak became so dense and deadly that Clostermann wrote "you could almost walk on it." By the end of the war, what he called "my morbid flak complex" had taken a heavy toll on his nerves and even his ability to fly. He had several crashes. He barely managed to live through the final year before the German surrender.

The Mole's View and the Panorama

A n American military historian interviewed thousands of soldiers after 1945, and described their experience in these terms: "Much of the time it is the fate of the men who compose the combat line to move blindly into battle like a colony of moles, and to grope for information."[20]

S. L. A. Marshall addressed problems of command, the inadequate "flow" of information on the battlefield, and the unwillingness of many soldiers to fire their weapons. His conclusions met with much disagreement, but he identified one of the most important features of the front: its opacity, and the radically circumscribed field of vision. Marshall's version of St.-Exupery's "field of consciousness" was dark. The front was the killing zone, a place where shock and chaos were deliberately used as principle. The battlefield was a place of fear and terror.

During the war itself, the challenges to a writer who wished to describe the front with any accuracy were often insuperable. Censors did not permit criticism of leadership. The presence of "Battle Police" or MPs—in other armies, the NKVD or *Feldgendarmerie*—could not even be mentioned.[21] Constant challenges included shock, the divided mind described by Billany and others, exhaustion, insanity, and wounds.

If the soldier at the front was a "mole," what, then, of the great "battle-piece," the epic panorama that described massed armies in a sweeping vision that included the fates of entire nations? Much of the war literature of the past, especially during the eighteenth and nineteenth centuries, has been characterized by two literary devices: the epic "battle piece," and the all-seeing eyewitness. Literary versions of great battles that changed the course of history have always been popular. It is a genre as old as Herodotus; the Battle of Waterloo, for example, was described by Stendhal, Thackeray, and Victor Hugo. They reconstructed the major battle with a strong emphasis on the outcome.

The Second World War was fought on a scale even broader than the battles described by these three authors or by Tolstoy in the nineteenth century. Its scale might seem to require a corresponding global sweep.[22] Of course the writer of fiction, especially adventure fiction, could do as he wished; a few works adopted a broad canvas, especially those written well after 1945.[23]

During the war years it was usually the military correspondents who tried to provide a broader context for actions at the military fronts, but probably they are the last writers we should turn to if we wish to know the real nature of the firestorm, and the concrete challenges of front-line experience. Accreditation of correspondents posed insoluble problems. Military authorities licensed journalists, giving them what were, in effect, monopolies, but monopolies subject to censorship. The rules were always hidden from their readers. Charles Lynch, accredited with Reuters, wrote bluntly: "We were a propaganda arm of our governments . . . We were cheerleaders. I suppose there wasn't an alternative at the time. It was total war. But for God's sake, let's not glorify our role. It wasn't good journalism. It wasn't journalism at all."[24]

Some correspondents had a sharp eye for visual detail, or an ear for vernacular speech; they tried to capture the sensations, the whiff and atmosphere of the front. Their interviews especially are valuable. But their front was rarely that of the soldier. They were outside his chain of command; and no matter how much they boasted of narrow escapes or brushes with death, they were shielded from danger. As John Hersey admitted, they were placed slightly to the rear, or to the side, or in a vehicle prepared for speedy retreat.[25] Censorship prevented journalists from presenting either what Marshall called the mole's view—so often tragic—or the many invaluable discoveries made at the front that had to be kept secret at the time for security reasons. In the words of Philip Knightley, whose *The First Casualty* is one of the best studies of war correspondents, they were incomparable mythmakers, propagandists, and even heroes, but their accounts were not accurate. The "first casualty" in Knightley's title was the truth.[26]

Some talented correspondents rose above the limitations of censorship, writing a fine mixture of well-observed nonfiction and fiction. Works by Chester Wilmot were widely praised, and Alan Moorehead wrote impressive panoramic descriptions from the battlefields in North Africa. Moorehead was present during a night attack by Rommel's Panzers that overwhelmed the Fifth South African Brigade; he wrote:

British soft transports had scattered before them and confusion more deadly than shellfire spread everywhere. Convoys of vehicles were scattered over a hundred miles of desert, not knowing where to go. Batteries of guns and groups of tanks were left stranded in the empty desert. Men who believed they were holding the end of a continuous salient suddenly found the enemy behind them. And north of them and south of them and all around them . . .

Men were captured and escaped three or four times. Half a dozen isolated engagements were going on. Both sides were using each other's captured guns, tanks and vehicles, and absurd incidents were taking place. A British truck driven by a German and full of British prisoners ran up to an Italian lorry. Out jumped a platoon of New Zealanders and rescued our men. Vehicles full of Germans were joining British convoys by mistake—and escaping before they were noticed . . . On the map the dispositions of the enemy and ourselves looked like an eight-decker rainbow cake, and as more and more confused information came in, Intelligence officers threw down their pencils in disgust, unable to plot the battle any further.[27]

Moorehead succeeded in rendering chaotic events taking place simultaneously, at cross-purposes. In reality, however, the events were more grim—far more grim than he admitted. It was actually a defeat and a rout. As the campaign progressed, more than three-quarters of the trucks in Rommel's possession would be captured British vehicles.[28] This was the time of multiple Allied defeats, when it was widely admitted "All's not right with the Eighth Army." Morale and generalship had become major problems.[29] Rommel was poised to enter Cairo. If he conquered it, the Allies would lose their control of the Mediterranean.

It is possible to admire Moorehead's description and, at the same time, notice what is absent. Moorehead's point of view is synthetic, comprising many actors and second-hand reports. If there is a dominant point of view, it is that of Headquarters and Intelligence. It was their map that resembled the multilayered "rainbow cake." As in many reports by correspondents, the picture of confusion is relatively sanitized, it had to be in order to pass the censors. Moorehead had his own vehicle for escape, significantly altering his sense of danger, point of view, word choice, and tone.

Crucial facts and the presence of defeat are not admitted. The point of view is not that of an individual participant or soldier. Anything comparable to Billany's fear, his exhaustion and lucidly described madness, is left out. The real danger and fear—ultimately, the real drama that was the most difficult to bear—was described by writers other than the accredited correspondents.

4

Discovery: Eyes and "Tongues"

English-speaking armies were not the only ones to censor and distort the nature of fighting on the fronts. Witnesses were often awed by the number of casualties the Russians were willing to accept. A German wrote: "the first waves were killed or left lying there, the second also, then a third wave came. In front of our positions the Soviet dead piled up and served as a sort of sandbag wall for us."[30] Germans complained that among the heaps of dead, a few Soviet soldiers would often manage to get through and outflank them. Soviet foot infantry regularly charged German tanks and artillery. The Soviet victory has been described as one of sheer volume.[31] Near the end of the war, the capture of the Seelow Heights in eastern Germany cost the Germans twelve thousand dead, the Russians thirty thousand. Bodies were still being discovered over half a century later.[32]

An observer claimed that the German-Russian front was so different from the others that "there were, in fact, two different wars . . . which might have been taking place on two different planets."[30] The novelist and correspondent Vasili Grossman noted cryptically in his *Writer's Diary*: "Once you're here, there is no way out. Either you will lose your head or your legs . . . Everyone knew that those who turn and run would be shot on the spot. This was more terrifying than the Germans . . . Well, there is also Russian zeal."[34]

The shock of battle proved too much for many soldiers in the ranks, so "blocking detachments" of the NKVD and Komsomol were used to prevent them from running away. However, the political officers would regularly give stories of the determination of troops to correspondents.

These "blocking detachments" were a second front or front behind the front, especially after the "Order No. 227," known commonly as "not one step backwards." Wholesale execution of men suspected of cowardice or desertion took place at the front. Tanks were deployed behind the forward positions; well-armed detachments of up to two hundred men each were present not to kill Germans but to shoot down any Russian who fled.[35]

A reader who expects to find explicit descriptions of this second NKVD front will be disappointed. The great heaps of bodies of dead Soviet soldiers were described by German, not Soviet writers. Trauma, wrote a historian who studied Soviet writings about the front, was foreign in general to writings under Stalin. The *Sovinformbureau* or Soviet Information Bureau did its best to keep the real world of the soldier out of sight.[36]

Events, often, were rendered in a kind of code. For example an author described a battalion crossing a river under heavy German fire, and noted: "only eight men reached the west bank of the Oder . . . Some political officers showed indecisiveness when crossing the river." The coded phrase implied there was panic, and they should have used their pistols earlier.[37]

* * *

Much of the censorship during the war itself was intended to bolster morale; it had to be used. We know that on all sides morale was subject to sudden and unexpected, dramatic changes. On the Allied side, morale and motivation were often among the most intractable problems of the war. These, too, were a major dimension and problem of the front. Leadership had to be alert to them, and deal with them quickly.

The fronts were places for hiding and for discovery. Discovery was one of the most important activities of the front. Discovery was a duel: the most successful fronts were able to carry discovery further—and more rapidly—than their opponents. A large number of actions were devoted to collecting information and intelligence. Aerial photography and the search for exact coordinates were always pursued, individual soldiers went on scouting missions. The front was a place of constant probes. These probes required genuine precision of observation: in the ability to see through disguise and, ultimately, use of words to communicate the observations to others. Each side tried to locate the other with evermore accuracy.[38] If the front was opaque and impervious, it was porous at the same time. Each side used all its resources to find openings, to see through it, to see around it, to see over it.

One of the most important tasks was to capture a live enemy soldier for interrogation. In the Soviet Union these enemy soldiers were called "tongues." Works by Victor Nekrasov, Vasili Grossman, and other writers describe the search for these German "tongues."[39] Intelligence and information at the front were probably as important as force, the two had to be combined. Discovery on both small and large scale was a constant process, without letup.

Marshal Zhukov wrote that a "good" front has many, many eyes.[40] Zhukov won a reputation for perfectionism. The front before the battle at Kursk was more heavily fortified, with greater concentration of artillery on both sides, than at any other battle of the war. Yet we know that at the same time the collection of information before the battle, by Zhukov's "eyes" and "tongues," was equally thorough and vast.

Elsewhere the process of hiding and discovery went hand in hand. For example, Pierre Clostermann always carried a camera on his airplane. He often made sorties just to take pictures. His squadron discovered the launching pad for the first V-1s or "flying bombs." Clostermann described it with remarkable precision:

> Out of the corner of my eye I watched the Hurricanes about to launch their attack. The target, carefully camouflaged against vertical photography, was visible in every detail at this angle: the high tension cables to the transformer, the concrete block of the control room with its curious aerials, from which the flying bomb is controlled. On either side, cleverly hidden in the undergrowth, the curious low ski-shaped construction whose function still baffled the R.A.F. technicians and Intelligence Officers for all their cunning, and, lastly, the launching ramp, 45 yards long, pointing straight at the heart of England. On the rails, a sinister cylinder, about twenty feet long, with two embryonic wings.[41]

Clostermann also discovered the underground factory where German engineers were manufacturing the new jet-propelled Heinkel 162. By 1944 the Luftwaffe had moved completely underground. Airplanes and hangars, entire factories in which the new types of airplanes were developed, had disappeared into reinforced mines, disguised quarries, and former road tunnels.[42] It was thought the new Heinkel might be produced near Neu Rippin. But the airfield there had been bombed many times, it was no longer used. Testing new aircraft was essential. But how could these aircraft be tested?

Clostermann's group discovered nearby a freshly poured straight stretch of a concrete autobahn. They reasoned—correctly, it turned out— that it was the trial runway for the new jet aircraft.

The panoramic battle-piece and all-seeing eyewitness were little used in literature about the front or the firestorm. These would have to wait well after the war, to wait even many decades.[43] They went counter to the experience of those who experienced the firestorm, and who risked their lives there. Contemporary descriptions during the war went in a very different direction. Panoramic views and omniscience yielded to the "mole's eye view," or rather to the tightly circumscribed yet alert, resourceful field of vision. It had its own kind of precision. It was fragmentary, confined, with countless frustrations and danger to human life. Most writers who experienced the front regarded omniscience as false. Their point of view—and their field of consciousness—was not privileged or omniscient in any way.

The front was intended to destroy and hide but it was also made to yield to discovery. The "good front" was the deadliest place of all. Yet it had many, many eyes.

IV
A World of Things: Occupation

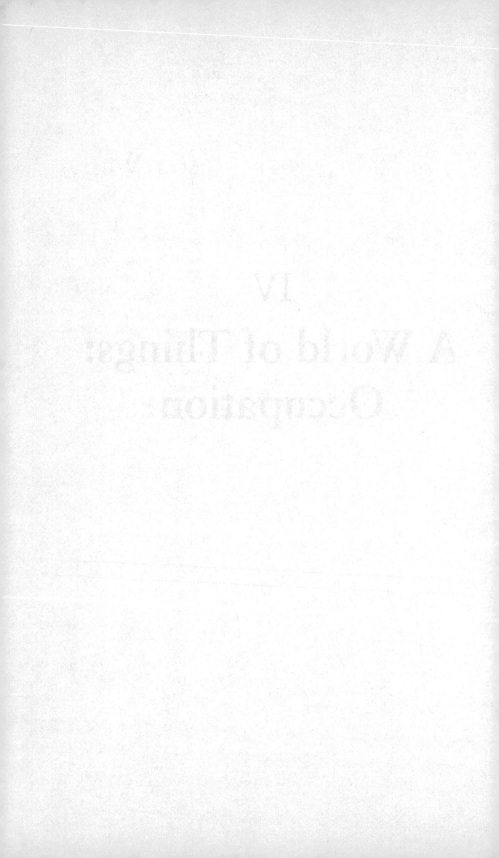

1

Scraps of Paper, Plaster Walls

*T*he number of civilians caught up behind the shifting fronts and the new frontiers of occupation outnumbered, by far, the numbers of soldiers. They were deprived of all relevant information; any communication, no matter how fragmentary or basic, suddenly acquired enormous value.

Any hard surface was enough to write a few words, to communicate with others. It did not have to be paper. A wall was enough, a wooden board, a plank, piece of furniture. Writing materials such as pencils or pens were often absent, so another instrument would be found. Something that could scratch, cut, or leave a legible mark.

* * *

A prisoner named "Mitard" records what it was like to discover words written on the wall of his prison cell:

On the walls are cries,
words scratched with a nail.

The despair, and the insane hope
of those who died before me—
I sense they are still here,
around me, and look at me.
Their eyes light up sometimes
in the blackness like stars.

And my head leans
on their shoulders of shadow.[1]

As he reads the words, scratched with a nail on the wall in front of him, he realizes he is not entirely alone. The words on the walls merge with the architecture and shadows around him. The words were written for a very small readership: the next person who would occupy the cell, and his successors. The "reader" in the cell does not know how many others may have already passed through and seen the words, nor does he know how many in the future will follow him.

Communication, and attempts to exchange information with others, became one of the most important activities in countries under occupation. Two acts of communication are included in the poem by "Mitard": a message was written earlier on the wall by a former occupant of the cell, then there is the poem itself—his own, originally written in French—and he describes his reaction to the message. The former occupants of the prison cell have disappeared, he doesn't know where, leaving only a few words scratched on the wall. He takes his bearings from these words. They become a physical presence and seem to merge with the wall, the words evoking dim shapes or images of those who wrote them, offering both hope and despair.

During the first twenty-two months of deportations and enforced relocation, walls and any available space became bulletin boards. Scrawled writings were found in trains, prisons, transit camps, holding areas, almost everywhere. One woman wrote afterward:

> To us, all was still chaos, without perspective. There was absolutely nothing of which we were yet sure. Of two individuals of identical habits, it was impossible to foretell which might disappear forever, without hope of return, and which might be told that his case was now completely in order and himself free to go home . . . Thousands of persons with infinite difficulty sent messages to tens of thousands of others, and not one of the messages was ever delivered by the person who had heard the original words."[2]

Messages were written in a variety of languages and they might contain a bare fact, a date, or a telegraphic notation. Usually the information was basic: a name, a place: "A mother and children, one an infant, husband escaped I don't know where."

Another message: "I am leaving for an unknown destination. I was in prison since March 6."

A third message: "Beware of two informers . . ." Two names followed, then two addresses where the informers were living.[3]

The first message provided no names, a wife and mother was searching for her husband who became separated from the rest of the family. The author of the second message was looking for anyone who might be included in his group scheduled to depart on "March 6." Perhaps someone knew their destination. The third message provided names and addresses; it was useful, practical, and could help a prisoner protect himself against informers. The knowledge might save his life.

Messages were frequently appeals for more information, and expressed hopes they would be passed on. They might eventually reach a person who knew a member of the family, people from a community or town. Some recorded the kind of sentence they were given, or where they were to be sent. The audience or readership of the messages was usually small. Most failed to reach the intended reader.

The messages remind us that when a prisoner arrived at a new place, his first encounter in a room or cell was often with written words. Many messages were found on walls at the French transit camps of Drancy and Fresnes; civilians and prisoners from many different countries passed through these transit camps and prisons, and after the war the messages were meticulously collected, photographed, and published. When seen in the context of the cells and rooms where they were written, they are strikingly concrete and vivid. The walls speak.

A number of the messages expressed regret, frustration, love, or anger: "*Les Boches sont foutus*" ("The Germans are screwed"). A message in English at a French transit camp: "Betrayed by a Frenchman." For many, acts of communication were greatly valued events, and the impulse to send a message to another living person was powerful. Most likely "Mitard," who read words on his cell wall, was unable to help the nameless writer who preceded him, but he sought something else: a basic act of communication with another person, and an act of solidarity. Those before him felt a need to communicate, and the same impulse was behind his own poem in turn. The poem records the moment when writing messages on walls became a theme in its own right. A communication process, and sending messages from one person to another, had begun. When was the final poem written? The poem does not inform us, eventually it was printed in a resistance anthology. The poem furthers the process of communication, showing how a message written with a nail found a recipient and reader, was passed on and given form in another work of literature.

Brief messages like these used words to question events as they were taking place. They are not works of "literature" as normally defined, and the audience was different from that of published books. The communication was intended for people in a situation similar to that of the writer. But sometimes the intended readers were conceived broadly: the message was "for the whole world."

Some messages were thoughtful. An Estonian wrote a maxim on a cell wall in the Soviet Union:

Forget what was,
Don't think of what is to come,
Take what you are given.[4]

Another was sententious:

Do not reject the beggar's bed and prison.
Entering, do not lose heart.
Leaving, do not rejoice.

Some messages have an important graphic interest. Written or engraved laboriously with an improvised tool or brush of some kind, they are often expressive.

One drawing took advantage of a whole wall[5], another of a whole ceiling.[6]

Most messages have a telegraphic quality that reflects the hard writing conditions. Usually the stress on concreteness and danger is vivid. The messages have an immediacy like no other narratives, and form a special genre. The difficulty and jaggedness of many of them—their very shortness and fragmentation—was part of the drama they attempt to communicate. The hasty act of communication frequently left out more than it included. The incomplete fragment, even after 1945, was maintained after the war by a few writers as a personal style.[7]

Military occupation immediately followed the fronts, and for civilians caught behind the fronts—then within new borders—all doors to the outside world were closed. Communication became an overpowering problem. Among the first inmates at the large Sachsenhausen concentration camp were entire faculties from the University of Strasburg and the Jagellonian University in Cracow; in occupied Norway, teachers were singled out by the Germans, rounded up, and kept in separate camps. At the very beginning of the war some of the worst massacres took place. After the first conquests German shooting squads would fan out, searching for Jews.

All prominent national and cultural leaders were at risk: judges, senators, professors, civil servants, lawyers, and political figures. Extermination was often based not on an individual trait but on membership with a certain group, for example, the intelligentsia of a conquered country. The famous mathematicians at the University of Lvov were executed in 1941; Simon Weisenthal has described how some five thousand people from the University of Lvov, artists and intellectuals were murdered by the Germans. The extermination of the Polish intelligentsia was another priority objective.[8]

The Soviet Union was equally harsh with the civilian populations it conquered. Both Stalin and Hitler were active in "decapitating" smaller nations (the phrase is Stalin's). In the Soviet zone of conquest, social criteria were stringently applied, and "decapitation" of professional groups was carried out immediately after the invasions in September 1939. Secrecy was more methodically carried out by the Soviet Union than by the Germans.

In late September 1939, retreating divisions of the Polish Army were pushed eastward by the invading Wehrmacht. Out of ammunition and decimated, the Red Army soon confronted them in their rear. Russian generals informed them they were "friends." Some fifteen thousand Polish Reserve officers were rounded up by Soviet forces, put in train wagons, and told they would be returned "to Warsaw."[9]

Several first-hand accounts have survived of the fate of the high-ranking Polish officers. They discovered their locked train wagons were traveling eastward. One soldier found several messages scrawled on the inside walls of the train wagon from an earlier trip: "They are taking us to Smolensk." Another written message warned: "They made us get off the train near Smolensk."[10] Four thousand four hundred top officers of the Polish Army were executed near Smolensk, at Katyn and Starobielsk. Secrecy continued until the very end, and they were buried in mass graves, pine trees planted on top of them.[11]

Throughout the Soviet zone, social class was considered to be hereditary. In *My Century* Alexander Wat described how members of the "intelligentsia" were among the first to be removed from prisons, secretly tried and killed. For example, a twelve-year-old boy whose mother was a school teacher and in a non-Russian group was at great risk. He could be threatened from either side, Soviet and German, for being a member of a professional class. The countless written messages reveal that for the civilian, an accurate assessment of personal danger was almost impossible. Careful Soviet deception and German camouflage—or *Tarnung*—were very effective while they were in place.[12]

The period from 1939 to 1941 was hectic, tragic, and chronicled in the literatures of the smaller countries. Invasions and deportations by the Wehrmacht, the SS, the Red Army, and the NKVD followed one another at breakneck speed. Confused movements of thousands of people—civilians of all ages from children to the elderly—were flung first in one direction then in another opposite direction with great loss of life.

By the late 1930s, the Soviet system of camps had become the largest in the world. Estimates of the population of their camps in 1939 vary greatly, ranging from three to ten million; the prisoners themselves arrived at a figure higher still.[13] As a result of the Hitler-Stalin Pact and the deportations of 1939–40, the Soviet camp system was enlarged even further. Germany invaded the western half of Poland on September 1, 1939, the USSR invaded the eastern half on September 17, the Baltic countries and Finland soon afterward.

This was a time when Soviet camps became what one writer called "a kaleidoscope of nations." Whole villages of farmers were packed into cattle cars and sent toward new camps that were receiving grounds for the deported populations. Railway lines led from newly conquered territories to new camps in the east. Largely ignored in the West at the time, the Soviet camps were not secondary products of war, they were central to the war in 1939–41, and an intrinsic institution or instrument of warfare. For twenty-two months after September 1939, this was the form taken by the Second World War.

As refugee civilians were sent east, the Soviet rail system was overloaded. Thousands spent the nights in the railway stations, on empty terrain nearby or local villages, lacking clothes, soon victims of famine and epidemics.[14] The railway system was transformed. Whole towns became "transit camps." The industrial city of Kharkov (Kharkiv, in eastern Ukraine) made a terrifying impression on observers. A Finnish writer, Unto Parvilahti, wrote that he was unable to find words for it, and with laconic irony he said it was "a huge traffic jam."[15]

Another writer described this large "city" as a sight to make one shudder:

Street after street, row after row of houses, crammed to the rafters with the pale faces, then staring eyes of prisoners. It was different in a gaol. A gaol was a thing apart, a place specially built to be isolated from the rest of the world, hidden behind walls and blind windows. But this was a town and at one time had homes and shops and schools, things like a town hall and cinemas. All that was defaced almost beyond recognition and overrun by the shuffling, emaciated mass of prisoners. It was like Atlantis, a dead city, engulfed by the gray waves of misfortune.

Here they did not bother to board or brick up the windows, as these did not look out on the world but only on this dead, underwater vegetation of starved people.[16]

During the first waves of deportations, desperate communications were thrown from train windows. A cup with words hastily scratched in it with a nail would be thrown to a passer-by. Or a book, with words hastily scribbled on the title page: "Merchants and manufactures were taken as hostages or exchange. Up to now the sentences ranged from 5 to 15 years. Death sentences have been changed to 10–15 years imprisonment. You are threatened for the smallest act of speaking out. Of those imprisoned, no one has yet been released . . ."[17]

In the course of the war many civilians experienced both German and Soviet camps as well as transit sites. The German attack against the Soviet Union in June 22, 1941, called "Barbarossa," reshuffled the alliances of the Hitler-Stalin Pact, and the result was a wave of new deportations. Almost all civilians who participated in these violent events agreed that sending messages to others was one of their most important activities.[18] For example, Margarethe Buber, who experienced both Soviet and German camps, wrote an excellent book, *Under Two Dictators*, largely about the many different kinds of messages that were sent and the various means, frequently ingenious, found to deliver them.[19]

What stands out is the wide extent and breadth of these attempts. It was difficult to find the most elementary materials for writing. A large number of messages were on improvised objects available by chance: metal, wood, oilcloth, or china. Many of the communications have been recovered, part of what is now called the "Riga Archive"; when the Germans attacked their Russian allies in June 1941 the NKVD hastily fled, abandoning the large collection of objects and documents they had confiscated from their prisoners.[20]

The messages were often accompanied by graphics, pictures, or documents, but the core of the communication was with words. At every stage efforts to send messages outside were challenged. Most difficult would be transmission of the message outside—to be followed by preliminary reception, reaching a destination, finding a reader or readers. Most messages disappeared, but with time some met with greater success. A few changed the course of the war.[21]

The struggle against disguise was to become one of the major "wars" of the years 1939–45. At first they reflected the application of the secret pacts and protocols; Germany and the USSR hoped disguise would work, that "friendly annexation" or "justified expansion" would be accepted as reality. It seemed that feeble efforts at resistance and communication with the outside world would have little importance.

For civilians, the need to lift the curtain of censorship and propaganda was overpowering. A deluge of different materials and devices were used to aid the process of communication—anything sharp could write, a nail, a pencil stub, walls were used in place of paper, furniture also served, wood, metal cups, china, furniture, cloth, raw lumber, even window shutters. The materials that were used for writing were inexhaustible. The great variety shows the strength of the desire to communicate, by any means possible, as writing was stripped to its most basic function.

2

In Medias Res: People as Things

Occupation by a foreign power was one of the most traumatic and formative experiences during the period 1939–45, and it drew a sharp contrast between the experiences in the occupied and non-occupied countries. By 1945 it was clear that the civilian experience in English-speaking countries was strikingly different from those under armed occupation.

The realization by a civilian he could be treated as an insentient thing often came suddenly. With some writers it occurred at the very beginning of hostilities, just after the first invasions. One writer described the attack on Poland in September 1939 in this way:

"I could reduce all that happened to me then to a few things. Lying in the field near a highway bombarded by airplanes, I riveted my eyes on a stone and two blades of grass in front of me. Listening to the whistle of a bomb, I suddenly understood the value of matter: that stone and those two blades of grass formed a whole kingdom, an infinity of forms, shades, textures, lights . . . Now I saw into the depths of matter with exceptional intensity."[22] More civilian than soldier, this was Czeslaw Milosz, winner of the Nobel Prize for Literature in 1980. Later he remembered, "A great simplification of everything occurs . . . Language is again an instrument serving a purpose . . . No one doubts that the language must name reality, which exists objectively, massive, tangible, and terrifying in its concreteness."[23]

The treatment of people as things was key to the widespread use of objects in writings that followed. Occupation brought the early discovery that civilians were treated literally as if they were insentient; if they felt pain it was unimportant, beyond concern. Ordinary people were open to arbitrary destruction, in practice as things. The term "occupation" for the subjugation that followed the invasions is misleading. It has been described as a "new world" where the treatment of people was uniquely brutal. Writers attempted to describe and explore this new world as their way of life radically changed. The traditional language of peace and independence had few words for the experiences of occupation.

One writer developed a way of writing that was particularly well suited to action *in medias res,* in the middle of events. She adopted a point of view that registers events and defies simple, traditional perspective; people are often interchangeable, they rarely have names and are referred to by pronouns like "she," "he," "they," or simply the impersonal "one." The texture of rapidly changing actions is constantly unpredictable, the individuals indicated in a rapid shorthand:

> They have run past,
> one is left behind.
> The man running in front of me is hit.
> The man running behind me is hit.
> We drag them by the feet
> and others run . . .[24]

> Mistakes are made. Who is hurt?
> Who is not hurt? Who was that person?
> They thought I was the one
> who fell on the street corner.
> I ran to the woman who fell,
> I wanted to take her away,
> but she was already gone.
> The body remained,
> looking a bit like mine.

People are often represented by what appears largest in the immediate range of vision at the moment. A boy crouches in shadow, holding his breath "as two boots thunder on the pavement, come closer." A scout "is eyes only." Or, "I was only a pair of hands." The body loses its integrity. It becomes part of the action around it, where it finds itself involuntarily.

The writer's procedure reflected actual events. Many of the poems by "Swir" (a wartime pseudonym) were revised after the war, with the intention of riveting her focus on the actual experience of wartime events as they unfolded. If people are treated as if they feel no pain, like insentient things—if people and things are interchangeable—it was the reality of daily life. The human being was one object among many.

Objects and people existed side by side, it was hard to tell one from the other:

A FINE PAINTING
A fine painting was dying in the mud,
bullets were making holes in it
people running under the bullets
were trampling it with their boots,
two boots came to a halt,
two hands seized it,
carried it under the bullets
until they dropped it in the mud,
blood started flowing onto the painting,
a body fell,
the fine painting died only later.[25]

The focus of the poem is a painting, and it takes on an independent life of its own. It has many characteristics of a living person, while the human beings who happen to be present are fragmentary, fleeting entities. Hands are detached from their owners as they reach out to grasp, but the rest of the bodies are omitted, they are outside the frame of the poem.

"A Fine Painting" presents dynamic action, and narrates the life span of a "protagonist," not a person but an object: the picture moves, it is carried, the perspective is low to the ground as if the picture were able to observe what is happening. This partly explains why the reader can only see hands reaching downward, and boots. The standard way of presenting people and things is reversed. Humans are usually the center of attention, objects or things are subordinate. Here the object is presented whole, while human beings are divided into limbs, legs, parts. The people are so diminished they are identified only by peripheral objects like boots. It is the painting that bleeds. It is shot full of holes and eventually "dies."

In another poem, the reader looks in vain for a whole or living person:

STILL LIFE
In a puddle of mud and blood,
between the half-charred body of a horse

and the half-charred body of a man,
near a broken-off drainpipe, an armchair with tassels, a teapot
and three pieces of shattered glass
lies the tatter of a love letter
singed along the edges:
"I am so happy."[26]

It is a world of objects. Nothing is alive within the poem. The objects are domestic or man-made, deliberately chosen for their associations with civilian life and peace: a drainpipe, an armchair with tassels, teapot, glass, a letter. Even the horse is a domestic animal and has human associations. Objects normally accompany human life at the periphery, now only broken fragments remain. No human being even appears to view the scene.

The fate of the letter, torn and "singed along the edges," belies its message about happiness. The irony is obvious, in stark contrast to the destroyed scene. The author of the letter and any whole living person is also outside the frame of the poem. The shattered objects and charred bodies in "Still Life" are on an equal footing, distinctions between them have disappeared.

The use of objects in these works should be called a language of protest. Comparisons with objects were a way of highlighting and protesting against cruelty, against the brutal treatment of civilians. With the exception of France, Germany treated conquered populations with unexpected cruelty. A prominent German general, von Manstein, wrote after the war that Germany's treatment of civilian populations was a major reason for its defeat. Germany could offer them only servitude and extinction.[27] It is well known that in a speech on August 22, 1939, Hitler told his military commanders to "close their hearts to pity and act brutally, with the greatest harshness." One of the war's secrets, revealed only after 1945, was Hitler's order to Heydrich in 1939 on "social policy": civilians under martial law were considered to be subhuman and under deliberate attack.[28]

In Swir's poems, cruelty is never far away. Atrocity blended seamlessly into the context of occupation. In "The German Soldier," she enters into the daily actions and sentiments of a German soldier: "Tonight you cried in your sleep / you dreamt of your children / in a far-off city . . . You got up this morning—uniform—helmet—submachine gun over the shoulder . . ." Prepared for the day "You went to throw into the fire, alive, / the children of others."[29]

The brutality in another poem is a cry of protest:
She whispered how he had loved her
and how he had departed,
the young woman with hair like a waterfall.
Yesterday
They cut off her leg.

She whispered about her happiness and despair,
she held my hand,
at dawn
when leaving I said:
see you tonight.

But that very evening
came that sudden moment
when the hospital ceased to exist.
And never again did I see
that woman without the leg, with hair
like a waterfall.[30]

The young woman and entire hospital were obliterated by a direct hit. During the war years a widespread revaluation took place of people, objects, and their relations to each other. Some writers admired the solidity of objects and even envied them. One advised his readers:

forget us
we envied
plants and stones[31]

Objects were admired for their solidity, they did not lie. They were concrete and tangible, stable, real. Objects were enlisted in a revolt against propaganda and rhetoric. One of the first revolts against rhetoric, and against ideology perceived as hollow, invoked concrete objects. In 1943, the French poet Francis Ponge wrote an entire volume about ordinary objects, *"Taking the Side of Things"* (*Le parti pris des choses*), and explained: "Objects convince me completely. Their concrete presence and evidence, their three dimensions, their palpable not-to-be-doubted look, their existence—is much more certain than my own. I am composed of their variety."[32]

But were material objects so invulnerable? They too could be destroyed with ease. An Italian writer, Natalia Ginsburg, noticed that a basic change in attitude took place toward a "home" when it had been fought for or struck with shells: "Someone who has seen a house collapse knows only too clearly what frail things little vases of flowers, and pictures and white walls are. He knows only too well what a house is made of . . . A house is not particularly solid."[33] The traditional notion of objects as solid is turned upside-down.

Once a realization was made that objects were not particularly solid, that they too were vulnerable like humans, the path was open to many new types of interactions. Some objects were life-giving, for example, life could be measured in terms of objects of food:

I was carrying two potatoes
a woman came up.

She wanted to buy the two potatoes
she had children.

I did not give her the two potatoes
I hid the two potatoes.

I had a mother.[34]

Some objects became unexpectedly precious. In the Warsaw ghetto, in 1943, one of the finest poets wrote that "celebrations" were to be made for the most useful objects, tools:

A cult will be made of objects
The spade, pickax, crowbar, and hammer.[35]

Many authors used objects to probe their experiences of deportation and the camps. For example, some objects were particularly close to the experiences of 1939–45. Trains affected the lives of everyone who lived under occupation; in the German zone of conquest a unified system of rails reached as far as Holland, Greece, and newly acquired territories in the East. The train regulated the lives of prisoners. It transported them, while prisoners laid the tracks. It was a common saying at the complex of camps in Kolyma in the USSR that a Polish prisoner lay buried under each tie of the railway that led there. In another version it was a Latvian. In Asia, prisoners repeated that under each tie of the Burmese "death railway" an Englishman was buried. In other versions it was an Australian, an American, or a Filipino. The Australian writer Ray Parkin calculated that a prisoner lay buried under every 17' 6" of the Burmese railway.[36]

The train became a protagonist in its own right in many stories, poems, and novels. In Heinrich Boell's *The Train was on Time*, the effect of trains on the lives of people becomes overpowering—all human relations, personal and official, are subordinated to trains and their timetables. In Jorge Semprun's *The Long Voyage* the narrator is identified with the train that takes him to Buchenwald; the ride lasts not several days but sixteen years.[37]

The stone, or pebble, appears in countless works about the years 1939–45. The stone comes in a multitude of shapes and forms.[38] Usually it represents a demarcation and limit—or benchmark—for inhuman, violent treatment. At work sites, men and women worked directly with stones. Micheline Maurel wrote in the women's camp in Ravensbrueck on August 15, 1944:

Lord my has soul become dried out . . .
If You make us wait any longer
for deliverance and return
You won't find anything to take . . .
You will find under the forehead
This divine and everlasting "soul"
As cold, as insensible and hard
As the stones that we carry.[39]

She compared the stones to her own exhausted body. In another poem she wrote she had become a "dried husk." The comparison had a special poignancy for prisoners at the women's camp at Ravensbrueck, where many permanently lost the ability to bear children.

Writings about objects were among the most original and unusual works produced during the war. Authors highlighted objects in most of the genres of literature—prose fiction and the novel, nonfiction, allegory, individual poems, linked series of poems. Many works resemble the *Metamorphoses* of Ovid as they dramatize the treatment, different uses and transformations of people—exploring the limits of what is human, what is not human.

3

"The New": The Shred of Platinum, the Explosion

"War literature" did not begin only in 1939, nor end in 1945. Its roots were deeper, it was not separate from national literary traditions nor was it outside the sequence of the history of literature. Traditional concepts of what was human and what was an object or thing were established earlier.

During the years of the 1920s and 30s, writers in the movements collectively called "Modernism" reacted against subjectivity and the emotional elements in the arts. Also they were influenced by the prestige and success of science. In American and English literature it is seen in the "Modernism" of Ezra Pound, T. S. Eliot, and T. E. Hulme, also in "Imagism." These writers associated concrete images and tangible objects with artistic form.[40]

A German movement called *Neue Sachlichkeit* ("New Factuality") also revolted against the emphasis on emotions of earlier Expressionism, and stressed realistic, factual detail. Ortega y Gasset defined a characteristic feature of new "modern" art as "dehumanization," and one avant-garde writer spoke for many when he claimed that the principal evolution of modern sensibility was a shift in creative effort away from the subject to the object.[41] Many writers were united in what they revolted against, sentimentality and diffuse subjectivity. But the conclusions they reached differed greatly.

There were different "Modernisms," often in stark contrast to one another. Two of them are summed up in works by two writers, Ernst Juenger and T. S. Eliot. The differences between them go to the heart of the history of the interwar period.

T. S. Eliot's essay "Tradition and the Individual Talent" is a well-known text of twentieth-century English literature: "It is in this depersonalization that art may be said to approach the condition of science. I, therefore, invite you to consider, as a suggestive analogy, the action which takes place when a bit of finely filiated platinum is introduced into a chamber containing oxygen and sulphur dioxide."[42]

When the two gases were mixed they formed sulfuric acid. "The mind of the poet," explained Eliot, "is the shred of platinum." During the creative act the mind serves as catalyst for the elements around it, transforming them. Eliot's comparison was fanciful but captured many of the aspirations of the time. Some of its ideas were already current. The comparison of men with machines had long been a stock-in-trade of the Futurists.

At about the same time Eliot wrote these lines, the German writer Ernst Juenger developed a similar analogy. Juenger compared the modern age as a whole to the working of an internal combustion engine. He thought the contemporary "technical" age resembled an engine that utilizes explosive detonations of gasoline vapor with maximum precision. It was at work in every field of life, part of a general process that Juenger called "Total Mobilization."[43] Juenger believed the history of civilization demonstrated the gradual replacement of men by things. He favored the process.

It is striking that two writers from entirely different backgrounds developed analogies with features in common: the appeal to science, the pursuit of impersonality, and the cult of precision. But the differences in their treatment of the analogy outweighed the similarities. Eliot admired precision but it was a means for finding a set of objects capable of expressing emotion, not destroying it. His intention was to produce a tangible work of art. Juenger's description was not really an analogy at all but a model for the whole world. It was prescriptive. He thought the desired transformation of society would be characterized by war, increased use of machines, unleashed vehemence, and pitiless discipline.

During the Second World War, Eliot and Juenger took different paths. Eliot was a fire warden during the Blitz, and wrote next to nothing. He did not apply his earlier laboratory image to the Second World War, or to any war. Juenger enthusiastically welcomed the war, and wrote about it at length.

He accompanied the invading German XI Army to Paris in 1940. In 1941, while eating at the famous Tour d'Argent restaurant in Paris, Juenger was surprised by an Allied air raid, and described the bombardment as seen through a glass of Burgundy wine. He enjoyed it thoroughly. The curved glass and the liquid were a "sea" distancing the author from the events on the other side of the goblet. His observation was an act of pleasure and delectation.[44]

The entries in the journals Juenger wrote between 1939 and 1945 have been called "hallucinatory prose poems"; Bruce Chatwin thought they were among the strangest literary productions of the war, comparable to works by Malaparte and Celine.[45] The main feature of Juenger's style was a deliberate intention to turn people into objects. An amateur collector of shells, stones, and insects, he affected a scientific—or pseudoscientific—attitude, applying it to the people he encountered in occupied France. He observed events around him with a "higher curiosity" that contributed to the willful depersonalization in his writings. The tone he adopted was that of a learned (*wissenschaftlich*) observer, looking at specimens.

Chatting one night with friends at a Parisian restaurant, they agreed that the main thing was not to be afraid, and Juenger had a vision: to eat, and eat well, gives a feeling of power. When Paris was again under Allied bombardment and eating with friends, he had a vision of the city submerged in the ocean: Paris was a coral reef. Another time he was dining and heard the sound of British bombers. "Sometimes the bombers flew rapidly above the houses like bats." Drinking 1911 champagne at the Tour d'Argent he compared the Allied airplanes to termites. Juenger shows an almost infinite ability to transform human beings and objects into something else.

What was ideological for others was for him an aesthetic, a style. He displays disarming ease and spontaneity in seeing things in the place of people. His study of the execution of a young German deserter in the Bois de Boulogne displays his method in an extreme form, especially his facility for making people disappear. A young German soldier had deserted. Hidden for several months by a young French woman, he was caught by the occupation police. Juenger presents the execution in minute, vivid detail. The trunk of the ash tree behind the victim is riddled with holes from earlier executions. One group of holes is from shots at the heads of previous victims, another group from shots at the heart. Inside the holes a few black meat flies are asleep. A fly crawls over the victim's left cheek. A medical officer pins a red tag the size of a playing card over the victim's heart. After the shots are fired, five small black holes appear on the card "like drops of rain." A fly dances in a shaft of sunlight.

The executioner, it turned out, was none other than Juenger himself, but we learn this not from Juenger. A young German soldier, Bernt

Engelmann, witnessed the scene. He watched, trembling, as the famous older German writer pulled on a pair of kid gloves before shooting the deserter in a spirit "of scientific curiosity."[46] By stylistic sleight-of-hand Juenger removed the main human protagonist—himself—`from his own description, leaving only a nameless, impersonal power. The victim was replaced by things: the holes in the tree, a colored card, the shaft of light, flies.

These substitutions could happen according to Juenger's whim, in any place or at any time. The procedure provided pleasure. It was also mixed with a portion of sadism, and disguised by a veneer of high culture. For the German writer it was an agreeable game of playful mental murder.[46]

In the 1930s, many observers had noticed there was an increasingly popular tendency to think of people as things. Michael Hamburger suggested it can be traced to the ideologies of the time that conceptualized large groups—social classes, and even nationalities—as things.[47] The trend was international. Writers noticed it in both Western and Eastern European literatures. Leaders, writers, and ordinary citizens spoke about groups and masses of people as if they were infinitely pliable, insentient collectivities. Individuals were frequently viewed only as representatives of the large groups.[48] Alexander Solzhenitsyn bitterly complained about strident Soviet administrative language that referred to people as "raw material," and entire social classes as "the nastiest of raw material."[49]

Albert Camus complained in 1943 in his *Letters to a German Friend* (*"Lettres a un ami allemand"*), "You speak of Europe, but the difference is that for you, Europe is a property, whereas we feel that we belong to it."[50] A historian, Robert Paxton, noted that at the highest level of policy Nazi Germany regarded the territories it conquered as booty.[51] In *A Thousand Shall Fall*, Hans Habe satirized the German occupation of northern France as an all-consuming quest for booty, but the "booty" was living people as well as things. Habe's satire became tragic when he showed how the quest for luxury goods led to the inexorable deportation of large numbers of French women into the German Reich.

The literalness of the treatment of people as things caused surprise at the time, and still causes surprise today. Juenger's pose of a scientific attitude and tone of a "learned" observer looking at specimens was not confined to him alone. During the Third Reich, technical efficiency and what has been called a "technocratic-hierarchical mentality" were adopted by the German state administration, the Foreign Office, the press, and academia.[52] The treatment of people as insentient things on an everyday level was facilitated by a corrupted German language that used words for "things"—*Stuecke, Figuren*—for living people.

Simon Wiesenthal recounted an episode that perfectly revealed, he believed, the kind of thinking that equated people with objects. A Russian bomb had torn a crater in a landing strip used by the Germans in Uman, near Kiev. The SS was ordered to repair it. Their mathematicians measured it exactly, and calculated that the bodies of 1,500 people would fill a crater of just that size. They procured the "building material" by methodically shooting the number of people required, threw them into the crater, covered them with earth and a steel mat, and the landing strip was as good as new.[53]

This points to systematic annihilation, and to the death camps.

4

"Books, Toys, and Everything . . ."

In a remarkable poem entitled "Things," a writer told the history of the Jewish ghetto in Warsaw in terms of their personal belongings, their "things." It is one of the most synoptic single poems about objects written during the war, and artistically one of the most accomplished. The "things" of the title are the entire range of personal objects that were carried, ranging from the unimportant—abandoned at the poem's beginning—to basic essentials, abandoned at the end. They correspond to stages in the lives of their owners, ending in deportation and Treblinka.

Between 1940 and 1943, German sweeps of the countryside forced more and more Jews into the Warsaw ghetto. At one point the crowded ghetto approached half a million people. They were forced to move from one place to another inside the ghetto, squeezed into a smaller area. The poem by Wladislaw Szlengel, "Things," has many stanzas, those placed at the left-hand margin alternate with those at the right. The left-hand stanzas name the streets along which they were driven. At first carts carried their belongings. Later they walked without carts, carrying what they could. The right-hand stanzas describe the objects they were forced to abandon along the streets:

THINGS

From Hoza Street and Marszalkowska
carts were moving, Jewish carts,

> furniture, tables and chairs,
> suitcases, bundles
> and chests, boxes and bedding,
> suits and portraits,

pots, linen and wall hangings,
cherry brandy, big jars and little jars,
glasses, tea pots and silver—
books, knickknacks and everything
go from Hoza Street to Sliska.
In a coat pocket, a bottle of vodka
and a chunk of sausage.
On carts, pushcarts and wagons
the gloomy band is going.

And from Sliska Street to Niska

all over again went moving:
furniture, tables and chairs,
suitcases and bundles,
linen and pots—gents, that's it.
Now there is no carpet,
of silverware not a sign,
there is no cherry brandy this time.
No suits or boots
or jars or portraits.
Already all these trifles
were left behind on Sliska.[54]

At the beginning of the poem the left-hand stanzas are short, the right-hand stanzas long describing many personal belongings that were taken with them. As the poem progresses these "things" are increasingly left behind on the streets. They were difficult to carry, inessential. As the poem continues the right-hand stanzas lengthen. More and more belongings are abandoned:

Then, from the apartment blocks to Ostrowska,
moving along a Jewish road,

with no big bundles or little bundles,
without furniture or chairs,
no pots for tea, no carpet,
no silverware or jars,
in the hand one suitcase,

a warm scarf and that's it.
Still a bottle of water
and a knapsack with straps,
trampling objects underfoot like a herd
they walked down the streets at night.

And on a cloudy day, at dusk, they walked
from Ostrowska to the Blockhouses.

A small suitcase, a knapsack,
no need for anything else.
Evenly . . . evenly by fives
they marched down the streets.
Nights cooler, days shorter,
tomorrow . . . maybe day after tomorrow . . .
to a whistle, a shout or command
on the Jewish road again.

The final destination was the railway terminal or *Umschlagplatz*. After that, Treblinka.

The last long stanza—all of it on the right—refers only to the abandoned objects. No people are in sight. It reads in part:

There are family photographs
scattered in a hurry.
A book lies open,
a letter in mid-sentence: ". . . bad . . ."
a glass half-empty
and playing cards, half a hand of
bridge.
Through a window the wind stirs
the sleeve of a cold shirt,
an eiderdown cover is hollow
as if someone nestled there.
Ownerless things lie around,
a dead apartment stands waiting
until new people
populate the rooms . . .

The understated word "bad" is bitterly ironic, contrasted to the real situation revealed by the abandoned "things."

What was it that led the writer, before he was killed by the troops of General Stroop in the April 1943 uprising, to describe the history of a large community of people in terms of objects? Much of the tragic irony of the poem and its pathos comes from the focus on the "things"—they are intimate foils for the people who used them in life and had a living relationship with them. The things are so varied that they evoke the life of the entire community. They are also a metaphor for the disappearance and death of the community.

Each object is still closely tied to its owner. The momentum and forward thrust of walking that continues for most of the poem carries over to the very end. The poet presents each object as if it was abandoned only a moment before. A book lies open as if it was still being read, but the wind turns the pages. Cards are dealt in the middle of a hand of bridge waiting to be played. Bedding, a down cover, still carries the imprint of a person nestling beneath for warmth. The "things," "books, toys, and everything," continue to evoke the life that animated them—but the life is no longer there.

This is true also of the poem, which was preserved; the author died in 1943 but some of his works still remain buried, deep under the rubble of the ghetto.

V
Animals

1

Flight

*L*ife could continue in captivity and under occupation. The treatment of the human being changed. The vocabulary of freedom, of home, security, and warmth, disappeared, many comforting illusions were abandoned. Conditions changed but life still went on. What was that life, how could a person describe it? The challenge was to find words for it.

Often it was a life of numbing physical labor. Many people found they were required to do the work of a domestic animal. One writer arrived at a forced labor camp and, on the first day, found a heavy wooden yoke placed around his neck. He had to heave, like an ox, against the yoke with all his strength.

Sometimes a person had the illusion that he was changed temporarily into an animal, perhaps a domestic animal, or an animal from a familiar species. But more often his situation could be best defined by a string of negatives: he was not this, he was not that . . . For better or worse he remained a person, he could not remove his skin, or transform himself into something else.

Most surprising were his own reactions. They were unmistakably his own. But in what category were they, were they "human" or something else quite different? How could he describe them to others, with words? How could he—or she—communicate them?

* * *

In a short story by a Czech writer, the protagonist is in hurried flight. It is a chase.

The whisper of stones disappears in white silence. Feet sink, fall behind, give way. But paws, brown, velvety paws, glide over snow, agile and light. They come with jaws, though . . . He had been on the run for several days and the border was still far. He skulked around lonely houses and farmsteads, slept in barns and haylofts, no, no one must see him, and he ate what he could steal: raw turnips, a handful of oats, and a few frost-bitten potatoes. He could not—dared not—ask anyone for hot food or a place to spend the night, no matter how he longed for hot food and a fire. He shook with cold and hunger, but he had to go forward. His was the hare's path, seeking always to confuse his pursuers. He had to be at once a hare and a fox, to glide through the silence and disappear into the snow. His hungry body cried out for sleep but his throbbing temples urged him onward. Onward, to where there is peace and quiet, bread and a hot bowl of soup; onward to where there is sleep in a bed, to the border. If only he could grow fur, white or brown or even russet; if only his heavy feet could turn into paws or perhaps hooves—it would have been good to be an animal. But in the thick of the hunt he was a man in a tattered greatcoat and cracked boots; he had to walk where he would have done better to leap, fly, or burrow.[1]

As he flees from unnamed pursuers, the man thinks of his actions more in terms of animals than of men. He thinks of himself as "I," and the images that pass through his mind are spontaneous, natural, and compelling. He focuses on flight in its most active form, as it unfolds in the present. He thinks of his own movements, his needs, and his hunger, with animal imagery. The reader is led to accept that the narrator is almost—though never completely—an animal. This was the form adopted by the Czech short story writer Jiri Weil to express an experience described in many writings from the wartime period: flight.

As with the writings that describe people treated as insentient objects, this was the experience of an ordinary civilian, one event in the lives of the countless people caught behind the fronts and changed frontiers, living in the world of occupation. It was always unpredictable, often deadly. The purpose of most of these comparisons with animals is to explore the "human" side of the comparison: the stress is on the reactions of the human person, caught up in "occupation" or captivity. As with the use of objects, it was often a language of protest against the treatment of human beings.

In the description of flight from unnamed pursuers, the greatest emphasis probably is at the end: "in the thick of the hunt he was a man in a tattered greatcoat and cracked boots." Despite his many thoughts about an animal world, he remained—for better or worse—a human person. There are many negatives in the passage: he is not this, he is not that, the narrator declares "he was a hunted animal, yet in this hunt he was not, could not be an animal." On the other hand what gives the passage its special force is the refusal of the man in flight to believe he belongs any longer to the "normal" human world. He has left safety, security, peace, all former comforts. His world is stripped bare. He is no longer human but something else, and the whole work strains toward what that something else is. Images suggest parts of animals, feet, paws, wings. But almost always he is *not* that.

Another writer might have given different concrete details about an escape, for example where he escaped from, which town, which prison, who arrested him and why. Weil chose a different kind of narration, and gives no circumstantial information about the man or the reasons for his flight; he provides only the man's vivid thoughts. For long passages he forgets he is a "man" at all. His needs and instincts are different from those of a human being in a normal world, but there is no one-to-one equivalence with a single animal. Rather he describes a range of behavior and instincts concentrated on the act of flight. In his thoughts he is a creature in the animal world. Later in the story the reader learns there is a bounty on his head, "for his blood." A bounty for a human being? Or for an animal? The question remains open, it is unresolved.

2

The Cracked Mirror

Jaroslav Seifert's "Song about a Mirror" describes a sudden explosion in an arms factory. The "Song about a Mirror" was an early poem by Seifert; who was to win the Nobel Prize for Literature much later in 1984. The explosion in the factory was unexpected, shook the ground, and took the lives of many civilian workers, most of them women:

> That time when the ignition cap factory
> was blown into the air,
>   clots of ash spattered the street
> from the bodies of working women torn asunder.
>
> Where did you lift your eyes, where did you turn,
> with nothing left to look on but despair?
>
>   The terrified birds
> forsook their rooftop nests in helplessness,
> but you were still more helpless than the birds,
> for you had no wings
>   and knew not where to fly.[2]

The images are careful and exact. At the sound of the explosion frightened birds suddenly rose in the air. The human participants in the event could not rise up like the birds, but their fears rose as if on wings. This is prefigured by the lifting of the eyes. The order of phrase and image, the use of questions and negations mimic the movement of the birds together with human fear at the same time. Both share the same impulse. The poet's reaction, his human fear and that of the women caught in the explosion, was a sudden impulse for flight. But ordinary human limbs were too slow, they were glued to the ground.

In "Song about a Mirror" Seifert focuses on a human experience, even a very human experience. It is not an act of close looking at an animal or birds but at his own human fear. The ending of Seifert's poem maintains a delicate balance with the focus on the person—"you"—at the moment he, or she, is characterized by an impulse toward flight.

Another author described the acute human need for safety and escape by developing a very different animal metaphor. She imagines she is a centipede.

I shall survive.

I shall find the very deepest cellar,
I shall shut myself up, let no one in,
I shall dig a hole in the earth,
with my teeth I shall bite out the bricks,
I shall hide in the wall, go into the wall
like a centipede.

Everyone will die, but I
shall survive.[3]

Who is the "I" of the poem? The speaker imagines that in order to survive she must disappear and blot herself out. She is both human and not human, both a centipede and not a centipede. The speaker focuses on the powerful instinct for flight and safety that characterizes both human and animal worlds. As in the short story by Jiri Weil, she wishes she could escape from her human body, find camouflage and safety. This is only a momentary wish as she forgets herself, wanting to obliterate herself and escape. "Man and Centipede" is a poem that expresses the human instinct for survival, and in a brief span the instinct takes the form of another creature that shares it.

Hunger was one of the most common and frequently felt needs during the war. It was nothing if not human. Often civilians and captives tried to highlight its overpowering intensity. The anonymous author of *The Dark Side of the Moon* described hunger in the large group of civilians deported to Kazakhstan: "Most characteristic of all was the animal sensation of hunger. Everybody was always hungry, all the time. Enormous strength of character, extraordinary vitality, were necessary to surmount the obsession all felt with this theme, and to speak or think of other things."[4]

Constant extreme hunger completely dominated the thoughts and the functioning of the human being. The same writer added that over a term of years, "the human being within the carcass dies progressively; a suffering, stupefied, and often barely complaining animal takes its place."

In a striking collection of short stories, *Men and Animals*, the French author Pierre Gascar described extreme hunger. Gascar wrote of a group of Russian prisoners confined by their German captors in a barn, and nearby a circus menagerie is driven from its regular quarters by an offensive front. The daily feeding of raw meat to the beasts proves an insurmountable torment to the men, who are starving on a diet of watery soup. The men begin to bribe the keeper with tobacco, and each day they are given a portion of the meat destined for the beasts: "As their own hell died down, another hell started up on the other side of the barn. It was the same hell: a wild frenzy that could never be allayed everywhere at once. The fury of the beasts condemned to hunger burst forth in a concert of growls and moans that left no peace to the inhabitants of the barn . . . The starving animals tore the floorboards of their cages with the spasmodic violence of creatures buried alive."[5] It was "the same hell," the hell of the animals and the hell of the men.

Events brought people into unexpected kinship with a variety of nonhuman creatures. The spectrum of animal life was always surprisingly broad, strict divisions or taxonomies tended to disappear. During peace hygiene kept many insects and animals at arm's length, but that had changed. The author of "My Lice" realized that her body was accompanied by other creatures. It seemed almost natural:

On my breasts under the blouse
move
the warm lice.

Only they and I are alive,
and that binds us.[6]

Many believed that the traditional division between humans and animals, including parasites, had broken down completely. A writer in a camp observed: "Head sunk deep into your body, it stands perpendicular . . .

Your blood shines through its skin."[7] In a gesture of revolt the poet Guenter Eich rhymed "Faust" with "*verlaust,*" a German word meaning "covered with lice." It was an irreverent joke, and by bringing *Faust*, the famous literary work by Goethe, down to the level of lice he was removing literature from any pedestal.[8] Animal life and fauna were almost never described for their own sake, they were not separate. The hierarchical model broke down, clichés and old stereotypes were abandoned. What we call "animals" were countersparts to human beings, and were used to express the shock that accompanied human recognition of a new situation. It was usually a result of direct experience.

In the labor camps, it was often the domestic animals that became benchmarks, or terms of comparison, for prisoners.[9] It became clear for many that they would be preserved barely above the starvation level. But domestic animals were better fed than the prisoners. A writer noted, "We did not have to wait any longer to see that even a domestic animal's standard of living was now an inaccessible dream for us. A dog, a horse, a cow that one washed and brushed down, and gave a dry sleeping place, an animal one nourished and did not strike except when truly necessary, had an admirable life in comparison with ours." The German writer Ernst Weichert tentatively used the comparison with animals to describe treatment of prisoners at Buchenwald then quickly rejected it: "These men are driven like cattle 'with the stick,' no, worse than cattle, since cattle have masters who are aware not of mercy but of profit. There is no farmer anywhere who looks upon his cattle with vengeful eyes."[10] They were not treated like a dog, or horse, or cow. How, then, were the prisoners to be classified?

One writer, Elinor Lipper, described an unusual event in a Soviet labor camp. A prisoner petitioned the camp authorities to be given the status of a horse. The prisoner was starving and had reached a point beyond caring. He would be better treated if he was given the status of a horse:

It's very easy to explain, Citizen Commander. If I were a horse, I would have at least one day off in ten. Now I have no days off.
If I were a horse, I could rest now and then while at work. As a prisoner I cannot.
If I were a horse, I would be assigned to work equal to my strength. As a prisoner I am always hungry, and when I do not meet my labor quota I get less bread, so that I do still less work, and in the end I get so little bread that I can hardly stand on my feet.

A horse has his stable and his blanket—I haven't had a new jacket for two years because my percentages are too low.

A horse doesn't have to work more than fourteen hours a day. But I am kept in the mines fourteen and sixteen hours, especially when I haven't met my quota.

If drivers beat a horse too hard, or drive him too much, they are punished. For a horse is precious in Kolyma. But who punishes the guards and brigadiers who beat and kick me because I've become too weak to do my work well?

What is a prisoner in Kolyma? Nothing. But a horse—a horse is something.[11]

As punishment for writing his petition the man was locked in solitary confinement for ten days. Lipper stressed the list-like nature of the petition; its faux-naif tone and its punctiliousness mock the camp's regulations.

The story was based on a real event in Camp Burkhala in October 1944, and became well known among prisoners. Varlam Shalamov probably heard it, and chose the form of parody for his version of the event in his short story "Caligula." A camp commander, choleric and completely drunk, flogs an emaciated horse because it has not fulfilled its "quota." Then, in a rage, he locks the horse in the camp prison. Shalamov notes that the angry commander "was panting like a winded horse himself." At a loss how next to insult the horse, he calls it a "swine." Then he shouts at the horse, "You can go to the punishment cells, damn and blast you, with all the other enemies of humanity. Seventy-two hours as it's your first time. On sheer damn water."[12] The event recalls the Roman emperor Nero who introduced his favorite horse, Incitatus, inside the Roman Senate. Here, the large horse is crammed inside a narrow punishment cell for humans.

These are bitter parodies about human behavior and cruelty. Another parodist used a broad array of animals to describe the real human behavior he observed. Curzio Malaparte began his novel *Kaputt* in the summer of 1941, continued it in Poland, Ukraine, and Finland as he simultaneously wrote news dispatches for the Italian newspaper *Corriere della Sera*. He put the last touches on his manuscript of *Kaputt* at the island of Capri toward the end of 1943. Malaparte played an intricate game of cat-and-mouse—of support and dissent—with Mussolini; he finally fell into disfavor because his dispatches were increasingly critical of the

Fascist Italian regime and its German ally. He was arrested on orders from Mussolini and sent to Regina Coeli prison.

Kaputt is divided into six parts, each named after an animal: "The Horses," "The Mice," "The Dogs," "The Birds," "The Reindeer," and "The Flies." These are fluid terms, referring to civilians and the landscapes they inhabit. "The Birds," for example, represent helpless civilians, above all Jewish women who live in a state of fear under German occupation and try to hide. "The Dogs" are real dogs, starving, abandoned by their owners and used by Ukrainian boys as grenade carriers.

In a chapter of *Kaputt* titled "Siegfried and the Salmon," Malaparte describes a "duel" in Finland between a German general and a salmon. It is a parody of the cult of the hunt, widespread among German officers who carried "hunting" terminology with them in their invasions abroad. Malaparte described a contest between an aging German general and a cunning salmon. The general tried to catch the salmon with a lure, but the fish was stronger and slowly pulled the general downstream. In full battle dress, his big Mauser dangling from his belt, the contest with the salmon lasted for three hours.

Finally, the general commanded his orderly to come and shoot it. The orderly waded into the water, following the line until he reached the fish. "He stopped, drew his pistol from its holster, bent over the brave salmon, and fired two shots point blank into its head."[13]

The scene is a sharp critique of Nazi-style behavior and the cult of the "hunt." It contains many direct references to the war. The shot fired point blank was the famous *Genickschuss,* a shot in the nape of the neck. The fish was treated like countless civilians in countries occupied by German armies, and with the victim's back turned it was a particularly cowardly type of execution.

Malaparte excelled in vivid scenes where German authorities with wives, dignitaries, and leading collaborators feast in sumptuous castles like Wawel, in Cracow, or in Finland. A real salmon might end on a silver platter, a little red Nazi flag with a black swastika stuck into its back. The heavily laden table often mimicked the hunt. Varied cooked game lay on platters with the head intact, pheasant, salmon, or young deer. In the Wawel Castle, where Hans Frank presided as "the king of Poland," the "etiquette of the hunt" continued to the end of the feast, the hostess carving the "fruits of the hunt" with a special bone-handled hunting knife.

According to Malaparte, the hunt was a thin cover for the joy of slaughter. It disguised this "joy" and at the same time directed it into "socially accepted" forms. Malaparte claimed that what most excited the Nazis was the defenselessness of their victims. In earlier centuries the hunt was a leisure activity favored by an aristocratic military class, but in Nazi Germany the old rules were completely transformed.[14] The fiction of the hunt erased the line between war and peace. The act of hunting needed no declaration, it also provided impunity from any religious sanctions. Malaparte believed it went to the heart of the Nazi enterprise. The traditional notion of "war" with fronts, concepts of defense and offense, became irrelevant. Malaparte raised a key question, whether he was really witnessing "war" with significant military objectives, or something quite different, unlike past wars. This was "the joy of slaughter," a phrase that Malaparte heard often from highly placed Nazi officials.

Mass behavior became a major theme during the war. Many were able to observe the behavior of large groups at close range. The loss of individuality, the compulsive merging in a larger group and "herd" behavior, was observed in different places by writers of different nationalities. Victor Frankl, a writer and psychiatrist, experienced at first hand the powerful temptation to stop thinking of himself as an individual. He described his own behavior: "He thought of himself then as only a part of an enormous mass of people; his existence descended to the level of animal life. The men were herded—sometimes to one place, then to another; sometimes driven together, then apart—like a flock of sheep without a thought or will of their own."[15]

Other authors used a combination of allegory and realism to describe mass behavior during the war. Some works were written after 1946 by Guenther Grass, Michel Tournier and others,[16] and Eugene Ionesco's play *The Rhinoceros* explicitly addressed the instinct that compels an individual to lose identity and merge with a large group. The best explanation of *The Rhinoceros* and its description of the transformation of human beings into a violent herd of animals is given in Ionesco's autobiographical study, *Present past Past present*. The experience of transformation is located at a specific moment: in 1940, in the country of Ionesco's youth, Romania. Ionesco was conversing quietly with a friend named "S." when they began to speak of politics. His friend was "of course" anti-Nazi, and hostile to the Romanian Fascist movement. But then his friend began to make concessions: "The Iron Guards . . . are not right on all points. However you must admit . . . they call for certain moral and spiritual values which . . ."[17] At this point Ionesco rose to his feet in horror. In the process of making concessions, his friend was becoming a fanatic without realizing it. He stuttered, became furious, shifted to the attack: "I see his skin get hard and thicken in a terrifying way. His gloves, his shoes became hooves; his hands became paws, a horn began to grow out of his forehead." He became a "rhinoceros."

Stanley Hoffmann, a professor and social scientist who was a boy in France during the war, described Ionesco's play in this way: "When I think back on that long nightmare from 1938 to the liberation of France in 1944 . . . there is one great allegorical play that embodies, for me, all the absurdities and tragedies of that long descent into degradation: Eugene Ionesco's *Rhinoceros* . . . The play captures the essence of the period better than any work of history or social science."[18]

Events made people look at the people around them, and at themselves, in a new way. A wide range of human behavior opened up: motivations, instincts, actions and reactions, the behavior and ways of acting of what some called "the human animal." These took forms that were new and old at the same time, raw, fresh, surprising. In the words of Pierre Gascar they "make us recognize, with an astonished sense of kinship, our own tortured likeness, as in a scratched mirror."

3

Animals, Angels, and History

Great conflicts between the animal and the divine are one of the most ancient themes of literature. Sophocles emphasized the contrasts in human nature, especially in the choral passages of his plays. In his *Pensees* Blaise Pascal showed man oscillating between the domains of the gods and of beasts. Contrasts between the animal and the divine have been a perennial theme in culture.[19]

The nineteenth century strictly hierarchized human instincts, vice and evil were associated with animals, subject to what were often called "downward comparisons." They were considered "lower" in an evolutionary sense. The novelist George Eliot used animals to show the debasement of some of her characters; the villainous Grandcourt in her novel *Daniel Deronda*, who is moved only by the will to dominate, is compared by the novelist at different moments to an insect, a crab, and a boa constrictor. For Dostoevski's "Underground Man" the "anthill" conveyed what it sometimes means in contemporary usage: mechanized social beings, deprived of freedom, individuality, spontaneity.

In the 1920s and 1930s, animal imagery and comparisons had become widespread in one country after another. In the USSR, rhetorical invective using animal references was used methodically in the press and even in the courts. State Prosecutor Andrei Vyshinsky denigrated a defendant as "a wretched cross between a fox and a pig . . . a beast in human form . . . a mad dog." This has been described as an official attempt to dehumanize the opposition, to animalize it.[20] Mircea Eliade and others described the popular use of black-and-white reasoning in the 1930s, and the widespread use of polarization and animal imagery; Zbigniew Brzezinski wrote of the the "metamyths" of the 1930s that tapped instinctual hatreds, aggravated by appeals to nationalist sentiment.[21] On a popular level, racist prejudices and doctrines had become widespread even though none had any basis in science.

In Asia, polarization was widespread. For Japan, the war for empire was based on concepts of race and ethnicity. The United States was a "mongrel" nation; Japanese printed media endorsed the thesis of the enemy as an animal or beast in an ingenious way peculiar to their ideographic writing system. To the usual characters for America 米 and Britain 英 they added a conventional radical or ideogram denoting bestiality 犭. In this way, America and Americans became 㹑, while Great Britain and the British became 㹈.[22] These were used in the 1920s and 30s, and during the war itself.

But after 1939, a shift occurred in a large number of English-language and non-English writings.[23] With increasing frequency, serious observers and writers rejected the rigidly separated categories of "people" and "animals." In response to the experiences of occupation and combat, many reevaluated the clichés of propaganda and popular concepts of psychology. The hierarchy, and separation, between humans and animals broke down. This can be seen in one work after another. The fusion of different domains can be seen in Jean-Paul Sartre's *The Flies*, staged in a clandestine performance in Paris in 1943. The "Flies" of Sartre's play were the omnipresent informers and denouncers in society at the time, made familiar in studies by Andre Halimi, Richard Cobb, and others.

One writer observed that "individuals and human societies constantly discover new dimensions that are accessible only to direct experience. We often apprehend these unintentionally, even against our will."[24] Writers discovered new dimensions in behavior, and sensed that they were confronting the most basic, essential human reactions for the first time. These produced a vivid shock of recognition. The great contrasts of human behavior were extended by writers in all directions: into history and ancient history, into religion, and ethics. The breadth of "human" actions, it turned out, was almost unimaginable in its range.

VI
Wall, Watchtower, Chimney

1

Sending Messages

*T*he most demanding challenge was to transmit information about the
camps. There were many different kinds of camps, and they became
one of the most widespread, ubiquitous institutions of the war years. Usually propaganda denied that they existed. During most of the war they
were carefully hidden. Thoroughly militarized, they were well guarded
and had strict security. Many were protected by great spaces, and distance
from urban centers. During the years 1939–45 it was extremely difficult to
transmit information about the camps. The risks at every stage of attempted
communication were lethal.

There were many different kinds of camps, and the features of the camps
changed constantly. They were not peripheral to the course of the war.
In 1939–41 they were central. After 1941 their importance did not
diminish. Information about the camps influenced some of the major decisions about the course of the war.

* * *

The two largest camps systems in the world—Soviet and German—
came into very close proximity in 1941. They almost collided. One captive
wrote:

When we were haymaking, a friend named Sadovski was asked
for his conjectures of the future. He took a few twigs, two hand-
fuls of hay and some berries of different colors, spread them on
the grass, and opened a fascinating lecture. In his opinion the first
four weeks of fighting would be decisive. While listening to official Soviet communiqués, it was necessary to keep before one's
mind the map of Russia in order to determine the speed of the
German advance.

It is a measure of the bestiality and despair to which the new system of slavery reduces its victims that not only the thousands of simple Russians . . . and minorities for whom the Germans were the natural ally in their struggle against the hated labor camps, but also almost without exception all Europeans . . . awaited from day to day with impatience and excitement the coming of Nazi liberators. I think with horror and shame of a Europe divided into two parts by the line of the Bug River, on one side of which millions of Soviet slaves prayed for liberation by the armies of Hitler, and on the other, millions of victims of German concentration camps awaited deliverance by the Red Army as their last hope . . .[1]

2

The USSR: Arrival

The first deportations eastward in 1939 left an indelible impression. A captive wrote, "Volumes could be filled with nothing but the story of the trains. And even then it would not have been told, for there are no words . . . One can enumerate the horrors but there will always be the distance of a universe between this imagination and the experience itself."

Security was tight. A soldier was in each car. Before entering the trains, fathers were separated from their families: "Regular inspections began by beating on the walls of the cars with their rifles, to make sure no planks had been loosened anywhere and nobody was contemplating escape . . . Always, in the last car of each convoy, there was a mounted machine gun. At night searchlights were lit on the roofs of the train."[2]

One woman wrote: "We saw the same scenes at each station: stretchers loaded with corpses of dead people. At first this horrified us, but then we got used to that, too, although we were always happier when the train stopped in the dark of night, because then, at least, we were spared these sights."[3]

This was the greatest happiness: not to have to look.

At every station prisoners were counted, surrounded by guards, weapons, and dogs. The guards had dogs on leashes, revolvers in their hands. The prisoners were told "a step to the left, a step to the right" would be treated as an attempt to escape, for this the soldiers had orders to shoot without further warning.[4]

A prominent theme in the writings about these deportations in 1939–41 was their sheer destructiveness. The loss of life, especially among the elderly and young, was on a vast scale and completely unnecessary. Another theme is equally prominent: the tight security measures. The deportees were alert for any possible means of escape or communication with the world outside, but the transports were thoroughly militarized. At the time they probably represented the tightest, most hermetic security in the world. There was no possibility of communicating with people from other transports who spoke their same language, or the home countries left behind hundreds of miles to the west. Escapes were nonexistent. Communication was completely blocked.

Narratives about imprisonment in the Soviet Union at the beginning of the war attempted to answer the basic question, Where were they? What was the nature of these "camps," were they recognizable "camps" at all with buildings or structures? The narrations are often built around questions: those of the writer, and imaginary questions of others. The descriptions are often explanatory as if they were a continuation of the many questions and fragmentary messages left at transit points. Where were they going? _This_—the description that followed—was where they went. After arrival they could finally answer questions of people they knew in their home countries about the destination of the deportations.

In Soviet nomenclature, these were neither "camps" nor even "sites" but something in between. The camp was a "camp-point," in Russian "_lagierny punkt._" A typical name for a camp was an acronym such as "L/P F," which meant "_Lagierny punkt F_" or "Camp-Point F." The shock of arrival was followed by other shocks in swift succession. Often the "camp" did not yet exist, it was a halt at an arbitrary point in space.

One writer described a large group that had traveled hundreds of kilometers: "When we arrived, a post was stuck into the ground and we were told: 'Now you can live here.'"[5] The camp was to be built by the prisoners themselves. The guards had a canvas tent they covered with moss and snow. The initial task of the prisoners was to build a wooden house, an office, kitchen and bathhouse for the guards. The author described how the prisoners dug their own "accommodations" in the frozen ground, and slept glued to it. He observed laconically: "Men died like flies, but new prisoners were brought to replace them."

A young Polish man fled the German invasion in 1939, like many others hoping to join an armed unit in the Soviet Union that would fight the Germans. Instead he was imprisoned then sent with a group to the far north:

At a certain moment, when we had come to a clearing in a wild and trackless forest, we were stopped. Stragglers were rounded up by the dogs. One of the guards stepped up to the thickest tree. He hacked off part of the bark, and drew the number "1" with red chalk on the trunk. Then he made a speech. This, he said, was where we were going to live. We were going to work here and help to build the Soviet Union. And that was our introduction to our labor camp which, as yet, did not exist.[6]

Further south, in Kazakhstan, they passed many established "sites" or settlements:

The whole is one vast NKVD state, divided into "zones," each territory enclosed within barbed wire, patrolled by armed guards and their dogs and made doubly secure by lookout towers and storks' nests containing sentries. Each zone covers hundreds of kilometers, and there is generally at least one camp on each kilometer. Thus camps take their names from the kilometers on which they stand, being called "on the hundredth kilometer," "on the thousandth kilometer," "on the fifteen-hundredth kilometer," and so on.[7]

At first glance the sites had the appearance of "colonies" in the wilderness. But captives soon learned that no effort was made to encourage families. The method of distributing food from different pots—the so-called "kettle system"—allotted larger portions to the strongest workers and was intended to kill the weak, elderly, and sick. One writer noted it would be incorrect to compare their camps to nineteenth-century British penal colonies, for example, in Australia, because they were never charged with any legal infractions. Basic questions remained. How could they be called "colonies" if no effort was made to sustain life?

Organization was strictly military, the deported civilians subject to the armed NKVD from beginning to end. When Margarete Buber worked in a Soviet agricultural camp or "sovkhoz" during the 1939–41 period she picked potatoes, a guard at the edge of the field training a machine gun on the workers. Unto Parvilahti wrote in *Beria's Gardens*: "I was one of the thousands of prisoners who, guarded by dog patrols, were transported for potato planting to the vast open fields. At the edges, machine-gun units were posted to prevent attempted escapes into the fields."[8]

An overriding question remained: What was the purpose of these militarized settlements? Was it "war" or something else, perhaps worse? Almost no effort was made to provide ideological camouflage. In the Soviet camps the word "war" was carefully avoided, phrases like "building the

USSR" used in its place. This was, however, the Second World War but a "war" dominated by militarized camps.

The prisoners were told they would pass their whole lives in their camp. Were the camps permanent? Would they ever change? A captive asserted, "There is no question of holding out within yourself for, say, three years, or even five or eight (in most camps, a physical impossibility anyhow) and remaining yourself, or some shadow of yourself, and then leaving it behind. *Nobody leaves lagier* [the camp] *behind*. Lagier is forever."[9]

There were no escapes or communication with the outside world, the blackout was complete, the camps would be permanent. Who could believe otherwise?

3

The USSR: June 22, 1941

When Germany attacked the Soviet Union on June 22, 1941, deportation trains filled with non-Russian civilians were still moving eastward, toward destinations inside the USSR. Camps in Siberia and Kazakhstan were filling up, and new ones created.[10] The railway system was clogged.[11] The attack on June 22, 1941, occurred at a moment of maximum vulnerability.

Inside the Soviet camps, the days after the German attack on June 22, were a time of shock and intense excitement. Most narratives by captives in the camps believed everything had suddenly changed. It would be a dramatic turning point in their lives. Countless conversations took place, each prisoner had two overriding questions: What did the event mean for himself? How would it affect the course of the war? Prisoners were aware that the enormous camp population must have a significant role in a war between the Soviet Union and Germany. What would that role be?

The author of *A World Apart*, one of the finest narratives about the Soviet camps during this period, wrote that "During the first few weeks of the war we talked of the fighting rarely and surreptitiously but always in the same words: "They are coming!"

As prisoners tried frantically to learn about the new events, something that seemed incredible happened: fresh contingents of young and healthy NKVD soldiers arrived at the camp to strengthen the garrison. But at the same time, the names of towns mentioned in wireless communiqués made it clear that the front was moving rapidly eastward. The official Soviet answer to the German invasion came quickly: "a declaration of war on all potential internal enemies." Which meant: the prisoners in the camps.

The reaction of captives was very different: "All German prisoners from the Volga settlements were treated with great respect by the Russian prisoners, who believed that they would soon be masters of the country."[12] More than a thousand miles to the east, in the gold-mining center of Kolyma, a Russian prisoner observed a similar rapid response to the bulletin about the invasion. He wondered what would happen to the prisoners, "As if in answer to my thought a detachment of guards appeared, marching with a quick step up the only street of the settlement. They disappeared into the gate of the camp, and almost immediately I saw two of them hauling something dark into the tower nearest to me. Looking at it hard, I managed to distinguish a machine gun."[13]

One Russian writer remembered the announcement of the attack:

Jumping from our bunks in the night of June 23 after being wakened by the furious firing of anti-aircraft guns, many of us congratulated each other on the outbreak of the war we had been expecting so long . . . Some now shook each other by the hand, hoping for liberation in the near future . . . These were men like myself who were outraged, ashamed, and helpless, who wanted to save their country, wrest it from the clutches of arbitrary rule, restore liberties and put an end to the constant mass terror."[14]

This was Dimitri Panin, who after the war became a friend of Alexander Solzhenitsyn and the model for the character "Sologdin" in Solzhenitsyn's novel *The First Circle*. Panin was a writer, and in his own book, *The Notebooks of Sologdin*, he described the initial reaction in his camp to the news of the German attack. He believed the majority of Russians outside the camps were hostile to the regime. If the Germans established a "provisional Russian government" in Kiev or another Russian city, he was certain they would give it their allegiance. An uprising would follow.

Throughout the summer and autumn the excitement at Panin's camp continued. A railway engine stood waiting, fired, noisily blowing off steam, preparing to evacuate guards and administrators if the camp was overrun. The presence of the steam engine ready to depart created a constant sense of suspense. Observers and writers agreed that the size of the camp population represented a huge vulnerability for the Soviet Union.

After the conclusion of the war, Alexander Solzhenitsyn dramatized the moment of the German attack in his play *Prisoners*. An anti-Soviet Russian soldier named Kolosovitov forcefully claimed that victory over Stalin was a fruit waiting to be plucked: "We should have landed forces outside the labor camps! All one needed to do then was to knock out the miserable camp guards and hungry hands would be stretching out for armaments. We would have had an army twelve million strong, and in the rear, what's more. But Hitler, that arrogant idiot . . . he was afraid to create independent regimes from us."[15]

In *Vanished without Trace*, Antoni Ekart described the same anxiety in a camp in the Urals, and the excited expectation that the prisoners' lives could change at any moment. "Imagine a crowd of prisoners, exhausted after work, living on the narrow margin between physical torture and the early prospect of death by exhaustion. They know perfectly well that their miserable situation is due to the Soviet system, yet they have to listen to an appeal to defend this system against an alien enemy. It is like a cat begging a mouse to defend it."

As chaos increased after the invasion, the hopes of Panin, Ekart, and others had real justification. The danger was acute, the constellation of forces transformed. Because of their sheer size—several times the size of the Red Army and the NKVD put together—the camps were an important variable. They were, of course, completely unarmed. News came that the Soviet Army was disorganized, whole units were surrendering. In the German encirclement of Kiev alone, 500,000 Russian troops were captured. By December 1941, it is estimated about 2.5 million Russian troops were taken prisoner, and 4.5 million were dead.[16]

When we read the few narratives that have escaped censorship, it becomes clear this was one of the most unpredictable and chaotic periods in the war. For the twenty-two months before the German invasion, the Russian people had been kept totally ignorant of German occupation actions and policies in lands to the west. Soviet newspapers and other media were without exception pro-German. For almost two years the Soviet press presented an idealized picture of German honesty, efficiency, and culture. German diplomats were regularly received in the Kremlin, Wagner's *Die Walkuerie* was performed at the Bolshoi Theater. After the attack on June 22, during the months of June and July, Russians fleeing areas occupied by German armies could be arrested and sent to camps just for saying that there was a war.[17]

Narratives vividly express the excitement, frustration, and helplessness of the unarmed prisoners during the German invasion. Speculations about a Russian provisional government, and German parachute drops near the camps, perhaps seem wild in retrospect, but when we recreate the real situation at the time—the locomotive ready to take guards to safety if the camp was overrun—they can be easily understood. The NKVD was speculating along similar lines. The drama of the summer of 1941 was real. It was impossible to foresee the outcome.

There is no evidence that Hitler ever considered the Soviet gulag in his strategy. Liberating slave labor camps was never on his agenda. The gulag camps even attracted Himmler's attention as a useful repository for *his* slaves. A military historian has written that Hitler made two of his greatest mistakes that summer: the first was his failure to take the huge population of the camps into consideration. The second was his continued brutality toward the Russian civilian population.[18]

The front was pushed to the outskirts of Moscow, then the Wehrmacht turned south.

As recruiting grounds the camps made important contributions to the Soviet war effort. Key decisions were made in August, a month and a half after the invasion: a pact was signed with the Polish government-in-exile in London, to recruit divisions of soldiers in camps inside Russia.[19] And Russian prisoners, many of them criminals, were drafted into the Red Army.[20]

On November 6, Stalin gave a speech describing German atrocities that were both widespread and real. The first retreats of German armies in early winter revealed the mindless German destruction and carnage to everyone.[21] By December, the methodical hangings of civilians, houses burned with families inside, children thrown down wells, large-scale killings of civilians and Jews—these became visible to all.[22] It was a major turning point, determined less by strategy than lack of it. Russian propagandists quickly seized the initiative. Newspapers became flooded with stories of atrocities. Morale improved. The danger of revolt effectively disappeared.

In his camp in the far north, Stefan Knapp noted only a small change. Before the invasion he was employed in painting slogans such as "Yesterday the Stakhanovites excavated so many cubic meters of soil"; after the invasion the slogan became "One cubic meter on the site, one German killed." Antoni Ekart wrote of his camp in the Urals: "Were it not for the primitive stupidity and brutality of the Germans in their occupation policy, Russia would have lost the war." For the remainder of the war the camps were secure.

In Russian literature the role of the camps in the struggle against Germany was a forbidden topic. Secrecy continued long after 1945. The alert reader, however, can find many oblique references in books published in the USSR. For example, Viktor Nekrasov wrote in his novel *In the Trenches of Stalingrad* that the orderly Valega—a major character in the book—"Did time. Did not complete his sentence. Released and volunteered for the army."[23]

We will never know the full extent of the contribution by Soviet camps to the war effort. The revival of the Soviet military and economy began in 1942. Even before the German attack, factories were constructed in the Ural mountains in "regime cities." A historian has written that "the villages of Siberia and Mongolia were scoured . . . to find fresh armies."[24] These were found at a time when German reserves were largely depleted. The camp system was turned into an asset. Dissenting writers were silenced.

Doctor Zhivago, by Boris Pasternak, was singled out when the Swedish Academy awarded Pasternak the Nobel Prize. It was published more than a decade after the end of the war, but even then the novel could not be published in the USSR, it was published in Italy. In his epilogue to the novel, Pasternak gave a moving description of how prisoners in Soviet camps welcomed the war:

> We cut trees. We harnessed ourselves, eight to a sledge, and we hauled timber and sank into the snow up to our necks. For a long time we didn't know that the war had started. They kept it from us. And then suddenly there came the offer. You could volunteer for front-line service in a disciplinary battalion, and if you came out alive you were free. After that, attack after attack, mile after mile of electrified barbed wire, mines, mortars, months after month of artillery barrage. They called our company the death squad. It was practically wiped out. How and why I survived, I don't know. And yet—would you believe it—all that utter hell was nothing, it was bliss compared to the horrors of the concentration camp.[25]

According to Pasternak the straight-forwardness of the danger was appealing. "The war's real horrors, its real dangers and the menace of real death, were a blessing compared to the reign of the lie."

* * *

Soviet literature was silent about the first two years of the Second World

War. Most fiction and poetry highlights the German invasion in June 22, 1941 as if it were the war's starting point. The finest works about the Soviet camps during the war years were by writers from the Baltic countries, Finland, and Poland. Accomplished books about Soviet camps were by Polish authors who were permitted to leave their camps after the Sikorski Pact of August 1941. Until then, the secrecy had been largely complete. A large-scale exodus went to the West by way of Iran, creating a major breach in the secrecy of the camps. In terms of communication with "the outside world," the exodus might be compared to the later escapes during the war from German and Japanese camps; it led to publications that brought information about the hidden world of the Soviet camps to Western countries.[26] Many of these narratives of the war years in Soviet camps had high quality as literary works. Decades later, they were echoed and confirmed by Russian writers such as Alexander Solzhenitsyn, Varlam Shalamov, and Vasily Grossman.

In one of his finest short stories, Varlam Shalamov wrote about the hope of the prisoner: "Hope always shackles the convict. Hope is slavery. A man who hopes for something alters his conduct and is more frequently dishonest than a man who has ceased to hope."[27] Shalamov was writing about the prisoner's hope for release, he referred also to the hope of broader reform that intensified in the Soviet Union during the war years 1942–44.

Stalin's speech to the nation on July 3, 1941, began with the words, "Comrades! Citizens! Brothers and sisters! . . . My friends!" In most Soviet war novels, the speech is dramatized, and considered to be very significant. Never before had Stalin addressed his countrymen in this manner. Hope for reform was immediately set in motion. Stalin's next speech in November, after the first German retreats, created hope for amnesty and general reform. The state had seized the initiative, mobilizing its many writers to spread a message of resistance and internal change. Hope arose, too, that the entire camp system might be disbanded.

Two fine writers discussed Soviet camps in probing, literary works, stressing the importance of hope and, above all, its manipulation. In his novel *Forever Flowing*, Vasily Grossman claimed that the camps were a "gigantic stage presentation" inseparable from the rest of Soviet and Russian history. This theatrical presentation was a continuation of the "Potemkin Villages" of the eighteenth century when Count Potemkin, Catherine the Great's overseer, erected empty wooden house-fronts along a river bank to be viewed by the empress from her royal barge. As soon as she floated past, the "villages" were dismantled and carried to another point, to be viewed by the empress once again. According to Grossman the widespread hopes for reform and amnesty encouraged by Stalin during the war were similar manipulated illusions. They were "a confidence man's tricks," modern "Potemkin villages."[28] None of the hopes were realized. Later Grossman came to hate this "gigantic stage presentation" and its "unfreedom." But he grudgingly admitted it was effective. It worked.

The writer Elinor Lipper also thought "the tradition of the Potemkin Villages" explained not only the camps but much of Soviet life and society. On a mundane level the practice of deception came from the methodical *"tufta"*—fakery—that characterized Stalin's regime, and this was also emphasized by Andrei Sinyavsky. Lipper thought its roots went deep into Russian history.[29]

During the war, Elinor Lipper was a prisoner at Magadan when two American dignitaries came to visit, Henry Wallace—a member of Franklin Roosevelt's cabinet—and Owen Lattimore. At the time the Magadan and Kolyma camps had the highest death rates of any camps in the USSR. Everything was prepared to fool the Americans. In a single night before the visit, the wooden watchtowers lining the access roads were taken down. The prisoners were given three days' holiday: the day of Wallace's arrival, the day of his visit, and the day of departure. Because the camp held hundreds of thousands of prisoners, and the American visitors might accidentally catch sight of them, movies were ordered to be shown to the prisoners from morning to night during the three days. One of the prisoners, squatting on a floor behind blackened windows, compelled to watch the films, was Elinor Lipper. As soon as Wallace and Lattimore left, the watchtowers went up again. In Lipper's words "the N.K.V.D. carried off its job with flying colors." Wallace described the "three hundred thousand inhabitants of Kolyma"—his figure was accurate—without noticing they were prisoners at all. He wrote in his book *Soviet Asia Mission*, "they are all pioneers of the modern age, builders of cities." In articles for *The National Geographic* Lattimore called them "scientists," and wrote that the camps "can be roughly compared to the T.V.A."[30] His message for the American public was that the camps should be imitated in the United States.

4

Japan: "Prisoners of War," a Contradiction in Terms

During the Second World War there were many different types of camps. In the years from 1939–41 the camp system in the USSR became central to the invasions and deportations that followed. Communication between prisoners and the outside world was nonexistent; no foreign country was likely to come to the aid of captives. But events that were completely unexpected at the time showed how the most perfect security in the world can be breached—badly breached—and forced to change.

In the course of their early, rapid conquests, Japan was confronted with a huge number of civilians and captured soldiers who came under their control. The country did not have a developed system to administer the great influx of people. Ironically, however, when a camp system was finally organized it became an international *cause celebre*, influencing decisions at the highest level of the war that changed the outcome. In the most dramatic way the Japanese camps highlighted the importance of communication between prisoners and the world outside.

In the first months of 1942, Japanese Imperial armies advanced rapidly south toward Singapore encountering one success after another. Soon some 320,000 prisoners had fallen into their hands. Japan turned native prisoners loose, leaving 140,000 Allied military prisoners. The Japanese did not consider Allied soldiers in uniform to be "prisoners-of-war" at all. They did not have this legal concept. Japanese soldiers were forbidden to surrender; military regulations stated that the only alternative to victory was death in battle.[31]

According to the Japanese code, the Allied captives were not supposed to be there at all. Their presence was an embarrassment, they were not human beings with dignity. General Homma explained after the war that

Japanese soldiers "despised beyond description" soldiers who allowed themselves to surrender. They were "genuinely surprised" the Allied soldiers had so little sense of shame. This attitude remained to the end.[32]

James Clavell put the matter succinctly in his novel *King Rat*. Peter Marlowe, the protagonist, humorously described the surrender of the Allied soldiers from their point of view: "They said we were without honor—the officers—because we had allowed ourselves to be captured. So they wouldn't consider us P.O.W.s. They cut off our hair and forbade us to wear officers' insignia. Eventually they allowed us to 'become' officers again, though they never allowed us back our hair."[33] The captives enjoyed relative freedom. Pierre Boule, a rubber planter in Malaya and author of *The Bridge on the River Kwai*, described the first months of inactivity as "a period of felicity."[34]

As Japanese victories became less easy, the treatment of the captives became worse. It took the form of revenge and, soon, arbitrary slaughter. After Major General King's surrender at Bataan in the Philippines, the Allied captives were driven on foot to the camp at Catanabuan, and along the road a systematic massacre took place with multiple beheadings. One American started counting bodies with their heads chopped off. At twenty-seven he stopped counting.

> They would see a man desperate for water, catch him throwing himself down at some filthy pond and chop his head off. They would kill a man even if they did not catch him drinking, bayonet him for having water stains on his trousers. They would bayonet a man squatting with dysentery, leave him bleeding to death, fouled, with his pants down around his ankles. They killed men for going too slow . . . The Japanese in the truck convoys made a game of throwing rocks at the prisoners, or else would whack at them with rifle butts . . . they appeared to be keeping score.[35]

What became known as the "Bataan Death March" made a lasting impression on all the prisoners. For another three years, however, the experiences were not communicated to the world outside.

The number of captured Allied soldiers grew rapidly. In June 1942, Imperial Headquarters in Tokyo made a new decision: the captives would be used as laborers for war-related projects and dispersed throughout the zone of conquest, from Java to the Philippines and Manchuria. They never gained the status of "prisoners of war," and their situation had many unresolved conflicts. Some captives clung to the concept of "prisoners of war" but it never corresponded to the reality of treatment. Another decision in Tokyo changed their situation further; many were sent north in the holds of ships to labor on the Japanese mainland until the end of the war.

Their status was unique. Their lives were considered without value. Of the Allied prisoners of war held in Germany and Italy, for example, only 4 percent died, but more than 27 percent of the Allied captives in Japanese custody would die. On the Burmese railway project the mortality rate exceeded 60 percent. David James, a historian and British captive himself, bitterly explained the statistics: "More British soldiers were killed . . . as prisoners of war than perished in fighting against the Japanese in battle during the entire campaign."[36]

Japanese camps were in the open, close to work sites. Usually they were referred to by kilometer designation on a road or path, called "camps" or "jungle labor camps" in a loose sense. They were only clearings, railheads, stages, or temporary squatters' camps. Jungle clearing was done by the captives, and as work advanced they moved to a new site, the jungle taking over the site just abandoned. The terms of labor were harsh. Prisoners were told "Work, or you will be shot." A Major Maida informed the captives at an agricultural camp at Davao, "Now you will learn about hard labor. Every prisoner will continue to work until he is actually hospitalized."[37]. When men fell sick their rations were removed. There were no "examinations" like those in Soviet camps, consisting of an NKVD doctor who gripped a fold of fat—Stefan Knapp called it the "stomach-gripping routine"—that determined the camp where each prisoner was sent.

In June 1942, the camps for Allied captives were transformed once again. Tokyo ordered the Southern Army to build a railway from Siam to Burma as a substitute for the sea route to Rangoon. The result was the crash program to build a Burmese railroad. About 61,000 Allied prisoners and a quarter million Asian laborers were impressed into construction. Some of the finest writings—by Australian, British, American, South African and French authors—are about work on this project. Even in its early stage, the mortality in these camps was high. From May 1943 onward a new policy called "Speedo" was enforced on the railway. A crescendo of violence was intended to spur the laborers to greater effort but in fact weakened them further and increased casualties. A British writer noted, "the cruder Japanese engineers boasted that each sleeper [tie] of the track would represent a dead prisoner."[38]

As the war spread, Asian laborers were recruited into the Japanese camps. Torn from their social settings by economic necessity and false promises, called "engineers" and paid trifling sums, Tamils, Burmese, Javanese, Chinese, and Malays came with their families and belongings, arriving in an alien environment where they had to fend for themselves. Without medicine and suffering from every conceivable disease, they lacked leadership or discipline other than Japanese beatings. It was one of the great massacres of the war. No roll of Asian workers was kept, no names were recorded. The total casualties under Japanese occupation can only be guessed. Estimates of the number of Asians who died under Japanese occupation in Asia are in excess of eighteen million.[39]

In 1943, cholera struck the railway camps. Men became violently sick. The bacillus entered the Khwae Noi or Menam Kwa Noi—"Mother of the Waters"—and flowed downstream from one camp to the next. Previously the dead were buried each day in pits, now they were burned. After the arrival of cholera, surrounded by the dead and dying, each man devoted his remaining energies to trying to stay alive.[40]

As work and disease took their toll, more of the prisoners thought about the possibility of escape. Even if chances of success were poor, the chances of survival in staying behind were also poor. Escape became the dominant thought and obsession in many narratives.

Prisoners who had been deported into Soviet camps had no redress— their home countries were small, under occupation and powerless. But England and the United States were large countries, actively pursuing the war against Japan. Australia, an ally, was not too far away. If a prisoner wanted to risk his life in an escape attempt, he could try.

The spaces confronting him were forbidding. As in Siberia or Kazakhstan, once outside the camp enormous distances had to be crossed. The country was under military occupation, densely populated, the roads patrolled. The Japanese were quick to torture and kill men trying to escape. Examples were made of them in front of the other prisoners, they were tied to a stake and bayoneted, or hung from a wire and beaten to death. The Japanese said they were willing to kill ten for every one who escaped.

Ernest Gordon wrote that the great spaces around the camps were stronger than any fence or barrier:

It was fairly easy to break through the flimsy twelve-foot bamboo fence. Guards were stationed at several points around the perimeter of the camp; others patrolled at regular intervals. They could be eluded. But if a man broke through, where was he to go? A thousand miles of jungle was the strongest fence that could surround any camps. To be caught outside meant death—immediate death at the hands of violent guards, or slow death by starvation. We were not deterred by the wild animals or by the multitude of poisonous snakes in which the jungle abounded (I'd had a cobra crawl over my arm and thought nothing of it). It was the jungle itself, impersonal, menacing, that restrained us.[41]

Ronald Hastain explained in *White Coolie*, "The odds were all against such attempts. From the map of the world it is difficult perhaps to realize the vast extent of this region. We were already thousands of miles from Allied lands and neutral countries. There could be no slipping over borders . . . And always one was a white man among colored people who would sell you for a bowl of rice."[42]

Dreams of escape and the desire to reach the Allied leadership, or to communicate some kind of record, went hand in hand. After the Burmese railway was completed in November 1943, survivors were transported north to Japan in the holds of "death ships" (Ray Parkin: "cargoes of old bones and dirty livers"); any communication from mainland Japan would be highly unlikely. The move made many of the captives rethink their plans. Those who had manuscripts, narratives, diaries, or drawings gave them to others for safekeeping, or buried them.

In most Japanese camps it was possible to keep a pencil and some paper. Laurens van der Post and his friends produced their own newspaper, "*Mark Time.*" Van der Post wrote: "As the supplies left behind by the Dutch were consumed, all our writings were increasingly produced on Japanese lavatory paper."[43] They managed to produce a collective "Memorial Book."

As events turned against the Japanese armies, camp guards treated the captives with increasing cruelty. Many thought it was a form of revenge. In Java, Van der Post learned of the secret order of Field-Marshal Terauchi to his commanders to kill all prisoners in their camps when the Allies began a final assault in South-East Asia. It seemed all attempts to communicate with the outside world had failed. The few escapes, messages sent by native allies and contacts by hidden radio transmitter, seemed to have no effect.

Van der Post decided to bury all his manuscripts. Drawings "were gathered together with my diary, material for our memorial book, and such camp records as we valued, and on November 26, 1943, they were tied in bundles, wrapped in ground sheets and buried late at night in different places in our camp. As far as I know only my diary, a small number of illustrations and some copies of *Mark Time* survived their interment in the dark soil of our camp. The bulk and by far the most precious part of what we had buried mysteriously vanished."

A number of excellent works in English were written about captivity in the many camps, and the works by Laurens Van der Post are especially noteworthy,[44] also outstanding are works by the Australian Ray Parkin.[45] The large majority of writings that we know were written in Japanese captivity were not recovered afterward, most were lost or destroyed. After the Japanese capitulation, Van der Post supervised a company of Japanese prisoners of war digging the soil of his old camp, looking for manuscripts he had buried. They were unable to find them. One hidden diary, with a London address inside the cover, had greater luck: "By some miracle the mildewed little book was recovered by an officer of the Indonesian Nationalist Forces who knew me and returned it to me, with some of the illustrations used in this story" (*The Night of the New Moon*).

A few fine poems by Ian Horobin survived, such as "Epitaph for Harokoe" and "In Memoriam," but others that made a powerful impression on his fellow captives—"Java Sunday" about the beheading of a prisoner by a Japanese officer—were never recovered.[46] John Coast paid an Indonesian to bury a long manuscript he had written, but when he returned after the war it was gone, probably taken by the man who buried it. Thomas Hayes, a doctor imprisoned in Bilibid Prison in the Philippines, buried his secret notebooks in the floor of the prison before he was shipped north in a ship's hold. He did not survive the war, but his son found the notebooks and published them as *Bilibid Diary,* in 1945.[47] This manuscript was exceptional. Most that were consigned to the humid earth quickly disintegrated.

In the last year of the war many prisoners were starving and sick, unable to walk, slipping in and out of consciousness. One wrote, "By the beginning of 1945 we were physically dying men." Prisoners traveling to a new camp rarely survived the journey. When the camps in Japan were finally opened in 1945, few prisoners were able to rise to their feet and walk out.

* * *

In 1943, ten prisoners escaped from the labor camp at Davao, in Mindanao. They successfully made their way to General MacArthur's headquarters in Brisbane, Australia. They were the first Americans to escape from the Japanese and reach the safety of Allied territory. They were also survivors of the "death march" in Bataan. Lengthy interviews with them made an overpowering impression on General MacArthur. Seldom in war has the escape of prisoners had a greater effect on subsequent military conduct and goals. Collectively, all of the prisoners were soon to become a major issue of the war. Their liberation became a priority of later military strategy.

Not only did primary witnesses escape, they brought with them their own written records. They arrived at the place—Brisbane—most likely to receive them with seriousness, concern, and willingness to act. It is difficult to say which method of communication, written or oral, was most instrumental in persuading MacArthur, and eventually the American public, of the danger to the captives as a group. The answer is probably a combination of both. MacArthur had a series of interviews with Captain William Dyess, who brought with him the diary he had kept throughout his captivity. Dyess also happened to be a fine writer. The presence of the diary, which he consulted during the interviews, gave extra authority and concrete accuracy to his words. Another book written by escaped captives, *Ten Escape from Tojo,* was vivid but hastily written.

Shortly after the interviews with MacArthur, Dyess sat down to write his own detailed narrative about his experiences for the War Department, titled *Bataan Death March.* Based on the diary he carried, it was a real act of literature. Its language was alert, fresh, and free of exaggeration, his insights into the minds of both captives and captors exceptional.

Permission to publish the book was denied at first. President Franklin Roosevelt personally suppressed the book, fearing it would have an incendiary effect on American public opinion.[48]. But he relented. When the book was released in January 1944, hundreds of newspapers and magazines serialized it and quoted it throughout the United States. It created a public furor.

During the war's last months, General MacArthur broadcast almost daily to the Japanese people warning them not to harm the prisoners of war. On August 30, 1945, after the surrender, MacArthur arrived in Japan on a C-54 with the name "Bataan" prominently displayed on the airplane's nose cone.[49] It was a declaration. Bataan was the place of the infamous death march; it was also the place where the Allied soldiers were abandoned—some said by MacArthur—to captivity.

A few days after the Hiroshima and Nagasaki bombings, President Truman justified the use of the weapons in a letter to the Federal Council of Churches. He underlined the importance for him of the prisoners of war: "I was greatly disturbed over the unwarranted attack by the Japanese on Pearl Harbor . . . and their murder of our prisoners of war."[50]

Events outside Japan were completely unknown to the captives themselves. A few had seen the flashes of the bombs from their distant camps. Ray Parkin wrote that by 1945 the captives imprisoned on mainland Japan "felt like Rip Van Winkels." Most of them were convinced all their attempts to communicate with the world outside had failed. They had no hope, and believed they were completely forgotten.

After the surrender Ronald Hastain, author of *White Coolie*, was transferred from his camp at Toyama in Japan to an American destroyer. His first encounter was with an American ensign. He asked for news.

> He stopped to look me fully in the eyes before replying firmly, but with a touch of conscious drama, "*You* are the news. *You* are the headlines. The liberation of you fellows is the only news that matters today. The whole world is waiting to hear from you."

> Allowing for the American proneness for exaggeration, this was still pleasant hearing . . . I made a disparaging comment, but he was bent on convincing me.

5

Germany: Factories of Destruction

In the course of six years the camps that were used took many different forms. They did not have a single model or prototype. The
most important feature of the many camps is that a majority were
intended for civilians. Other major features were secrecy, militarization,
and frequent location at a great distance from the home population or
in a foreign conquered country. The Soviet camp system was probably
the most varied. The Japanese camps went through several different
stages, transformed by events on the ground and by improvised decisions in Tokyo.

The camps in Germany were developed at an early date, in 1933. What
was called "preventive detention" was used as a device against the Nazi
regime's political opponents, and in the following years German camps
took on a bewildering variety of forms. In the areas of German conquest,
camps multiplied quickly with different functions. Between 1939 and
1944 they became what has been called "an SS-owned arsenal of compul-
sory labor."[51] Some became factory-like extermination camps. A historian
has argued that these were not "camps" in a literal sense at all because
there was no intent to accommodate prisoners for any length of time.[52]
Some camps were hybrids of the two.

In the areas of occupation, German camps had competing purposes.[53]
Among civilians in the conquered countries, awareness of danger
developed gradually. As in the Soviet areas of occupation, large professional groups—judges, senators, professors, civil servants, lawyers,
and political figures—were exposed to great risk. An accurate assessment of personal danger required observation, trial and error, multiple
experiences, informed speculation, and luck.

In 1941, Jews began to realize they were in particular danger, but the awareness was never uniform. Michael Marrus referred to the German "procrastination" of the period 1939–41; Christopher Browning has written of the "thirty-month stay of execution" for Jews after Hitler's invasion of Western Poland in September 1939.[54] The creation of ghettoes had an improvised character, proceeding in fits and starts, making accurate estimates of danger extremely difficult. When a conference was held at Wannsee in January 1942 deciding the "Final Solution," it was a tightly held secret.

Observers like Emanuel Ringelblum and Chaim Kaplan were among the first writers to be alarmed that Jews were singled out for especially harsh treatment.[55] The historian Sebastian Haffner wrote, "Hitler's mass murders were committed during the war, but they were not acts of war. On the contrary, (they) impeded the war. He used the war as a pretext."[56] The war was cover or *Tarnung* for other intentions; at the time it was difficult to think the war might be subordinated to other aims.

In December 1941, during a savage German raid on the ghetto in Riga and a massacre in the nearby Rumbuli Forest, the historian Simon Dubnov exhorted witnesses to "Write and Record!" (*Schreibt un farschreibt!*). His imperative was a call to write, to "write at once, and to write definitively." The directive applied to all observers irrespective of profession.[57] Like Ringelblum, Dubnov was a professional historian. If it was impossible to defend oneself or save one's life, at least a record of the events could be preserved for others. It was the written word, above all, that should be used to record an event. It would make the record permanent, it could be transmitted it to others.

Sometimes violence coincided with the determination to write. This can be seen in the work of Yitzak Katznelson. A teacher of Hebrew, a dramatist and poet, Katznelson was already in his fifties when he was driven by the Germans in 1939 from his home in Zgierz, near Lodz, to Warsaw. For about a year in the Warsaw ghetto, Katznelson ceased writing entirely. Then, after a particularly violent German raid or "*Aktion*" in the ghetto, he began to write again and produced some thirty literary works in succession between June 1940 and the beginning of 1942. From 1942 to the beginning of 1943 Katznelson wrote ten more important works, and switched from Hebrew to Yiddish; he deliberately chose a language that was widely spoken and read, and would have an immediate impact on those around him.[58]

For both Dubnov and Katznelson, an act of particular violence awakened a resolve to set it down on paper. It was as if writing was reinvented; not only was it a way to reach those nearby, it also became a means to communicate with others—any others—in the future.

German sweeps in the countryside drove more and more Jews into the Warsaw ghetto. It became desperately overcrowded, holding 450,000 people at its peak. It has been called the largest "city-camp" in Europe.[59]

In the many ghettoes and camps of Eastern Europe, periods of inertia were often followed by what observers called "turning points." A change occurred that was psychological and social at the same time. In 1942, Marek Edelman, a physician who became a commander in the Warsaw ghetto uprising, wrote of "our own terrifying apathy." This was followed by a realization that a person was not a mute or passive object with no ability to resist. It was possible to assume an active stance. Edelman thought the "psychological turning point" was one of the most important events in the history of the Warsaw ghetto. It led to the armed revolt of 1943.[60]

The "turning points" were often closely connected to a resolve to commit words to paper. The decision to bear witness by an act of writing had to be made by the individual, on the other hand it could be widespread and even collective. Emanuel Ringelblum described the mood in the Warsaw ghetto: "Everyone wrote . . . Journalists and writers, of course, but also teachers, public men, young people—even children. Most of them kept diaries where the tragic events of the day were reflected through the prism of personal experience."[61]

People of all ages wrote, not only diaries but sketches, satires, poetry, and other genres. It might seem surprising that poetry, sometimes considered a subjective genre, could take root in such unfavorable conditions. But observers attested that ordinary people felt an instinctive faith that "poetry would escape unharmed"—the phrase comes from *Konrad Wallenrod* by Adam Mickiewicz, the nineteenth-century Polish poet and dramatist, and was adopted as the title of a major postwar anthology of writings from the concentration camps and ghettoes.[62]

Many who made a decision to write had no training or literary background at all. Michael Borwicz described an elderly manufacturer in Lodz named Silberstein who began a new habit—to the surprise of his wife and children—of waking late at night and writing poems in Yiddish. He paid no attention to rhythm or rhyme, but with time became aware of problems of form. Other works in Lodz were written by a master baker named Hiler, a shoemaker named Czechowicz, and a locksmith, Vogelman. "Typical of these nonliterary authors was a tailor from Lvov, a brow-beaten husband and father who, besides tailoring, had betrayed no sign of ambition or aspiration whatsoever. He came and asked some questions about what was going on—or so it seemed. Then without waiting for a reply, he took a manuscript out from under his jacket. 'I have written some poetry,' he said."[63]

The Lvov ghetto was a target of a massacre by the SS, and the violence brought forth a written response from Maurycy Szymel: "In a ruined burrow in the Lvov ghetto he lay on his side among debris, broken water pipes and puddles of water, reading aloud one of his poems by the light of an anemic candle. He was completely concentrated, the words taking on the rhythms of the dripping water, candle, and smoke."[64]

The desire to write was reinforced by the growing realization they were completely cut off. Security around the ghettoes, camps, and prisons was tight and had acquired permanence. Those trapped inside wanted to communicate with the outside world. Writing became a *pis aller* born of confinement. People wanted to break through the barrier.

As conditions became worse, many were convinced that a living messenger might communicate orally with the outside world more effectively than a written message. The best "message" was a human being who could speak; this required an escape. Many prisoners were obsessed by a desire to escape, less to save their own skins than to transmit, as effectively as possible, information about murders in the camps to the outside world. The desire for an escape became universal, and is powerfully expressed in most narratives. For example, at least six books by survivors from Auschwitz describe the daring escape by a young Belgian "runner" named Mala Zimetbaum. During the two days after her escape the entire prisoner population went through agonies of hope, exhilaration, and anguish. She was finally caught near the Slovak border, returned to the camp and executed. Escape attempts had varying results. Rudolf Vrba, author of the book *I Cannot Forgive*, escaped with Robert Wetzlar and successfully crossed the Polish-Slovak border near Zakopane. Soon they were able to communicate all they knew about the Auschwitz crematories to the Slovakian Jewish community. A Papal Nuncio was sent from Bratislava to interview them. But their information was ultimately suppressed.[65] Similar escapes by Czeslaw Mordowicz, Arnost Rosin, Rudolf

Reder (from Belzec), and others had little effect. A representative of the Polish Home Army, Jan Karski, was smuggled inside the Warsaw ghetto dressed as a German officer, and also into the camp at Majdanek where he observed conditions. Then he traveled to London and New York where he spoke with world leaders, describing what he had seen. He was met with skepticism.

The resolve to write sometimes coincided with a decision to resist with arms, a decision that was usually tragic. An excellent description of a personal turning point leading to armed resistance was written by Gusta Draenger. She decided to join the resistance and, at the same time, to leave a written testament. The two decisions were based on the loss of illusions, the deaths of family members, and a determination to take her life into her own hands. She explained:

> After a German "action" exterminating a large number of families, they—the combatants—were free. Those last threads that attached them to daily life were broken. Thus the one who up to this point had hesitated, not knowing if he should abandon his younger brother, his only sister, his elderly parents, now discovered after the action that his hands were free, he could throw himself into underground activity without any reservations. It was a moment of liberty, born in the ruins of family life.[66]

This is a lucid formulation of motives that led from avoidance of danger—and concern for relative safety—to active resistance. Draenger was captured by the Germans and sentenced to death. Denied paper and pen in prison, she managed to write a remarkable psychological study of the underground, *Memoirs of Justyna*, on toilet paper, posthumously published in 1946.

A historian of the literature written in the ghettoes, David Roskies, has described the moment of decision and called it a "breaking point":

> What a detailed, sequential study of ghetto writings shows is the precise breaking point and the way in which writers began to apprehend the Holocaust . . . It happened in 1942 when all the old strategies had already been tried: when . . . even subjecting the most recent counter-traditions to irony failed to produce an adequate response. It happened when they took away the

children, because without the children there was no hope whatsoever.[67]

There was hardly a camp that did not produce written works: Auschwitz, Janowa (Lvov), Plaszow (Cracow), Majdanek (Lublin), Treblinka, Sobibor, Skarzysko, Ponary, Pustkow, Szebnie, Bialystok, Stutthof, Buchenwald, Sachsenhausen, Mauthausen, Gusen, Dachau, Ravensbrueck, Leipzig, Drancy, Fresnes, Natzweiler, and others. Many of the works are brief and truncated, usually because the authors did not survive. There is a remark-able continuity between them and postwar works by survivors. Their forms, motives, and themes were expressed more fully after 1945 in works by Primo Levi, Elie Wiesel, Sim Kessel, Jozef Bor, and others.

Inside the Warsaw ghetto, few expressed the combination of the two motives at the same time—to resist with arms and to write—better than Wladyslaw Szlengel. Several of his poems and an essay about him were included in Ringelblum's archive, buried underground and dug up from the ruins after the war. An excellent illustration of Draenger's observa-tion that armed resistance could be accompanied simultaneously by an act of writing, Szlengel threw himself into the armed struggle. One of the strongest exhortations to revolt—armed, fierce revolt—can be found in his poem "Counterattack." Several survivors claimed this poem was one of the most widely read and popular in the Warsaw ghetto. The inten-sity of the call to arms is maintained from beginning to end. The poem reads in part:

A sky-blue uniform is lying
On the spittle-covered stairs
Of Jewish Pavia Street
And does not know
That at the Shultz and Toebbens factories
Bullets are dancing in a joyous burst of song:
Revolt of the meat,
Revolt of the meat,
Revolt of the meat!
Meat spits grenades out the windows,
Meat coughs out streams of scarlet flame
And clings to the edges of life!
. . . Listen, O German God,

How Jews pray in their "wild" houses,
Clenching in their fists a bar, a stone.
We beg You, Lord, for a bloody battle,
We implore You for a violent death.
Before the end let our eyes
Not see the train rails dragging away
But give the hand unerring aim, Lord,
To stain the blue uniform with blood.[68]

In another poem, "Call in the Night," he dedicated the collection of poems he wrote in the Warsaw ghetto, *What I Read to the Dead*, in this way:

I dedicate these poems . . .
In the whirlwind of events,
In the dance of chance, of connections, of death
To those who remembered to rescue
Not only members of their family,
Not only friends, not only money
But the few remaining last of the Mohicans
Whose entire capital, whose only
Weapon is the word.
To those who are reached by my

CALL IN THE NIGHT

Szlengel was killed in the uprising of April 1943. To the end he retained his sense of irony. His only remaining "capital," his one weapon, was—the word.

6

Communication across Time: The Boxes at 68 Nowolipka Street

Until 1945 the secrecy of the German extermination camps was given the highest priority. Huge efforts were made to maintain the framework of camouflage and semantic cunning. General Jodl boasted that the concealment of the Final Solution during the war was "a masterpiece."

By 1943 it became clear inside the camps and ghettoes that they were sealed off from the outside world. Escapes were few. The failure of attempts to communicate with the outside world had a profound effect on the way captives in the ghettoes conceived of the act of writing, and what kind of reader—or audience—they might write for. The possibility arose that someone using words might avoid the present, by-passing it, and communicate with a reader in the future. It resembled the imperative to write and record, but had a major difference. Communication was no longer directed at readers in the present.[69]

In early 1943, inside the ghetto of Vilnius, the Lithuanian capital, the poet Abraham Suckever described his activity in a poem "Grains of Wheat":

Manuscripts, I bury them and sow them here . . .
And when I am struck by despair
My thoughts take me back: to Egypt,
And the tale about the grains of wheat.[70]

Suckever recounted the story of an Egyptian king or Pharaoh who built a pyramid on the banks of the Nile. Inside he placed golden urns containing wheat grains. Nine thousand years passed. When the urns were opened, the grains of wheat were exposed to rays of the sun, and began to grow. The poem ends:

Perhaps, some time, a person will excavate
These words and expose them to the light,
And at some fated hour they too
Will burst into bloom?

Like the primeval grain
That changed into an ear of wheat
Perhaps these words will give food,
Perhaps these words will fall among
The people in their eternal march.

With Suckever's "Grains of Wheat" we observe a new kind of communication taking place. His intention was not to reach a living reader but to wait after his own death. He claimed he could wait nine thousand years in order to be read. It was a form of posterity, but nevertheless alive and concrete.

Suckever literally buried his manuscripts. Hidden in the earth, they would not die but eventually be preserved by a finder and reader. Suckever also buried bound books. The occupying German Army was about to transport some 20,000 volumes of special value from the Jewish libraries of Vilnius to Germany, and twenty people were selected as experts to locate the books. Suckever was one of them. They took the most important works in the Strashun Library and YIVO collections, sealed and buried them under the ground so they would be found after the war.

Suckever succeeded in escaping the Vilnius ghetto by way of its sewer system. One of Suckever's finest poems is *Secret Town*. About 150 pages long, it describes his experiences hiding in the sewers and being hunted. Literally going underground had become the surest means of preserving life.

After the armed revolt in the Warsaw ghetto, writing activity took extreme forms. In some cases the writer thought of his manuscript as a substitute for his physical body. For example, Koppel Holzman carried a manuscript with him from one place to another, each time burying it anew in the hope it might be preserved:

One thought tortured me: if someone found my hiding place, he would find my notebooks too. I buried them. I could not sleep at night, trembling at the thought that humidity would attack the paper. I took out the already moist papers, on which one could barely make out the pale writing. After verifying them I took all possible precautions, and surrounded them with absorbent tissue. Like a mother who presses her child against her breast—her only treasure—thus I firmly held with my two hands this document that was the only goal of my life.[71]

The author did not survive the war, but his manuscript was found and published posthumously.

The desire to write did not mean composing a carefully wrought work of art. The intention was different: to complete an act of communication from one living person to another person not living in the present. The author might be an excellent writer like Szlengel or Suckever, or an ordinary person simply using the words of everyday speech. The intention was not to produce literature destined for admiration or to be set on a pedestal, but to create living, human communication. Many "testaments" were written. The genre recalls other testaments written during Medieval plagues, for example, by Francois Villon.

David Grabner wrote a "testament" dated August 2, 1942:

We have decided to write our testaments, to gather some material about the German *Aktion* and bury it. We are constantly in a state of uncertainty. We must hurry. Yesterday we worked late into the night . . . With what joy we received each new manuscript! We had no fear of the risks we were taking. We were aware we were perpetuating a piece of history, and this was more important than the life of an individual. We were ready to let ourselves be cut into shreds rather than betray our secret.

In a note written later the same day, at four o'clock in the afternoon, he added: "The neighboring street is already under attack. All of us feel the atmosphere of danger. We are preparing for the worst. We are hurrying. We are going to dig the last hole for the containers. May we have success in burying them!"

The writer was concerned exclusively about his manuscript, an act of communication that was intended to travel across time itself. It was successful. Like Holzman, Grabner died but the manuscript survived.

Further to the west the writer Yitzhak Katznelson was sent to the French transit camp at Vittel. Katznelson sensed his life was still in peril, and decided to bury two manuscripts he had recently completed, *Vittel Diary* and *Song of the Murdered Jewish Nation*. A friend has described how Katznelson selected a spot on the Vittel grounds, near a football field and a pine tree, to bury his manuscripts: "Katznelson stood guard while I dug up the ground, but as soon as anyone appeared he signaled to me, whereupon I would throw my coat over the hole I had made, and we both pretended to be reading the newspaper."[72] Katznelson did not survive the war. But the manuscripts were found and preserved.

In some works describing camp life, words were accompanied by pictures and portraits. Alfred Kantor kept a picture-journal that documented life at Theresienstadt: "Sketching took on a new urgency. I was determined to keep a continuous record, even though I knew there was no chance to take these out. I started to sketch almost without interruption anything that came to my eye. It was not so much that I wanted to draw my own story, but rather to capture this extraordinary place so that I could show the world something of it, when and if I was ever free."[73]

Another artist, Zoran Music, felt a similar urgency: "Tomorrow may be too late. For me, life and death depended on these sheets. But will these drawings ever be seen? Will I get out of here alive?" An artist at Gusen, Aldo Carpi, wanted to preserve his drawings and wrote: "The risks we were running, my papers and I, augmented our misery. It seemed all that was good was in these papers." It is hard to imagine a more complete identification between an artist and his works: "my papers and I."

Hanna Olomucki recalled how the subjects of her drawings felt a similar concern: "My fellow prisoners wanted me to draw but for a different reason: 'If you live to leave this hell, make your drawings tell the world about us, we want to be among the living, at least on paper.'"[74]

In 1944 and 1945, attempts to leave a record of life in the camps intensified. It was clear the Germans were methodically destroying all evidence of killing in the camps. They were waging a war not just against people but against evidence. With the Wehrmacht retreating on all fronts, colossal efforts were made to destroy buildings and documents in full view of the prisoners. The crematoria were dynamited, their foundations dug up.[75]

The killing of witnesses increased. Mass graves of the buried dead were exhumed, their contents burned on high pyres with gasoline and railway ties in an effort to obliterate them. Efforts were even made to destroy bones by grinding them into small bits. One heavy grinding machine operated by the SS General Bloedel called *Sonderkommando Fuenf* ("Special Commando Five") was captured by the Russians and can be seen in the military museum in Kiev.[76]

Seeing these actions only increased the prisoners' determination to leave a record. The squad of prisoners who operated the crematoria at Birkenau buried a cylinder in the courtyard, near the chimneys, that contained detailed explanations of what they had seen and done. Filip Mueller described the efforts to leave "for posterity" a record of events at Auschwitz and Birkenau before they were killed.[77] Documentary proof and accuracy took priority over any literary embellishment; Mueller carefully peeled the label from a Zyklon B container, sketched the crematoria complex of buildings, and gave statistics of the killings. For good measure a second copy of the buried record was sewn into Recamier chairs the prisoners were repairing for the wife of a certain SS officer Bach, then sent to her outside the camp.

Works by artists and writers were hidden inside barrack walls, buried in the ground, concealed in bunks and lofts, under floorboards, tucked into torn clothing, smuggled out by prisoners leaving on transports. Coded messages were written on thin paper and inserted into hollowed-out candles, empty fountain pens, cigarettes, keys, and innocent-looking objects. Every possible means of drawing or writing was used: cigarette paper, matchbox covers, posters and medical reports, one artist used the blank margins of postage stamp sheets for miniature drawings. The painter Esther Lurie used wrappings from cotton rolls saved for her by a doctor in the infirmary. Others used old bed linen, burlap from potato sacks, and rough flour bags as substitute surfaces for their works. An exquisite miniature painting on lacquered egg-shell has survived.

After the end of the war a note was found at Auschwitz, stuffed into a German aluminum canteen with a metal stopper: "Dear finder, search everywhere in every inch of soil. Tens of documents are buried under it, mine and those of other persons, which will throw light on everything that was happening here. Great quantities of teeth are buried here. It was we, the commando workers, who expressly have strewn them all over the terrain, as many as we could, so the world should find material traces of the millions of the murdered." If they could not communicate what they knew while alive, they sought a way to do it after death.

Even after the liberation of most camps, and the certain defeat of Germany, the intense struggle against evidence continued. Former prisoners, now wearing civilian clothes and mixing with crowds of refugees on the roads, were still pursued. In one chilling narration a liberated prisoner was foraging for food when, suddenly, an SS officer appeared with a Wehrmacht general. They lined up the refugees and demanded "anyone who had formerly worked in the Auschwitz KZ to step forward." The former prisoner, now wearing civilian clothes, wrote: "My blood froze in my veins. No one knew me here. There was complete silence as the seconds ticked slowly by. And then they left. I had won again."[78]

Many liberated captives and writers—Filip Mueller, Gisela Perl, Reska Weiss, Krystyna Zywulska, and others—thought they were safe when they left their camps and began the journey home. But they did not know a lethal war continued, this time against witnesses. Each narrowly escaped.

The war against survivors and witnesses had a chronology of its own. The battle at Stalingrad took place in 1942 and the battle near Kursk in 1943, but it was also in June 1943 that new German administrative decrees made the camps even more destructive.[79] Large amounts of rolling stock, railway cars, locomotives, use of tracks, personnel, supplies, whole military units urgently needed at the front were diverted to destroy prisoners and records. This other war—against witnesses, evidence, and the written word—had its own momentum, increasing to a crescendo at the end.

* * *

Emanuel Ringelblum collected an archive that represented the activities of the entire community of the Warsaw ghetto from 1939 to 1943; it included original works written in many languages, Yiddish, Hebrew, Polish, Hungarian, and Czech. During the violent uprising of April 1943 Ringelblum decided to seal his archive in large rubberized milk containers, and sink them deep in the earth. In 1944, Ringelblum was killed together with his family.

In 1946, a Historical Commission was established to try to locate the archive. They thought it was buried under many deep layers of rubble. In order to find the exact location the commission members had to make complicated calculations, then clear the enormous amount of debris that had piled up after two different insurrections. They dug a shaft or "chimney" downward, leading into the cellars of another time.

They excavated, square meter by square meter. A historian who took part in the search wrote:

> Where was the buried archive? We stood there, the members of the Historical Commission—Wulf, Blumental, Wasser and myself— looked at each other, and with our eyes only guessed the same thought each one of us had: it isn't here at all.

> Suddenly a shovel struck something hard. After further digging, the first metal container appeared. Then others. Eight in all. In the neighboring room, two more.[80]

After months of drying the papers and careful restoration, "The objects began to speak."

Some of the preserved objects, like a tramway ticket in Ringelblum's archive, teeth buried in the ground or the label peeled from a Zyklon B container, have purely documentary value. They are intended to communicate a way of life that was obliterated to the future. A few postwar writers have complained that many writings do not go beyond traditional communicative language, but a demand for "literary" or "heightened" language implies different writing conditions. Greater elaboration of the experiences of the camps would come later. The language of 1943–44 was that of essential communication. It was directed against "the lie . . . which had gigantic technology at its disposal, and was protected by unbounded violence."[81]

Are we the future readers foreseen in these works? They sought transtemporal communication that might leap over a generation or even many generations into another entirely different world. Suckever wrote that the gap in communication might last nine thousand years.

Many of these works are strained—as if with a bow—toward a reader living at a distant point. This can often be seen in the texture, or in small touches, just a verb tense. For example:

I had a house. A small nook.

Or:

Once I was called Stanislaw George Lec. I had my home and my mother, my home and my wife.[82]

Or, the last poem of Robert Desnos:
It is left for me
to become the shadow that returns and returns again
in your sunlit life.[83]

Or:

How can I throw a bouquet
on a grave scooped out of air?[84]

Or:

The stars ask me: and where are you going?

The words have a strong future orientation, like seeds, or like the grains in Suckever's poem, cast outward.

VII
The End of Time

1

The Riddle

*T*ime was one of the great discoveries during the Second World War. The way it was imagined, and experienced, suddenly changed, and changed radically. It could be transformed on very short notice, or with no notice at all. This included the short units of time—seconds, minutes, hours measured by a watch or clock—and the longer units, calendars, important dates, historical benchmarks.

Every nation that took part in the war experienced defeat at one point or another. Time during defeat could pass with agonizing slowness. Defeat could destroy hope, the future, the possibility of defense and time itself. During captivity and occupation, the passage of time was often felt as if it was outside history, outside recorded time altogether.

Many discovered that other people they encountered during the years 1939–45 had different calendars, different concepts of time and very different notions of history from their own. Many participants and writers felt compelled to devise their own narrations and interpretations, their own versions and structures for the events they experienced. Often these put the notion of "narrative" itself, and the sequence of events in time, into question.

* * *

Retreating under the blows of a seemingly invincible army, a hard-pressed general paused in the midst of intense fighting. He consulted with a battalion commander, and surprised him by asking a totally unexpected question. It was a riddle.

"What is it that is the longest thing in the world and yet the shortest, the fastest and yet the slowest, something that people waste more than anything else, and yet regret most when it is gone?"
The commander could not guess the answer right away.

The general was pleased that he was puzzled. He took out his watch and held it up.

"Here it is! Time! Our job now . . . is to gain time, to take it away from the enemy. See me off."

We clambered up the steps out of the dug-out.[1]

Defense, retreat, and the clear likelihood of defeat gave time special urgency. Time in the riddle is the time necessary for successful defense: time that is more valuable than ever before, time that is crucial for avoiding defeat. But it is also time in the lives of ordinary individuals. Both are the same time measured by a watch.

The conversation comes at a dramatic moment in a novel. Time was running out, German armies were advancing rapidly, and the general explains, "Our job is to hold the roads. If the Germans break through, our troops must be right there on the roads in front of them. That's why I took a battalion away from here. I wanted to take yours but you cover an important road."

They had to use every means in their power to prevent the use of roads by the Germans. Above all the task was to gain time.

Alexander Bek emphasized the incident in his novel *Volokolamsk Highway*, elaborating it into a guessing game and riddle. The sequence of actions occurred in the summer of 1941. Only very recently the Soviet Army was put on the defensive. But a variation of this "riddle" could have been described in other places on the globe where defense suddenly became essential, survival doubtful. In one work after another a writer would stress that the value and real nature of time was a discovery. The new awareness came as a surprise, with the force of an overwhelming, belated revelation.

According to Pamfilov's riddle, time is tragic. It is rarely appreciated. People are forgetful spendthrifts. They do not value time until too late, until it is gone. Only then are previously accepted assumptions called into question or abandoned. Time is the longest thing in the world and yet the shortest, the fastest and slowest, what "people regret most when it is gone." Time is heedlessly squandered.

In another very different part of the world, an observer described an event where the passage of time was crucial. In his narration, the shortest units of time—seconds—are emphasized. The observer is counting seconds and looks through binoculars. In the distance a companion is crawling toward an enemy outpost:

He checked with his watch again. Less than twenty seconds. Each one seemed to be stretching out elastically into great lengths of time. Sweat salted the corners of his mouth and he could feel his heart beginning to thud against the cage of his ribs . . . Then the tension squeezed his mind dry of every scrap of emotion, and he was only conscious of the strengthening beat of his heart measuring out the count-down.

"Ten seconds . . . Nine . . . Eight . . . Seven."[2]

The writer slows the action deliberately, the crawling companion is magnified by the binoculars, the rhythm slows and the words also slow, tension increases. The observer's consciousness narrows as it is now his heartbeat that measures the slowly passing time. Probably he had never measured time this way before.

As the seconds are counted, the passage describes a frustrated act of communication—the scene almost takes place among deaf-mutes. The men cannot speak with one another or share the count-down of seconds. The man with the binoculars is reduced to anguished silence. Suspense continues to build. Many events—both spoken and unspoken—hang waiting upon the passing seconds.

In Francis Clifford's novel *A Battle Is Fought to Be Won*, the narrator looks at his watch, and time has slowed almost to a stop. But as he raises his eyes time accelerates again. Then, as he picks up his binoculars and looks through them at the magnified image, it slows again.

The experience of passing time varied greatly from person to person, from action to action, from place to place. John Steinbeck recounted a small-scale action in which three soldiers were in close proximity, yet their worlds, and their temporal dimensions, were entirely different. In a dispatch from Italy dated December 8, 1943, Steinbeck described interviews with several soldiers. He tried to establish the most basic facts about the event. What happened? What ground was covered? When did it begin and end, how long did it last? Because the men were together it seemed that these could easily be compared and discussed. But they were unable to agree on the most simple, basic facts. It was impossible to establish a single time frame. There were many time frames, all different, and contradictory. The men had been together but did not agree on when the action began or when it ended. Communication failed.

Steinbeck wrote: "There probably is nothing in the world so elastic as time. There is no way of knowing how long the action took . . . It may have been half an hour and it may have been three hours."[3]

Time, both with and without clocks or watches, was a new discovery during the wartime period from 1939 to 1945, it underwent constant transformations. For active participants, the prewar assumptions about time often seemed false. There was no single, homogeneous time, there were no universal standards or benchmarks to apply to events as they occurred. The basic units for measuring time—both small and large—that once seemed unvarying could no longer be taken for granted. Problems of communicating time to other people, through spoken or written words, loomed larger than ever before. Communicating the significance or the "real" nature of time—a new narrative of time—suddenly became urgent. The failure to do this was the source of some of the greatest mistakes made during the war.

Time was monolithic, gigantic. But it was also completely elastic, contradictory. Time was malleable. Its passage had endless variations and conflicting perspectives that were constantly reshuffled. In one written work after another, time became a major theme. Time, of course, has been a perennial theme in every language and every age, but between 1939 and 1945 it acquired overwhelming urgency. It was not abstract. It required action, it was concrete through and through.

2

Clocks

The clock or watch was used in many passages that stress the urgency of passing time, its drama and its suspense. They were literal reference points, indispensable for planning and synchronizing action, instruments not only for measuring time but communicating it to others. In the hands of a skilled writer they could have an even larger function.

Events as they were experienced by a participant, and also memory, rarely obeyed mechanical time. The flow of time was uneven if it was a "flow" at all, except in a limited, technical sense. More than ever before, time concealed risk and danger. Time was unpredictable. In some writings the importance of a watch or clock was magnified so it became part of the narrative action, an important actor in a drama. On the other hand, in some writings the watch or clock is noticed only to be rejected. It fails to show information that is relevant .

In James Jones' novel *The Thin Red Line*, it is a watch that mediates between a character, his surroundings and events. Captain Stein, severely wounded, lying on the ground, hears an overpowering "booming and banging" in the air. He tries—and fails—to distinguish friendly from enemy fire. His eyes accidentally fall on his watch. "What time was it, anyway? Stein looked at his watch, and its little face stared back at him with an intensity it had never had before. 6:45, a quarter to seven in the morning. Back home he would be just—Stein realized he had never really seen his watch. He forced himself to put his arm down. Directly in front of him his reserve Third platoon were spread out and flattened. Most of them were looking at him with faces as intense as his watch's face."[4]

The passage puns on the meaning of a "face," shared by his watch and by humans. The description is faithful to the thoughts and perspective of Stein, and the watch is of no use to him. He shouts to his men but no one hears him, he can hardly hear his own voice. He dies, and an hour later another soldier sees another watch on the arm of a dead soldier. Ironically the watch is still running.

One feature of the front was that action came sporadically, in fits and starts. Periods of waiting were followed by sudden events too rapid to follow, they had different rhythms and different kinds of "time." During lulls in action there were ample opportunities to think about the past and the future. Each individual, whether soldier or civilian, had his own past, his own concept of the future, and brought these with him. Time was measured in terms of his own personal life and biography.

One writer, a soldier in a dugout, recalled he had a completely different sense of time when he was younger. The future seemed endless: "He had always felt that a thousand years of living stretched ahead of him. He had rarely stopped to think about the way he lived through a day, for there would be innumerable days ahead. Now, ahead of him, there stretched no years, but only the time separating him from the German attack; and all his life would have to be contained within this time."[5] In another novel, written three years later, the same author observed that events in the past were not less vivid or concrete than those of the present. On the contrary: "Time passed according to its own laws during the war; things that happened a long time ago sometimes seemed near and clear, as if they were yesterday, while the longest, slowest, and most never-ending was what was happening at the moment. It seemed as if he had spent half his life sitting on the burned-out hill." Temporal perspectives had changed. In unexpected ways they were telescoped, reversed, transformed. Which perspective was the right one? How to measure it? Were there any laws or rules governing time at all?

As the war continued, time for many—for soldiers, prisoners in camps and civilians under occupation—was stretched to the breaking point, and beyond. Ties to the past, and shared experiences with people at home, became increasingly dated, strained, and painful. Communicative links with the past were broken. As a character in Cecil Lewis' novel *Pathfinders* reflected in 1944, "The pre-war life seemed something that belonged to another planet."[6]

The clock in many of these works is a device for communicating time to others. With vivid regularity, the communication of a common sense of time is a failure. A pilot exclaimed: "Over the radio I heard Control calling me back . . . An hour already! Everything seemed to have happened in one second."[7] Typical was a moment when a writer was lost in thought, sitting in a dispatch room and staring out the window: "Suddenly a completely ridiculous image came into my mind. I thought of clocks out of order. All the clocks of France—out of order. Clocks in their church steeples. Clocks on railway stations. Chimney clocks in empty houses. 'The war,' I said to myself, 'is that thing in which clocks are no longer wound up.'"[8]

In Kurt Vonnegut's *Slaughterhouse Five*, the passage of time is described as absurd. It is also perverse. "Somebody was playing with the clocks . . . The second hand on my watch would twitch once, and a year would pass, and then it would twitch again."[9] Vonnegut was writing about the operations of time in memory, and the involuntary leaps from one temporal setting to another. Memories were rarely synchronized with each other. The passage of time in war, its "clocks," were not synchronized with those of peace. Time did not follow a straight line, like an arrow. It was not linear.

Captivity altered the normal sense of time, and played havoc with it. The absence of watches and clocks in captivity had disastrous psychological results. Time could not be differentiated, this robbed the present of its reality. Viktor Frankl noted that small units of time seemed endless, while the longer units passed quickly. Odd Nansen wrote: "Every day may seem miles long to get through, but the weeks nevertheless gallop into eternity, and before one can turn round a whole month has passed, and summer with it. What became of the summer, all told?"[10]

Completely amorphous time was psychologically intolerable. Over a long period, it was a danger to sanity. Any device or improvised "clock" that could be found to mark the passage of time was welcome. It helped the prisoner to structure his life, provide for the future, and unite him with the outside "normal" world.

A prisoner who improvised one of the most unique "clocks" or time-keeping devices was Christopher Burney. His experience was like that of few other captives. The length of his solitary confinement was unusual. Burney spent 526 days alone in a cell in Fresnes prison in France, he had no cellmates or communication with other people. It was a deliberate form of torture. The Germans hoped to obtain information from Burney about his mission to the French underground. He came close to madness.

He wrote afterwards,

Patience is a matter of anticipation . . . Nobody can say sensibly to himself, "I am going to sit still for fourteen hours," and no more, because before the sentence can mean anything to him, the hours have to be given substance. But he can look at his watch at ten o'clock, say his sentence, and wait quietly until the hands pass twelve o'clock for the second time.[11]

That is, if the man has a watch or clock. But Burney had none.

Before long his legs felt like wooden sticks. He could hardly speak because his muscles for speech were becoming atrophied. Time was an ungraspable blur.

Then, he found relief in an unusual sequence of events. He wrote:

I discovered a sort of clock. On a sunny day I could just see through the frosted glass of my window that while the main part of the wall opposite was of a light color, a shadow was cast by the gable on top of it, and this shadow lengthened slightly as the sun rose higher. After the zenith there was a period when I had no sign at all, but late in the afternoon the sun sent one tiny beam on to the wall of my cell above the skylight, and this again cast a shadow, which crept upwards for an hour or so and then dissolved.

In the architecture of his own prison building he had found a sundial. In short, a clock. With this "clock," and with its measurements and divisions, came patience and a degree of sanity.

When we read of these invented clocks, and discover how important they were for survival, we remember how little information most prisoners were given. The prisoner's ties to the outside world were nearly nonexistent. For example, Burney heard an important bit of news, from tapping on the walls of his prison cell, that a certain general had just won a great victory. He guessed from the name—Eisenhower—that the general must be a German.

3

Narration

Many writers felt there was an unbridgeable clash between military and civilian life. Alexander Baron wrote in his novel *From the City, from the Plough*, "There were two worlds in which men lived, Norman had come to realize; the world which was summed up by the word 'home'; and the world of the soldier."[12] They had different rules, different ways of feeling, psychology, and concepts of time. Yet they co-existed. The conflict between the two would never be resolved.

In *From the City, from the Plough* a colonel, lying flat and hidden on the ground at the front, is distracted by vivid thoughts of home and his family. Then, "He watched the second hand of his watch crawling round; an object of attention, an alternative to thought . . . The watch ticked on. But I am a battalion commander, he thought. Men are watching me. Men are waiting for me . . . He rose to his feet. He could see the upturned faces all about him, he could feel the suspense of the men waiting in folds and crannies in the ground." It is a reminder that the face of his watch has the same word as the human faces looking at him, and it is the same in both of the "two worlds." The struggle to reconcile the experiences of military life and personal or family life was universal in the years 1939–45. A large number of works describe the search for forms that could express these clashes and discontinuities, that could salvage some sense of connection.

Unexpectedly, in unusual places and often in the midst of fighting, many writers recalled their childhood. Childhood proved to be an important, universal benchmark. Following an association of thoughts about rising early in the morning, St. Exupery sat in his cockpit:

Again I was reminded of school. Of a time when I was very young. How long ago was that? I—
"Captain!"
"What's up?"
"Er . . . nothing . . ."

Of school, yes. When you are a little boy, in boarding school, they get you up too early. They get you up at six o'clock . . ."[13]

The voice interrupting his thoughts came from the gunner. The author's lack of attention was perceptible to others. But for St.-Exupery, his thoughts had real importance. Probably it is not an accident that after this recollection of childhood, when he went into action with his airplane, he felt a sudden fierce concentration and anger at the enemy.

Childhood and early consciousness was a determining measure, or unit, in the life that followed. Each soldier brought his past with him into the airplane cockpit, tank, or ship, wherever he was. These were the ties to his personal past. Each individual had his own sense of time based on concrete experience. The number of ways in which present and past could be fused was infinite. They could lead to a passionate determination to wage defensive war, or—on the contrary—not to fight at all. There was no formula governing the way past and present would come together. If the present was hostile and unpredictable, the author sought for a point of support, a solid foothold, however small, in the flux of events. This support was no trifling matter.[14]

Narration, and the telling of a story, has always been an essential element in prose literature, it is important both in fiction and in nonfiction. A literary historian has written of "a basic need in the moment of existence to belong, to be related to a beginning and an end . . . Human beings instinctively require intelligible ends. They try to find consonance between the end and the middle in critical points along the way."[15] Narration answers to this essential need: it speaks of a life in relation to time.

But rarely have beginnings and endings been more difficult to locate than during the Second World War itself. A great, sometimes bewildering variety of narrative forms are found in literary works about the period 1939–45. Forms of narration were strained to their limits. When a contemporary reader encounters early narratives of the war, he often finds them awkward, their temporal frames broken. Consonance between middle and end of a narration is rarely present. Narratives in English—especially about experiences of multinational armies fighting far from home—are among the most awkward and complex of all.

The future was impossible to predict. In his novel *Flesh Wounds*, David Holbrook describes two students stirring porridge together over a stove in 1942. They are not sure if they are in love, or not.

"But look how we talk," Paul went on, warmly, seizing a large wooden spoon to help her. "We talk as if there was a future, but we can't even be sure of that."

They stirred thoughtfully together.

"I suppose one is hoping for that, in going out, and fighting."

"One couldn't dare think of there being no future at all."[16]

In the delicately balanced scene, many questions come together. Should he join the army or not? Should he join now, or should he wait? And how long would that be?

In much British and American fiction about the war, the question arises if a young couple should marry or not. In this scene from *Flesh Wounds*, the question becomes more subtle still. Anxiety about the future leads the two young people to question more carefully what they really feel. They become uncertain. Concern about an "ending" was not just the province of the narrator or writer, but of the characters themselves, the practical decisions they make. It was woven into the fabric of daily life.

Where, then, was the critical point in time that knits past and future into a single fabric or plot? Where was the beginning, middle, or end? In *Flesh Wounds* the crucial moment occurs when the future's uncertainty is clearly expressed. The two decide they will not marry. Joining the army takes precedence, and the need to assure another, more general future. When he returns at the end of the war, they will not marry then either.

A similar relationship between two young people is described by the American writer Vance Bourjailly in his novel *The End of My Life*. The main character, "Skinner," decides he will not finish college. He also decides not to marry the girl he loves because the future is so uncertain. In his words, "We can just as easily be married tomorrow as not. That's the trouble with it."[17] He joins the army, but then lives together with his girlfriend for six months in New York City before he is shipped abroad.

Bourjailly emphasized the disjunction of this six-month period by placing it in a long flashback in the middle of the novel. The flashback is one-third of the novel's length, a sizable narration within a narration. The sections before and after it describe events that occurred later in chronological time. This was Bourjailly's way of emphasizing that the episode was central. It was out of sequence with the "beginning" and the "end," but was more important than either. His novel is not a cumulative succession of chronological events, and is characteristic of much wartime fiction.

According to postwar taste, accustomed to a smooth temporal sequence, it is jagged and awkward.

Surveying only British war fiction, a historian distinguished nine very different types of narration about the wartime period, and admitted his list represented only a few of the attempts to construct a time frame around war experiences, "to reduce . . . the tangled mass of phenomena" to a pattern. No one form was more successful than the others.[18]

Writers were challenged by countless difficulties. The war was international. Alliances brought people from different countries into close contact. Alliances spanned the globe, soldiers from different countries worked together, and by necessity depended on one another. But they represented different societies, and very different pasts. Novels that included people from several countries in a single narrative—like *The Pathfinders* (1943) by Cecil Lewis, who described a Lancaster bomber with its international crew—found characterization difficult, because the backgrounds of the characters were so dissimilar.[19] If the author wanted to do justice to their formative years, it required constant breaks in time sequence, and much awkward exposition. *The Pathfinders* is one of the more accomplished novels about international bomber crews—there were many— but the temporal sequence was repeatedly broken. To compensate, the characters were simplified and made two-dimensional.

Authors of narratives set in World War II sought new devices that could synthesize experiences from different times. Linear time, and its assurance, was frequently broken and lost. Participants in the war writing before 1945 were especially hampered by lack of knowledge of the war's ending; there were great gaps in their information and a frustrating perspective that was too narrow, a version of the "mole's eye view." Many works were speculative by necessity, resembling science fiction.[20] Authors strained their imagination as they guessed what a postwar world would look like. H. G. Wells, so fertile in imagining the future in *The War of the Worlds*, *The Time Machine*, and *The Invisible Man*, wrote in 1943–44 in one of his last works that he saw little chance for humanity to survive; there was no progress, only regression.[21]

But postwar writers also had disadvantages. If they projected their postwar knowledge backwards in time onto wartime experiences, they risked falsifying them. In narrations written after 1945 there is often a double temporal sequence, the real time of a past that was experienced earlier, and a "narrative time" imported by the author into his text that includes, in varying degrees, postwar knowledge. If his "present" was 1950, or 1955, or 1965 or later, events would change as new layers of time were incorporated.[22]

The conflicts in time become a major international theme, a hallmark of narration. Marc Bloch wrote in 1942 that "war and defeat have had upon Europe the repercussions of a Time Machine in reverse," and he was referring to the time machines of Jules Verne. World War II narratives were rarely concerned with the progress of technology or science, exploring the disjunctions and conflicts in time instead. Time, and the experience of time, often remained a riddle without a single linear direction—a beginning, middle, and end—but multiple beginnings and juxtapositions.[23] Writers sought forms that could communicate the extreme dissonances of the years 1939–45: the clash, the gap, the break.

4

Calendars, Defeat, and the End of Time

Many of the longer units of time sanctioned by tradition were questioned or abandoned during the years 1939–45. It was clear that the world had changed. Almost everything had become unpredictable, security was nowhere to be found. In the journal he kept throughout the war, Harold Nicolson wrote in early June 1940: "How strange it is to have no knowledge of what is about to befall us. In ordinary times one seldom thinks how odd it is to have no knowledge of what may happen even within the next hour, but now the consciousness of this ignorance becomes acute. I see the future only in terms of color:"[24]

The calendar—the Gregorian calendar—was the normal device in Europe and America for counting years ever since the Renaissance. But accelerating events required new ways for measuring the passage of time. Older time schemes and calendars were inadequate. During the Battle of Britain, Winston Churchill adopted a new shorthand calendar for events. For example, in his notation "Z + 18," "Z" meant the beginning of the war—September 12, 1939—plus eighteen months. It was a convenient method for calculating production for defense, and the dates when products and supplies were planned to come on stream. Churchill often called the future after the war "the after-time."[25]

Earlier, in the 1920s and 30s, new methods of counting years suited the new conceptions of time and ideology. In Fascist Italy, all official pronouncements carried a date in Roman numerals indicating years elapsed since 1922 when the Fascist party seized power. 1922 was counted as "Anno 0." Only when Mussolini resigned—in "Anno XXI"—did official dates in Italy return to the old system, 1943.

The German "Third Reich" began in 1933, and some organizations in Germany dated events from that year. The Third Reich was also the "ThousandYear Reich"; time was adapted to ideology that had its own calendar, benchmark dates, and luxuriant mythology. The millennial claims of National Socialism went back to the Middle Ages. In Oswald Spengler's description the Third Reich "was the Germanic ideal, an eternal tomorrow to which all great men from Joachim de Floris to Nietzsche tied their lives—arrows of yearning for the other side of the river, as Zarathustra says."[26]

Japan adopted a special calendar during the war. In the year 1940, the Japanese wartime calendar celebrated the 2,600th anniversary of the beginning of Japan's history. This mythological calendar dated the imperial lineage back to the Sun Goddess, Amnaterasu Omikama. According to the Japanese national anthem "Kimigayo,"

The Emperor's reign will last
For a thousand then eight thousand generations
Until pebbles become mighty rocks
With moss.[27]

William Owens, author of a fine book about the liberation of the Philippines *Eye-deep in Hell*, criticized the widespread American view that the Japanese were "inscrutable" Orientals: "The few who had read the Tanaka Memorial—with its boast that the invasion of Manchuria was the beginning of a hundred years' religious war with the aim of bringing the eight corners of the earth under one roof, with the mperorgod at the roof pole—ignored or refused to believe what they read."[28]

In the USSR the Second World War, called "The Great Patriotic War," was said to begin on June 22, 1941. The preceding years were supposedly a period of friendship treaties and peace. But the 1930s were far from a period of "peace" in the USSR. Roy Medvedev quoted a writer: "In the thirties we felt as if we were at war with the entire old world . . . While the conflict was on, a conflict to the death, it was necessary to maintain iron discipline no matter what. That's always how it is in a war."[29] An international consensus on the importance of specific dates rarely exists. Time, its benchmarks and inflection points, is measured differently in different places. In a study of time in history, the philosopher Raymond Aron concluded that time is, above all, the expression of human nature.[30]

Few countries during the years 1939–45 did not experience military defeat. Millions of Europeans and Asians fell under the occupation of foreign regimes that promoted their national versions of history, and had their own calendars to measure it. Conquest was enforced with arms, and required adaptation for survival. People often worked side by side with others who lived according to entirely different concepts of time and different calendars.

The violent invasions and occupations of 1939–41 seemed to be outside comparable events and outside any calendar. The question arose with increasing urgency: in what kind of world were they living?

The historian Marc Bloch reacted to the defeat of France in 1940:

The privations resulting from . . . defeat have had upon Europe the repercussions of a Time Machine in reverse. We have been plunged suddenly into a way of life which, only quite recently, we thought had disappeared forever. I am writing these lines in my house in the country . . . We have gone back thirty or forty years! It was as though the two opposed forces belonged, each of them, to an entirely different period of history. We interpreted war in terms of the spear (*assagai*) versus the rifle, made familiar to us by long years of colonial expansion. But this time it was we who were cast in the role of the savage![31]

Bloch, a professor, author of several books on the Middle Ages and editor of the distinguished *Annales Historiques*, had fled Nazi-occupied Paris. He wrote these words in 1942, and knew nothing of the camps. He was killed by Germans in 1943.

Captives tried to improvise their own personal calendars for the longer periods. In a camp in the Soviet Union, Elinor Lipper found a solution with a simple matchbox: she calculated that five years were sixty months, or sixty matches. Each month she removed a match from the box. One day, however, she threw away her last match—it was 1942—and nothing happened. She had become an "overtimer." That was all.[32]

A partial substitute for a calendar was the passing seasons. Celebrations of Christmas produced a large number of writings by Christians; Christmas commemorated the passage of one more year. The Norwegian poet Arnulf Overland, sent to Sachsenhausen, fell silent for most of the war, but mustered enough energy to write a poem each Christmas, reading it aloud to his assembled compatriots on Christmas Eve.[33] For Jewish prisoners the secret observation of holidays had particularly great significance.[34]

Defeat became a common experience that was shared by many, either earlier or later in the war. Writers who were captives, or in occupied countries, were often struck by the sense of regression to a more primitive state. This required a new "calendar" to date the present, a new concept of time and history. As the first ghettoes were formed, many thought of the Middle Ages. In his book *The Pianist*, Władysław Szpilman described reactions in late November 1939 to the first barricades and barbed wire of what would become the Warsaw ghetto, and the demand that Jews wear armbands: "Not in our most secret thoughts would we ever have suspected that such a thing could happen . . . So we were to be branded publicly as outcasts. Several centuries of humanitarian progress were to be cancelled out, and we were back in the Middle Ages."[35]

With increasing frequency writers came to believe that the Germans' "New Europe" was an abrupt regression in time and history. It was technologically advanced and primitive at the same time. Andre Malraux also believed he was living in a period similar to the Middle Ages; in his last narrative, *The Walnut Trees of Altenburg,* he describes how he found himself imprisoned in a camp near the Cathedral at Chartres, its stained glass windows and ancient statues looming over the ragged captives. "In the earliest days of the war, as soon as his uniform had blotted out a man's profession, I began to see these Gothic faces. And what now emerges from the wild crowd that can no longer shave is not the penal settlement, but the Middle Ages . . . Perhaps because the Middle Ages undertook to represent men, and we are not in the sort of place that yields gods."[36]

Malraux imagined that the present, and France under occupation, were transported back in time when the statues of Chartres Cathedral were first created. The physiognomies of living, captive Frenchmen were the same faces he saw on the sculptures.

In Germany, Eugen Kogon, author of *The Theory and Practice of Hell,* noted "the predilection of the National Socialists and the SS for early Teutonic history, reenacted in castles and cathedrals to torchlight by night." He thought the SS were basically illiterate; their psychology "differs little from that of the Praetorian Guard in ancient Rome, the followers of Mohammed's immediate successors, the Mongol shock troops of Genghis

Khan, the dervishes of Mahdi . . . Only in the matter of social origins did the S.S. bring a modern note into the picture."[37]

Many who were imprisoned in the USSR also thought they were living in a version of the Middle Ages. One writer, arrested by the NKVD in Eastern Poland after the Soviet invasion of September 17, 1939, thought he was transported back in time. "While in jail, I frequently asked myself whether my entire life was not merely a dream, whereas in reality we dwelt in the Middle Ages except with modern techniques of torture." At about the same time, the writer Alexander Wat described the Zamarstynow Prison in Lvov: "In this prison we always had a feeling of a return to the Middle Ages: the way we were treated, the prison itself. This is how medieval prisons, mental asylums or leprosaria must have looked."[38]

The Russian writer Vasili Grossman thought of the Mongols. The only valid concept of history, he wrote, was "the law of the conservation of violence." "Violence is eternal, no matter what is done to destroy it. It will not disappear and will not diminish but will only be transformed. It once took the form of slavery. Then of the Mongol invasion. It moves from continent to continent, and sometimes it takes a class form and then is transformed into a racial form."[39]

In Asia the captive John Coast evoked an earlier past as he worked on the Burmese railroad: "The two thousand pre-dynastic slaves of Wan Po built the entire railroad in 17 days!" The sense of reverting to an ancient past was widespread. Also working on the Burmese railway, Ray Parkin wrote: "It is humid and we are hurling rocks down the hillside. Scraping them out with our hands, crowbars, picks and shovels. We strain on great ropes, for all the world like the slave pyramid-builders of Egypt."[40]

They seemed to be plunged into the past and chaos. The whole sweep of time had no distinguishing benchmarks. The "pack of cards" series of bridges at Hintok collapsed three times before they were finally made to stand in September 1943—and they were never strong enough to support rail traffic. The bridges required no European engineering (*pace* Pierre Boule), and the immense project had no metal parts except wire binding and staples. The labor of the prisoners was lost in waste, chaos, and a mounting crescendo of violence.

The poet Yannis Ritsos rejected any concept of linear time, and in a poem written under occupation in Greece in 1942, he noted the date simply as "Before Man."[41] These writers were not indulging in intellectual exercises; their beliefs about present and past grew out of their concrete experiences. Defeat and surrender, brought an acceptance of the end of historical time as they had known it.

Tadeusz Borowski was well-read in history and Western literature, and the experience of captivity led him to question them in their entirety:

We are laying the foundation for some new monstrous civilization. Only now do I realize what price was paid for building the ancient civilizations. The Egyptian pyramids, the temples, and Greek statues— what a hideous crime they were! How much blood must have poured on to the Roman roads, the bulwarks, and the city walls. Antiquity— the tremendous concentration camp where the slave was branded on the forehead by his master, and crucified for trying to escape! Antiquity—the conspiracy of free men against slaves! . . It is we who pulled the oars in galleys and dragged wooden ploughs, while they wrote dialogues and dramas . . . We were filthy and died real deaths. They were 'aesthetic' and carried on subtle debates.[42]

This was the experience of "slavery" that Camus and Solzhenitsyn believed had become the main characteristic of the twentieth century. Borowski's reaction was outrage. He thought the so-called "classical" tra-ditions, complacently accepted and taught before the war, were hollow. A forced laborer like Borowski was not predisposed to think the Roman patrician, or slave-owning citizen, was a model to be followed. Borowski adopted the plural pronoun "we" for all slaves, in the present and past, as a gesture of solidarity.

Few wartime writers—Weichert, Kogon, Primo Levi, or Borowski— thought the contemporary world owed a common debt to Rome or "stood on its shoulders." The Oxford historian Ronald Syme reinterpreted Rome on the eve of the war in his most famous book, *The Roman Revolution,* and instead of focusing on the ideals or constitutional structure of the empire, Syme stressed the lust of the emperors for power and money, comparing them to the European dictators of the 1930s.

The most systematic attack on the Latin and Greek classics, and the historians who used them as models for an idealized past, was probably made by Simone Weil. She fled from France to England in the early years of the war, and died there in 1943. Weil had visited Germany in the 1930s; she observed how Rome served as a model for National Socialism and an imperial Germany. She sharply criticized the stereotyped role of Rome as a model in her own French culture. As a scholar she knew the Roman historians well, and had a modern awareness of propaganda. She distrusted most Roman historians as insincere, servile, venal, directly supported by imperial patrons. Ennius, Virgil, Horace, Cicero, Livy, even Tacitus "wrote always with political bias and, whatever their policy, it was always imperial. They have had their deserts." Neither history nor literature were neutral accumulations of documents; they were characterized, rather, by the destruction of documents and texts, and the creation of new ones. "Documents"—she wrote in *The Need for Roots*—"originate with the conquerors."[43]

Simone Weil had a special interest in the destroyed civilizations of the past. She thought free Europe was about to be similarly destroyed. "No compassion," she wrote, "is felt for things that have been utterly destroyed. Who is there who accords any to Jericho, Gaza, Tyre, Sidon; to Carthage, Numantia, Sicily under the Greeks, or Peru before the time of Columbus? . . . We know nothing about them because they have disappeared. No attention is paid to the defeated. They disappear. They become naught."

Weil's 1939–40 essay "The Great Beast" was a study of the imperial and predatory state. Her most moving pages are devoted to these destroyed civilizations. Her description of Carthage—"a civilization that must have been at least as brilliant as the Latin"—is well-informed, vivid, the deportation and enslavement of the city's inhabitants described from the Carthaginian point of view. After deputies pleaded with the Romans against deportation, "the scene that followed, as related by Appian, is tragic on a Shakespearian level and resembles a far more atrocious version of Hacha's visit to Hitler." Hacha, President of Czechoslovakia in 1938–39, had been forced to surrender to Germany.

Weil analyzed slavery as an institution that derived from war. In a brilliant essay "*The Iliad* or the Poem of Force," she showed how armed force transformed human beings, turning both those who use it and those who submit to it into objects or things. As for her native France, defeated as completely as Carthage, she thought it would suffer a similar fate and disappear from the map.

Both Simone Weil and Borowski identified with the victims of Rome, not with Rome itself. The shift was significant. It meant defeat and the end of meaningful history, of time. Weil knew that the more powerful victors, whether Germany or Rome, wrote the history of the nations they defeated. It always happened that way. The written records of the defeated would effectively vanish. No longer would they have their own history, in a version written by themselves. Others would write it in a condescending, jeering manner, and they would become "naught." History was not cumulative. A new "history" of lies and repression would supplant the old.

In defeat, the linear narrative for one nation after another broke down. Old historical sequences and tenets of belief collapsed, becoming meaningless. All the countries at war during the period 1939–45 experienced defeat, without exception. This would be obscured only later, with the arrival of postwar national pride. American and British armies suffered defeats too numerous to list. There were error-filled periods of "lethargy, myopia, order, counter-order and disorder," of bad generalship and defeatism.[44]

A writer described the attempt to pick up soldiers after the tragic failure of the Allies—Canadian, American, British—at Dieppe in August 1942:

> The men we took aboard *Garth* looked as if they had learned some terrible lesson that was still too vivid to them to express it clearly either to themselves or anyone else; but that was because they had learned it so thoroughly. "Never glad, confident morning again"; many were badly wounded, all were suffering from shock and exhaustion. They had the gray, lifeless faces of men whose vitality had been drained out of them; each could have modeled a death mask. They were bitter and resentful at having been flung into a battle far more horrible than anything for which they had been prepared, and as they came aboard one heard the oaths and blasphemies, the cursings and revilings, with which men speak of leaders by whom they feel that they have been betrayed and deceived. I thought that this is what a beaten army looks like.[45]

The defeat seemed irreversible, and had a strong effect on subsequent Allied strategy. The description is a warning, as if to say: This is what defeat is. This is the end of illusions, of rhetorical self-deception. A whole army has been decisively defeated. "Beaten." A coda.

One of the worst periods for the Allies was when Rommel, repeatedly dominating the battlefield, was poised to enter Cairo. British headquarters burned official papers during what was ironically known as "Ash

Wednesday." Mussolini had prepared for a grand entry into the Egyptian capital; he flew a white stallion in a transport plane to the North African coast, intending to ride it into the city.[46]

In his novel *Stalingrad*, Theodore Plievier described the German Army in prehistorical terms. Their technology was modern, but the contemporary events in which it was used could have been occurring thousands of years ago:

This thing in the night was not some beast pursued by primitive man, not some mammoth stung by stone axes and mad with pain; it was a DaimlerBenz truck powered by a ninetyhorsepower diesel engine, with three axles, frontand rearwheel drive. Howling it fled through the night, sagged into holes, bounced over bumps. All this took place not three hundred thousand years before our era, but on the night of January 12, 1943.[47]

Technology is consigned to unimportance and prehistory. The traditional calendar, with its myths and notions of progress, its accumulation of linear time—what has been called "time's arrow"[48]— is mocked and held up to ridicule.

One of the finest evocations of defeat and the end of time is by the Japanese novelist Yoshida Mitsuru. If most nations experienced defeat at one time or another between 1939 and 1945, few expressed it as well as Yoshida, author of *Requiem for the Battleship Yamato*. The *Yamato* had the distinction of being the largest battleship in the world. Its cannons were capable of hurling a shell thirty statute miles, further than any other existing ship.

During the Battle of Okinawa in April 1945, the *Yamato* was struck by torpedoes from American aircraft. It listed to one side, shaken by a series of explosions. The author, on the battleship, was thrown into the water.

Around me it becomes quieter and quieter.
Though there is no letup in the sounds of destruction hastening
the end of the fighting, I am oblivious; only a gentle silence touches
my ears.
Everything I see shines with a white light. I gaze in wonder, as
if my eyes were seeing things for the first time.

Have my eyes become crystal clear to their very depths?
Space comes to a stop before me; time freezes around me.
I am I and yet not I.
Barely a few instants, this interval.
Again, the voice from inside my chest presses me, virtually out
loud.
"You, I pity you. Finally given in to death?"
The voice, with a derisive laugh: "You fool. Judging yourself
even as you are being engulfed in the stench of death! Still deceiving
yourself even at this late hour?"
"Leave me alone. Don't take this last brief moment of ease too from me.
I'm sinking: where am I going?
"Please kill me. Rescue me from this fathomless terror."
"Kill me."[49]

Under the force of shock, time comes to a complete stop. The speaker
sheds his identity, he is no longer "I." The defeat is total, the name, the
individual, time, history, calendars—time anywhere—all reference points
are abandoned and lost.

VIII
Defense

1

Armed Resistance

*S*ometimes *an awareness of the urgent need for armed defense was instantaneous. But just as often the need for defense was not apparent at all; it did not crystallize until it was too late. Frequently the motivation for defense was completely dormant.*

Many times between 1939 and 1945 the instinct for defense was activated and amplified with astonishing force. Armed defense required communication—every form of communication, all avenues of the media—in order to be effective.

Defensive warfare was different, even qualitatively different, from offense. Defensive battle gave rise to some of the most fierce fighting in the entire period of the Second World War.

* * *

When Finland was invaded by the USSR its defense was remarkably effective, even though the country was small and the invader many times its size. A Finnish writer evoked the spirit of this defense:

The Ghost Patrol

They ski like ghosts through the night
they slide like apparitions in the moonlight,
cautious, a chilling surprise—
who would dare confront them.

There were not many of them, no,
when on skis rose a flock dressed in white.
Only a flock, whose tracks were taken by the wind
as many in number as cousins of the spruce.

But from where did this group appear,
why is the skiing so strange?
why aren't there even shadows on the snow,
the skis don't leave tracks, even the pole marks don't shimmer.

Now joining the skiers are
all who ever skied here through the years
all the woodsman and guerilla crews,
even the cold moon fears the sight of this group.

Thousands of ghosts, patrols
from centuries past, still looking for the enemy
with rifles, spears, bows, and clubs
they fight in the deep woods of Finland.[1]

Many of the themes of armed defense can be seen in "The Ghost Patrol" by the Finnish writer Yrjo Jylha. The use of weapons—any and all arms, including wooden clubs—is deliberately stressed. The poem, by a writer from a small country, is a template of other works that praise active, armed defense against a larger enemy. The "spears, bows, and clubs" indicate that all the resources of defense without exception must be brought to bear. In addition the poem advocates courage; pride in small numbers against unfavorable odds; defense of familiar territory and a well-known landscape, "cousins of the spruce"; discipline; and pitilessness toward the invader. The defenders have supernatural qualities: they have no shadows and leave no tracks. The writer feels an identity with the country's dead and with its history. "The Ghost Patrol" defends an entire national community.

One of the most significant lines is the ending, "They fight in the deep woods of Finland." An invasion is not threatened but already occurring. The poem is based on the realization that the enemy has penetrated far inside the home country. It has become a war for one's home, one's own life. The motivation sharply contrasts with works glorifying expansion or battles in a foreign country. It is a battle not just for your home but *in* your home.

Jylha's poem expresses some of the qualities of successful armed defense in what was called "The Winter War." The USSR invaded Finland on November 30, 1939, in accordance with the Hitler-Stalin Pact. The adult male population of Finland was equivalent to that of the city of Leningrad. Finland withstood the attack. Despite its small size it waged one of the most successful and earliest defensive battles of the Second World War. During a hundred days of fighting the Red Army suffered great losses and was forced to retreat. Then a massive military draft was ordered in the USSR to redress the situation. The condition of the poorly equipped, badly motivated Red Army was noted at the time by German observers in Finland; they brought it to Hitler's attention.[2]

The instinct for defense could be remarkably powerful. Armies often fought harder the closer they were to home, outfighting numerically superior invading forces. It was defense that motivated some of the most ferocious and unforgiving battles of the Second World War. But sometimes armed defense failed; it was the cause of the greatest misjudgments of the war. The paradox of defense was that an accurate assessment of threat often crystallized in people's minds too late, only with the invasion itself.

Defense required a collective decision. Personal history and national history came together suddenly in a compressed period of time. Hesitation about the need for armed defense was present in England during most discussions reflecting disbelief described in Chapter I. Distinctions were often made between minimal defense, hoped to be adequate, and more serious armed defense. The debates were bitter, abrasive, self-righteous, dividing families, turning friends into enemies and taking up the small margin of time available. Defense depended on a shared belief in its necessity. It depended on communication in the broadest sense, and participation of the media. Discussions about defense became one of the most crucial "battlefields" of the war.

Defense was never automatic and it was not formulaic. There were no rules, and complacency was its great enemy. It was fragile, it could evaporate. Or on the other hand it might become a huge, overpowering presence and belief. This depended on an awareness of threat, the accuracy and conviction with which the threat was expressed, and the likelihood of attack. Always differing points of view were held, the "disbelief" highlighted in Chapter I was a potential hurdle and cause for failure. The stress we have put on writings made during the war itself—before 1945 and before an outcome could be known—highlights this fragility of defense.

In "The Ghost Patrol," intimate, concrete features of national life were key elements. Culture, and all the many features of history, of lived history, were essential to defense. In Finland, references to skiing, snow, and

195

fir trees evoked instant reactions. The poem, by a writer whose traditions were different from those of an English-speaking reader, reminds us that patriotism takes many different forms. Traditional themes can be felt by a reader in one society as basic, as intense, but not necessarily in another. The forms can appear "nationalistic" in the context of an unfamiliar country. But a narrow parochial interpretation would be a mistake.[3] In "The Ghost Patrol," several features of Finnish culture are deftly brought into the poem: the coniferous landscape and spruces, sights and sounds, familiarity with skiing and its equipment—Finnish mail carriers used cross-country skis—the characteristic winter clothes.

In this chapter we show how defense was composed of the ties that knit together the most basic cultural allegiances of society, what we call "ties that bind." Some of the finest writers of the wartime period wrote about them in compelling ways, often producing superb works of literature.

Many works describe anger and even rage, the special concentrated anger of defense. It was very different from the euphoric motivation of expansion, with its carnival atmosphere. It is rarely euphoric.

The surge of anger characteristic of defense was well described by St.-Exupery: "A wave of something strange went over me . . . A kind of anger was going through me. A beneficent anger. God knows, no ecstasy of sacrifice. Rather an urge to bite into something." Other writers expressed comparable anger, Clostermann, Hillary, and the many others who took part in defensive fighting. A Polish poet wrote in 1939, "Oh, seize the sword of history and strike! and strike!"[4] Szlengel wrote in his "Counterattack": "We beg You, Lord, for a bloody battle, / We implore you for a violent death."[5] The likelihood of the author's own death is welcomed. In the Finnish poem, we find pride in small numbers and high casualties. In many defensive battles all stops were pulled out in what became the most savage and violent fighting of the war.

2

Ties that Bind: "City, City"

When a large city came under direct attack, no inhabitant could remain indifferent. A country's capital dramatically symbolized national institutions and historical continuity. Many large cities were objects of all-out attack during the Second World War. They often became a focus for defense, a catalyst for the decision to take up arms. It was the city that represented civilian life in its most concentrated form. Personal and national life overlapped in the city; in some literary works the city assumed such importance that it moved into the foreground, becoming a major presence or protagonist in its own right.

Even when an ancient capital fell into enemy hands, it might still remain a symbol of cultural continuity or resistance. This was the case of Prague, one of the first major European capitals to be conquered in 1938. A major theme in Czech literature between 1937 and 1945 was the city of Prague as symbol of independent culture. Vitezlav Nezval, Jaroslav Seifert, Frantisek Halas, K. J. Erben, Vladimir Thiele, and Vladimir Holan all wrote moving poems about Prague during the war years; a Czech literary critic has written that the Czech state was subject to many changes throughout its history—its territories were disputed, religion, culture, and language persecuted, its form of government abolished in 1938—but what remained was Prague.[6]

But if no effort was made to defend a capital city, its fate could be different. Paris fell in mid-June 1940; the "open cities" provision of French capitulation meant that French cities would not be bombarded but their administration was to be transferred to Germans by "due process" within forty-eight hours.[7] The city had no material destruction. But more than any other major city, Paris became a symbol of impotence. In a poem written in 1943 "To Kill," Paul Eluard described a conquered city:

Tonight there falls
a strange peace over Paris
a peace of blind eyes
of dreams without color

that hurl themselves against the walls
a peace of useless arms
of vanquished faces[8]

In the same year Marcel Ayme wrote a short story "The Man Who Could Walk through Walls." The story became well known because it archly satirized a mentality prevalent in France during the war years. Ayme described a man who had a magical ability to walk through buildings, walls, and floors. But one day he forgot to take his "medicine"; he became trapped inside a wall. The story was an allegory about wartime opportunism. Ayme used the city as a symbol of those who adapted to enemy occupation and took advantage of it, advancing their careers but becoming ensnared in collaboration.[9]

Many Parisians were happy their city escaped the destruction of Warsaw, or of Vippuri (Vyborg) in Finland, the Karelian capital bombarded by the Red Army in 1939–40.[10] Paris was not even subjected to attack. But for that same reason, it never became a symbol of resistance.

The fight to save Warsaw in September 1939 was particularly savage. Although it fell there would be two more revolts in the city against the Germans before 1945. Several major Polish writers singled out the destruction of Warsaw in books about the war. The collection of poems *Building the Barricades* by Anna Swirszczynska evoked Warsaw as a living presence[11] Tadeusz Gajcy wrote:

over the furrow of letters you still see
my image: I am walking through the air, and my city
walks behind me.[12]

In "Song of the Walls":

How can one not love the shattered walls
of this city, which flows away at night . . .
the Warsaw which is dead, and the living.[13]

In perhaps the finest book about the insurrection of 1944, Miron Bialoszewski asked himself several times why he was unwilling to leave the dying city.

I don't know what we expected. After all, I think it was known that those stumps of Krucza or Wilcza were only stumps and nothing else . . .On top of that, there's the destruction of protective structures. If the building should collapse, if it disappears, then our chances become worse. Or it could shrink even more. And more. Go somewhere else? Where? Houses are dwindling every-where. And the crowding. People are dying. That's true. But houses are dying too.[14]

Bialoszewski's book was about the city and its people; in the course of his narration the two become interchangeable. He remained in Warsaw until the end, when the Germans ordered all inhabitants to leave. Almost simultaneously the Germans retreated and the Soviet Army advanced into the ruins of Warsaw on January 17, 1945. The city that had housed 1,289,000 inhabitants six years before did not contain a living soul. Ninety-three percent of the dwellings were destroyed or damaged beyond repair. Bialoszewski's book concluded with a simple sentence: "I set eyes on Warsaw again in February 1945."

Czeslaw Milosz wrote "In Warsaw" in 1945:

How can I live in this country
Where the foot knocks against
The unburied bones of kin?
I hear voices, see smiles. I cannot
Write anything, because five hands
Seize my pen and order me to write
The story of their lives and deaths.[15]

The poem shows how the destruction of a city, its transformation into ruins, could be endless. Together with Dresden and Hiroshima, Warsaw was one of the most completely destroyed cities during the war.

During the war the legend and personification of "London" was created by several British writers. The city became a major presence in a collection of poems by Dylan Thomas, *Deaths and Entrances*. Four poems about the Blitz—"A Refusal to Mourn the Death, by Fire, of a Child in London"; "Deaths and Entrances"; "Dawn Raid"; and "Ceremony after a Fire Raid"—were among the finest in the book, and London became a single collectivity. Thomas wrote of those "wounded on London's waves," and of "many married London's estranging grief." He claimed he was giving the city a "tongue."

In a long, stately poem, "Ceremony after a Fire Raid," Thomas mourned a young girl killed in a bombardment, "Laid in her snow / On the altar of London." The mode of lamentation was rhetorical, nevertheless the poem is moving, reaching a crescendo in the final third section with an image of the city transformed into a sea of fire:

> Into the organpipes and steeples
> Of the luminous cathedrals . . .
> Over the urn of sabbaths,
> Over the whirling ditch of daybreak
> Over the sun's hovel and the slum of fire
> And the golden pavements laid in requiems,
> Into the bread in a wheatfield of flames . . .
> The masses of the sea
> The masses of the infant-bearing sea
> Erupt, fountain, and enter to utter forever
> Glory glory glory
> The sundering ultimate kingdom of genesis' thunder.[16]

Contemporary novels and poems used bombed landmarks such as St. Paul's Cathedral and the House of Commons for scenes that expressed strong defensive resolve. The ending of Hillary's 1943 novel *The Last Enemy* had an important London setting, as did Eric Knight's *This Above All*.

A volume in Evelyn Waugh's trilogy *Officers and Gentlemen* began with an animated description of London burning:

> The sky over London was glorious, ochre and madder, as though a dozen tropic suns were simultaneously setting round the horizon; everywhere the searchlights clustered and hovered, then swept apart; here and there pitchy clouds drifted and billowed; now and then a huge flash momentarily froze the serene fireside glow. Everywhere the shells sparkled like Christmas baubles. "Pure Turner," said Guy Crouchback, enthusiastically; he came fresh to these delights.[17]

Despite the ironical "enthusiasm" the scene is by no means lighthearted. Guy Crouchback had returned from abroad to his native land,

and to London when it came under attack. He was in the place where he wanted to be.

Cities played a prominent role in the defense of Russia, but only in the middle years of the war, after June 1941. Moscow, evacuated in 1941, had negligible importance. Konstantin Simonov and Ilya Ehrenburg both wrote that defeatism in Moscow reached epidemic proportions.[18] Stalin made a decision in 1942 to defend another city, the city on the Volga named after him. A lesson had been learned in Moscow. Stalin personally prohibited the evacuation of civilians from Stalingrad, calculating the troops would defend the city with greater motivation if the civilians remained inside.

Two cities, Stalingrad and Leningrad, were key to a strategy of defense and counterattack. Leningrad had a passive defensive role; it was besieged for nine hundred days, from August 3, 1941 to January 18, 1943. During the period much of the armaments industry was evacuated to the Urals and armies regrouped in the East. In popular consciousness the link between what were called the "hero cities" of Leningrad and Stalingrad was kept alive; the poet Olga Berggolts broadcast on September 20, 1942 that "an umbilical cord" united Leningrad and Stalingrad.[19] The siege of Leningrad was lifted only after the successful defense of Stalingrad. In Leningrad, between eight hundred thousand and a million civilians died.

In a deliberate campaign the defense of the two cities was orchestrated by writers and propagandists. Aliger was flown in to the surrounded Leningrad in order to write about the siege. Many writers and journalists continued to live in the city. Their works were quickly published and reached a wide national audience.[20] Olga Berggolts wrote in 1942:

In the mud, darkness, hunger, and sorrow,
With death's shadow dogging our heels,
We were so happy,
So wild with freedom,
That our grandchildren would surely envy us.

The introduction of freedom was new. Freedom and defense turned out to be a powerful combination.

Leningrad was a city of civilians, the military presence negligible. As the siege continued the city was without electricity, fuel, or water, daily rations were below subsistence level. As many died from starvation as from bombing or shelling. Muscular dystrophy crippled thousands.

The city was compared to a submerged town in which the manner of walking of its starved citizens was so slow "they seemed to be moving through dense water . . . It was as if I was reading some fantastic novel about the earth's last days, about life's extinction . . . cities standing devoid of life and covered in snow."[21] Berggolts saw the city as a necropolis. Personal relations took on a special dimension.[22] Dogs, cats, birds, glue, and belts were eaten, Ales Adamovich wrote that people ate whatever they could lay their hands on "everything from the birdseed to the canary itself." When loaves of rye bread were brought across Lake Ladoga they became objects of reverence, "sacred," "whiter than snow."

The defense of Stalingrad was also a holding action while Soviet armies were repositioned to the east and north. As fighting became intense, civilians were driven from contested districts; in Simonov's novel *Days and Nights* a commander tells his men they can retreat only when the ground under them is so hot, literally, that they cannot stand it. Victor Nekrasov wrote they were expected to "dig themselves in, surround themselves with wire and mines, and hold on."

Stalingrad stopped being a city in a meaningful sense. When the hero of *Days and Nights*, Saburov, returned to his battalion after an eighteen-day absence "The three buildings which Saburov's battalion had been defending no longer really existed; they were only foundations on which the remains of walls and the lower parts of windows still stood in a few places. They all looked like children's toys, smashed and broken. To the left and to the right of the buildings ran unbroken lines of ruins. In some places the chimneys were still standing. Now, at night, the rest dissolved into the darkness and looked like an uneven rocky valley. It looked as if the houses had disappeared into the ground and as if burial mounds of brick had been raised over them."[23] The city had been turned into trenches, dugouts, burial mounds, "cairns haphazardly raised over houses which had gone underground."

It was during this period that General Chuikov was reported to say, "Time is blood." Some of the finest Russian novels focus on the events of the battle of Stalingrad: Victor Nekrasov's novel *In the Trenches of Stalingrad*, Konstantin Simonov's *Days and Nights*, Yuri Bondarev's *Hot Snow*, Vasili Grossman's *For a Righteous Cause* and *Life and Fate*.

Interpretations of the meaning of the victory at Stalingrad varied greatly. The phrase "the spirit of Stalingrad" became popular, indicating the determined defense of the city. What was this "spirit"? Many episodes in Viktor Nekrasov's novel, published in 1946, express a palpable sense of revolt against authority.[24]

Vasily Grossman was explicit on the meaning of this "spirit" in the closing pages of the novel *For a Righteous Cause*. Communications between a small defensive unit and headquarters were severed, rank suddenly had little importance. The differences between regular, conscript, and penal troops disappeared. The "spirit" of Stalingrad, according to Grossman, was democratic with strong elements of revolt. In the later novel *Life and Fate*, Grossman made his most forceful statement of all about the nature of the fighting for the city. Everything at Stalingrad had "a new intensity" that impressed all people, old party men as well as ordinary soldiers, "There was something about the relations between people here. There was a true sense of dignity and equality on this clay slope where so much blood had been spilt." Young people in their teens were caught up in this spirit. "Nearly everyone believed that good would triumph, that honest men, who hadn't hesitated to sacrifice their lives, would be able to build a good and just life."[25]

To dramatize his interpretation of the battle of Stalingrad, Grossman chose a dangerous combat situation at "House 6/1." This pocket of resistance was surrounded by German troops and cut off from headquarters, as in his earlier novel *For a Righteous Cause*. The telephone cable leading to the house is repeatedly cut. There is ambiguity about this: how, and by whom, was it cut? The army command is worried about reports that discipline has broken down in the group fighting at House 6/1, that the group's commander, Grekhov, has refused to write official reports. The members of the tiny detachment are of different ages and backgrounds; they hold meaningful discussions, Grekhov speaks in favor of liberty and sharply criticizes Lenin. An adolescent girl falls in love for the first time. After a long period without communication from headquarters, Krymov, a narrow-minded older Bolshevik, comes to reassert discipline. He is met with mockery and hostility. He makes threats, and lectures the group. Grekhov fires a shot in his direction and orders him away.

Later, before the end of the battle of Stalingrad, the "handful of men" at House 6/1 are overrun and killed. Grossman interprets the scene categorically: "Freedom engendered the Russian victory. Freedom was the apparent aim of the war. But the sly fingers of History changed this: freedom became simply a way of waging the war, a means to an end." Victory sprang from the spirit of equality and liberation that characterized much of the fighting at Stalingrad, but that spirit became the first casualty once victory was secured. Grekhov died, and Krymov lived on.[26]

The Battle at Stalingrad became known in the West as a remarkable feat of arms and a turning point. In late 1942, a Chinese leader wrote that Stalingrad marked "a turning point in the whole history of mankind"— this was Mao Tse-tung, writing for the *Liberation Daily* in Yenan.[27] But major works about Stalingrad suggest it was a different kind of turning point from what Mao had in mind. In Stalingrad there was a strong element of revolt against authority. It was the defensive battle that inspired morale and determination during a crucial period in the middle of the war. For a brief period the city, reduced to rubble, became the powerful symbol of the freedom of an entire nation.

3

Ties that Bind: Farms and Fields

The densely inhabited metropolis or capital became a potent catalyst for armed resistance, but so did the traditional farm holding or farmstead. It was a vital way of life, an institution that went far back in memory and time. It linked men to historical traditions and to one another. Those who lived on a farm were united by ties to past and present in a rich living texture, and these ties became a presence of great importance during the war. They were concrete and visceral, they evoked familiar aspects of life and the surrounding landscape. Different countries had varied rural traditions and ties to the countryside, villages, and peasantry, but they all proved to be remarkably strong. Writers evoked them repeatedly in calls for defense.

An excellent example of the strength of these traditions can be found in a work by Andre Malraux. He was a French intellectual with almost no peasant or agricultural origins; he had traveled widely, flirted with Marxism, and suddenly found a justification for defense not in an abstract idea or ideology but an epiphany while staying at a peasant farm. Malraux was surprised at his own strong emotion. He recorded the experience both in *The Walnut Trees of Altenburg*, written during the early war years, and his later *Anti-Memoires*.

Malraux was called up after the German invasion of France. Captain of a tank crew, he raced toward the attacking Germans. After several days of mishaps and frustrations, exhausted, the tank stopped at a small farm so the crew could get a few hours of sleep.

When he woke the next morning, Captain Malraux saw the farm with fresh eyes:

I can hear in this picturesque profusion, the hum of the centuries buried almost as deep as last night's darkness: these barns bursting with grain and straw, these barns with their beams hidden by husks, full of harrows, canes, poles, wooden carts; barns which consist only of grain, wood, straw, and leather (everything in metal had been requisitioned). Surrounded by the dead fires of refugees and soldiers, these are the barns of the Gothic Age; our tanks at the end of the road are filling up with water, monsters kneeling at the wells of the Bible! O life, how old you are![28]

He walked past the door of the barn, left open by the family in their flight, and saw a looted room, old tools, carts, empty ovens, washing, and linen. Malraux felt suddenly in the presence of an unaccountable gift: "All this might never have been, might never have been as it is. How these individual shapes harmonize with the earth!" Two old peasants were sitting outdoors on a bench and spoke to him in resignation, tank turrets in the background gleaming with dew. This prompted a reflection: "I now know the meaning of the ancient myths about the living snatched from the dead. I can scarcely remember what fear is like; what I carry within me is the discovery of a simple, sacred secret. Thus, perhaps, did God look on the first man."

The epiphany is presented as it occurred. The effectiveness of the scene depends on the contrast with the chaotic hurried tank fighting that preceded it; in a sudden, unexpected revelation all doubts are resolved. The purpose of the chaotic military actions of the previous days is made clear: to preserve the lives of the elderly farming couple seated before him, the lives of the other villagers who fled. It could be a scene from the New Testament with Malraux as one of the Magi. Many echoes from the past are crystallized in the description of the setting of the small farm. Malraux suddenly becomes aware there are no barriers between what happened long ago and what is occurring in the present.

The rural past was a powerful unifying force in the history of many countries that mounted powerful defensive movements during World War II. With Malraux it had a bookish aspect. Other writers who were more closely rooted in rural conditions had similar experiences. These might be more subtle and less rhetorical, even occasions for humor. For example, a novel by Pentti Haanpaa, *War in the Wilds* (1942), describes a line of Finnish tanks coming on several homesteads destroyed by invading Russians. They reach a village. Their reaction is as intense as that of Malraux, but there are differences.

The farms and groups of houses filled them with stupefaction. There were colorful walls, windows that sparkled, a village complete and intact, in the middle of the gleaming snows of March. Look, over there, a dark mound of manure emerged from the snow, a real pile of manure just like at home. So here, too, they were confident that next summer the wheat would ripple in the wind . . . It was worth more than the most patriotic speeches or military marches. These people did not want just to fight. They wanted to live.[29]

Together with humor the passage contains familiarity and deep feeling. Many of the soldiers were themselves farmers. This made their reactions especially powerful.

The novel by Haanpaa also presents a darker side of armed defense. When the column of tanks passes many destroyed farmsteads, the narrator reflects: "The rest of the world would learn with stupor that here one had forgotten arithmetic. The healthy man acts and does not hesitate when there is fire in his house." The spirit of the Finns in the defensive Winter War was unique. They were willing to accept extremely high casualties, and took pride in their accomplishment against superior numbers: pride that they could disregard the "arithmetic" of their own small numbers.[30]

One of the finest novelists of World War II, Vasil Bykov, was Belorussian; he developed the theme of attachment to a small farmstead in several short novels. In *Sign of Misfortune* a farm is associated with the historical past, as in Malraux's narration, and with the New Testament. In this powerful work the associations are entirely tragic. An elderly peasant couple has terrible luck: their farm is chosen as billet for a German motorized battalion. The collaborationist Belorussian Polizei—a few still wear Red Army uniforms with insignia torn off—choose their farm, and the couple is unable to resist. They hope the Germans will eventually move on without inflicting too much damage. The farm is on "a god-forsaken hill" once called Golgotha. The name remained "precisely defining the grim reality of that patch of earth, so unsuitable for raising bread, and consecrated by tears, toil, and a years-long peasant cavalry."[31]

The German soldiers force the old couple to live in a small boilerhouse behind the farm, treating them like servants. They beat the spirited wife, Stefanida, and bray with laughter as they throw apple cores at the husband, Petroc. The soldiers shoot their cow in the head, and chop it up with an ax. They fire indiscriminately at hens, and kill a local boy. The couple tries to hide their last pig in a badger hole but it escapes and disappears. The local collaborationist Polizei turns out to be as bad as the Germans, motivated by envy they slowly strip the farm of anything of value. Ultimately it

207

is destroyed in a conflagration. In Bykov's novel there is no propaganda or sentimentality. The Golgotha theme is handled skillfully, associated with lethal struggles of resistance and collaboration that leave no way out.

Farms had different features in different parts of the world, yet were consistently associated with defense. One of the finest works about resistance to German occupation was a play set in the context of a farm, Kai Munk's *Niels Ebbesen* (1942). Kai Munk, murdered by the Gestapo in 1944, was one of the most talented Danish writers of his generation. Before the war he was known for his play *Ordet* (1932), made into a film by the director Carl Dreyer. A clergyman, Kai Munk was by no means a pacifist; he advocated active resistance to the Germans.[32]

Niels Ebbesen was the name of the owner of a farm not far from the Danish-German border. The first act presents the farm in its physical setting: a meadow, women washing clothes, a man digging with a spade. A ditch is being cleaned and a swamp drained, people tend to everyday chores. The play is about the change of heart in a man who tries at first to cooperate with the Germans. Nominally set in an earlier century the play is dedicated "To Our Young Soldiers of April Ninth," the date of the German invasion of Denmark in 1940.[33]

Niels Ebbesen is aware of his own vulnerability and weakness. One of the most eloquent speeches at the beginning of the play is an argument *against* resistance. "Listen, there are my children playing down by the river; and there are my men cutting the first grain . . . War means that I and my tenants will get our arms and legs cut off, and that we shall never again follow the plough or wield the scythe."[34] The traditional farmstead was completely defenseless. Exposed and easily destroyed, it could become hostage or handed over to others. It provided as many reasons against resistance as for it.

But as Niels Ebbesen sees how one concession leads to another, he is made to wallow in his own shame. There is no end to the process of abasement. Gradually he is forced to change his mind. The play is modern despite its historical setting. The problem of military occupation is given a concrete context and made timeless, the plight of Niels becomes like that of others under German domination.

As in Hillary's *The Enemy Within* but with a very different setting, *Niels Ebbesen* ends with a conversion: a tortured, difficult conversion, and a call to arms. In Kai Munk's play the conversion takes place on a farm, what is to be defended is a countryside filled with similar farms. The setting acquires

ncreasing importance as the decision for full-fledged, armed defense
becomes crystallized; typical farm implements, the organization of field
workers, the maintenance and cultivation of land, all become part of the
decision. Niels vows at the end never to return to his home, plough, and
children until freedom is won. "Free we must be, if we are to live."

In different parts of occupied Europe, farms and crops took different
forms as the landscape changed. In Yannis Ritsos's long poem *Our Lady
of the Vineyards*, written in occupied Athens and published in 1945, he
described a setting of vineyards. It is a resistance poem. Although Ritsos
was a communist this did not prevent him from invoking the Madonna
and, further, identifying the Madonna with armed soldiers:

The olive tree reads to itself
The petrified gospel
And in the vineyards anger boils wine for the great
Chalice of the struggle.
. . . The Holy Gate thunders:
"The forty days of bitterness and fasting are over,
No more memorials for the dead, the Madonna is armed."[35]

The vineyard is generalized, the Madonna becomes the guardian of all
vineyards. The Greek landscape, rural life, and folk religion are fused in a
call for rebellion.

In his wartime poems Ritsos was particularly skillful in evoking the
specific Greek landscape with its traditions. His epic poem *Romiossini*
(1943), later set to music by the composer Mikis Theodorakis, is a tour
de force of nature evoked in its many forms, all of them sympathizing
with the local, clandestine resistance movement, hostile to the invaders.
The natural landscape has its own will, supporting the region's long-time
inhabitants and tillers of the soil.[36]

In all of the areas of combat, attachment to productive land and small
farms was a potent motivating force. It proved true in Eastern and Western
Europe, and also in Asia. Invading armies often disregarded farmers,
thinking they presented no danger, but frequently they were surprised by
the "embattled farmers" when they were given arms. In a Japanese novel
about the invasion of China, a Japanese soldier could not understand the
peculiar, unmilitary behavior of Chinese soldiers fighting against his unit.
They were barefooted, many had no uniforms, fled the disciplined Japanese

but then regrouped and unexpectedly came at the Japanese again. "'They must be farmers from this region,' Miki said to Takeo . . . 'Since they are defending their own lands, they must be stronger than soldiers.'"[37]

Farm and countryside evoked a history even older than that of the city. They were intimately associated with religion, myth, and history, their symbols evoking the most deeply held popular values.

4

Which Past, Which Future?

When national survival was threatened, the concrete features of people's lives and culture took on special meaning. They were based
on frequent contact and familiarity, and had developed over time. They
expressed the most intimate ties to nation and history. Raised to a universal
level they had great power. The more familiar they were, the more important they became as catalysts for self-defense.

Many works of literature about occupation and resistance developed
these ties as themes. Communication of them to others—both orally and in
written forms—was crucial to defense. Many of the writers who explored
these ties between the past, the present, and future were among the finest,
and most influential, of the wartime period.

Landscape. The values of a national literature were frequently focused
on specific places, and concrete landscapes. The frequency of this might
cause surprise. But the emphasis on landscape, the sense of a need to
defend it, was widespread among resistance writers. Italo Calvino wrote
of the Italian resistance, the *Resistenza Armata*: "The Resistance represented the fusion of landscape with people."[38]

The observation is borne out by works produced in almost every occupied country. It can be seen in the far north, where a Finnish poet wrote
in "Cornflowers":

As through the grain we crept along
in our helmets we plucked the flowers,
flowers, yes, cornflowers,
remembering our homes.
In the cornflower petals
shows the home sky blue,
deep blue.[39]

The Norwegian Tarjei Vesaas wrote in "Snow and Spruce Woods":

Home!—
snow and spruce woods
mean home.[40]

And the same emphasis can be seen in the Mediterranean south, where Yannis Ritsos described spices and lavender growing in rock crevices as if they participated in the struggle against the invader. References to arms and national feeling did not have to be expressed in general terms to be understood. Concrete terms were highly effective, and skillful writers gave them great resonance.

Language. After invasion and lengthy occupation, even the spoken language of a country could be menaced by extinction. This was felt acutely in the smaller countries. Milada Souckova's poem "Village Name" ("*Kalady*") was written in Czechoslovakia during the ominous month of September 1938:

Words of my mother tongue, hide in the name
of a village.
The place must be given some name
and even if it is distorted you will somehow
still live in it, even if unrecognized
you will still breathe, die, and carry on life.

Words of my mother-tongue. When it goes
hardest with you, do not hide on the bank
of waters, do not hide in rock or in a tree.
Hide in the name of a small village.

The children will not even know
how they learned your name, and even
in direst need you will never be discarded.
Perhaps some wanderer will pass, and stop,
and bow, and ask his way . . .[41]

At this time the Czech language, and speech, was being methodically replaced by German. Roman Jakobson called Souckova's poem "the succinct culmination of the centuries-old tradition of 'apologies' for Czech speech."[42] The poem was a warning that German pressure on language would become so great that only "forests, rivers, towns, and villages could refuse to change their Slavic names."

Haanpaa too wrote of the importance of language for the native Finnish soldier: "It was for him that the earth was green and the forest breathed in the wind. It was his land. It was here that he first heard the Finnish verb, the word that hits exactly, that goes straight to the heart."[43]

Childhood. A surprisingly large number of passages about childhood are found in literature about the war, above all those written during harsh occupation and active fighting. As a reason and motive for active defense, childhood often fused with language, landscape, and the past. At first glance the recollection of childhood might appear to be an escape from pressures of fighting. But passages about childhood often occur in the midst of action and are associated with defense. Recollections of childhood coincided with a sense of affirmation, often triggering determination or anger.

Fellowship with the Recently Dead. An awareness of the presence of the dead was dramatically expressed in many works. The dead were an important dimension of the collectivity. In Hillary's *The Enemy Within*, the narrator helped remove a woman and dead children from a bombed house, and it was at just this moment he suddenly became aware that others, many others, were near him. "They were there somewhere, all of them around me; dead of course, but not gone." The enumeration that followed—a lengthy one—was an act of solidarity with the dead. It was followed by his new personal determination to take the war to the enemy.

In *The Big Show*, Clostermann describes a group of pilots listening to a radio announcement of victory celebrations in London and Paris in 1945. Inexplicably, one of them throws a bottle in anger at the radio set, breaking it. Why the anger?

"From the smashed wireless still came a feeble whispering noise. I looked at Ken. No need of words, we both understood. Half an hour passed, an hour perhaps. And then, suddenly, I swear I felt they were all there, round us in the shadow and the cigarette smoke, like kids who had been unjustly punished. Mackenzie . . . Mouse Manson . . . young Kidd . . . all those who had set off one fine morning in their Spitfires or their Tempests and who hadn't come back."[44]

The Past. One of the most unexpected efforts to resuscitate the past began with Stalin's speech to his nation on November 6, 1941. It was the twenty-fourth anniversary of the Soviet revolution, but Stalin exhorted the nation this way: "May you be inspired in this war by the manly images of our great forefathers: Alexander Nevsky, Dmitri Donskoy, Kuzma Minin, Dmitri Pozharsky, Alexander Suvorov, and Mikhail Kutuzov." Of the six "forefathers" mentioned, two were grand dukes, three were princes. One was a Tsarist general, another a wealthy merchant. This was an abrupt change in direction, and extended to all sectors of society.[45]

Stalin praised Tchaikovsky and Count Leo Tolstoy, Glinka (composer of *A Life for the Tsar*), and generals Kutuzov and Suvorov who led the tsars' armies to victory. At this time the national anthem of the "Internationale" was abolished. Tsarist epaulettes were introduced into the army. The Orthodox Metropolitan Sergius was crowned in the Moscow cathedral, recognized as the Patriarch of all Russians on September 12, 1943. Most of the Stalin literary prizes during the war went to works about the prerevolutionary past; the communist past was relegated to a subordinate level. Roy Medvedev recounted how Stalin composed the text of his November speech in the apartment of an old Bolshevik, Elena Stasova. A doctrinaire Marxist, she was horrified at the Tsarist allusions and generally non-Marxist tone of the speech, but according to Medvedev Stalin was adamant, replying, "We will never rouse the people to war with Marxism-Leninism alone."[46]

In Yuri Bondarev's novel *Hot Snow*, a Russian general named Bessonov was about to face the German generals Manstein and Hoth at the approaches to Stalingrad. On the wall of his underground bunker, Bessonov had a picture. It was not a portrait of Stalin but an icon of a saint. Bessonov directly questioned the icon: "What do you know about it, saint? Where is the truth? . . .What do you know about Manstein? About his tank divisions? If I were a Christian, I would pray now, of course. On my knees I would ask for counsel and help. But I don't believe in God and I don't believe in miracles. Four hundred German tanks—that's truth for you!"[47]

It is a moving scene. Believer or not, what is important is that an icon was hanging on a headquarters wall in December 1942, and the commander directly addressed it before a major battle.

The past was revived in most of the defensive wars fought between 1938 and 1945. In Yrjo Jylha's poem "Ghost Patrol," Finnish troops on skis were joined by others from the past "as many in number as the cousins of the spruce." In England the Arts Council made a deliberate effort to activate the literary past. Shakespeare was widely published and read, and soldiers carried their "Pocket Shakespeares" in bombers. The plays were performed in factories, mining villages, parish halls, remote gun sites, and aerodromes. Performances were often treated as if they were about current events. Ivor Brown was watching *Macbeth* with Sybil Thorndike in Burnley when he suddenly realized the people packing the hall "were not just waiting to see what a famous player would do with a familiar speech. They were gripped with curiosity, wanting to know what happened, and how it ended."[48]

A poet living far from England also thought of Shakespeare during the Blitz of 1940. In "To the Londoners," the Russian poet Anna Akhmatova imagined Shakespeare as still alive and a contemporary, composing his plays. Her poem was an unusual act of solidarity when the USSR was still allied with Hitler:

Time is writing now with impassive hand
Shakespeare's black play, the twenty-fourth.
What can we do, who know the bitter taste,
But here, by the leaden river, re-enact
Those tragic lines of Hamlet, Caesar, Lear?[49]

In ghettoes in Eastern Europe, Jewish writers searched for models in the past that could serve as guides in the present. In ghettoes where insurrections took place such as Warsaw and Bialystok, poets and dramatists evoked the revolt against the Romans at Masada, in 1941 a dramatized version of Yitzhak Lamdan's poem *Masada* was presented in the Warsaw ghetto.[50] Yitzhak Katznelson wrote *By the Waters of Babylon*, invoking historical disasters and precedents for the World War.

Liberation and Self-Determination. Novels and poems about liberty were written in all the occupied countries of Europe. These works sought not just the expulsion of an invader, but a more general liberation and social revolution. Most resistance movements were animated by the desire for self-determination and social justice. Frequently they expected some form of social liberation and reform to coincide with the end of the war.

In the USSR, Alexandra Kurosheva wrote with conviction: "There can be no return to old deeds and thoughts; All has been cremated in a monstrous conflagration."[51]

Many Russians shared this attitude. Probably the defense of the USSR should be grouped with the other wars for liberation, even though it was manipulated by Stalin, and the wartime reforms were all withdrawn.[52] Many works, like Vera Panova's *The Train*, evoke the optimistic anticipation prevalent during the years 1943–44: that after the war one would be able to do—or be—anything.[53]

Isaiah Berlin wrote that the wounded sense of national identity is "like a bent twig, forced down so severely that when released, it lashes back with fury . . . After years of oppression and humiliation, there is liable to occur a violent counter-reaction, an outburst of national pride, often aggressive self-assertion, by liberated nations and their leaders."[54] Joseph Brodsky went further: "war proved to be a blessing for Russian prose and poetry." He was referring to the defensive war after the German attack: "For the first time in three decades, they were allowed to address tragic subjects and deal with them in considerable depth. Monstrous as this may sound, the war as a theme offered Russian literature a welcome break from the one-dimensional glorification of building socialism."[55] Even Solzhenitsyn called the months after June 1941 "a strange brief interval of freedom which no student of society could have foreseen."[56]

A movement for social reform in Britain coincided with the first attacks. Harold Nicolson vividly described a dinner during the September Blitz with a retired Major General who had served in India and his wife.

> We listen to the news while distant bombardments thump and crunch over the hills and plains of Kent. Priestley gives a broadcast about the abolition of privilege, while I look at their albums of 1903 and the Delhi Durbar and the Viceroy's train. Priestley speaks of the old order which is dead and of the new order which is to arise from its ashes. These two old people listen without flinching. I glance at the pictures of the howdahs and panoply of the past and hear the voice of Priestley and the sound of the guns.[57]

Hatred. Hatred characterized much of the fighting on both offensive and defensive fronts, for example, the bitter warfare in the Pacific. Hatred in resistance movements was closely tied to anger and an awareness of the brutal treatment of civilians, those in prisons, deported and in camps.

Hatred as a motivating force was often deliberately orchestrated. The writer and filmmaker Alexander Dovzhenko wrote in 1942:

Today, as yesterday and tomorrow, the newspapers are glutted with accounts of such cruelties, such inhuman deeds committed by the enemy, that the mind boggles and one does not even feel anger, only an ordinary reflex of disgust . . . These events cannot be contained by the mind . . . They are like cries of pain or groans of despair . . . The country has experienced enough evil for ten generations.[58]

The USSR revived the old concept of "Holy Hatred." By January 1942, the official doctrine for nearly one thousand Soviet correspondents became hatred of Germany. Ilya Ehrenburg, correspondent for *Red Star*, produced three to five articles a day with titles like "Bottled Spiders," "An Eye for an Eye, a Tooth for a Tooth." Vladimir Sholokhov wrote "The Science of Hatred" and "The School of Hatred."

These works must be read with care. Originally, hatred was a doctrine of aggression and offense, not defense. The same Soviet writers like Aliger and Tvardovsky who expressed hatred for Balts, Poles, and Finns between September and December 1939—recommending even their "extermination"—expressed hatred in remarkably similar terms, but in an abrupt reversal, for Germans in 1942.[59] Some serious writers were motivated by a tragic sense of the newly discovered atrocities, and their works have value, avoiding propaganda.[60] But among other writers, as Dovzhenko indicated, hatred took on a shrill, collective form.

Friends. What Albert Camus called "the unique brotherhood of those years"[61] was an important feature of every resistance movement. The ties between soldiers in a unit, formed over time and in battle, became extremely strong and provided the structure of many narratives.[62] Civilians in resistance groups developed powerful ties to one another. In many cases resistance movements were embryo forms of postwar governments, both in Europe and in Asia.[63]

Family. The presence of family members often discouraged revolt in occupied countries; they were registered with the police, and when the police wanted to capture resistance members they always began by pursuing their families. In his 1942 book *Army of Shadows*, Joseph Kessel insisted that members of the resistance had to forget their families.[64] Many collaborators defended themselves by arguing that collaboration was the only way to care for their families.[65] Tragic decisions were forced on families: Was it safer for the family to stay together, or should it separate? Were the children safer with their parents, or with other adults somewhere else?[66]

But often family members could give one another crucial support, gathering information from a variety of sources, and maintaining shared values from before the war. In nonfiction and fiction, examples abound of family members giving one another invaluable help. They sometimes worked in close proximity but just as often were far from one another, even on different continents: one in Stockholm and another in Kolyma, one in New York and another in Riga, one in London and another in Brazzaville.[67]

Ties that contributed to resistance and effective defense were countless. Many of the finest works of literature during the period 1939–45 dealt with these ties, the need for defense and attempts to carry it out. They were innumerable, and covered a broad range. The "ties that bind" were shared above all among civilians, and were based on language, education, shared values, religion, culture in an inclusive sense, both "low" and "high culture," and on history. They could be positive, sometimes very positive, appearing in a revelation or epiphany. Motives for defense might be powerful in the context of one country, weak in another. They were subject to state involvement, they could be manipulated, amplified, or ignored.[68] Much depended on accurate, effective communication and organization.

Armed defense was never a purely tactical or strategic issue. The countless ties that motivated defense and morale were among the most powerful forces unleashed by the war, provoking casualties and some of the most lethal fighting—the worst "arithmetic." The strength of these ties often determined a country's future and the direction it would eventually take. Ultimately they were the ties uniting people to life, and the future.

IX
"Write and Record!"

1

"Dear Reader . . ."

The narration "A Year in Treblinka" was one of the earliest reports about Treblinka, it was also one of the finest. Connected by a rail link to the ghetto in Warsaw, Treblinka was one of the war's most tightly guarded secrets. Written by a craftsman and "a carpenter by profession," the narration addressed the reader directly: "Dear Reader." Treblinka was never supposed to be described by the written word. Those who were inside, or had seen it were killed. With its crematoria it was built with the intention of killing all of the ghetto's inhabitants.

The narration is meticulous and objective, vivid, and above all concrete. It was written immediately after the author's escape from the camp. Originally written in Polish, it was translated into Yiddish and then from Yiddish into English. Like many other works of witness it was hastily translated, and the English version contains some obsolete words and phrases.

Parts of the narration make painful, extremely difficult reading. That the author escaped, was still alive and able to write his narration, was nothing less than "a miracle."

* * *

The cremations then got underway. Again the corpses of the old, children, women and men were exhumed . . . It turned out that women burned easier than men. Accordingly, corpses of women were used for kindling the fires. The sight was terrifying, the worst that human eyes have ever beheld. When the corpses of pregnant women were cremated, the abdomen would burst open, and the burning of the fetus inside the mother's body would become visible. However, this made no impression whatsoever on the German killers, who stood around watching, as if at a badly functioning machine which produced little.

I am not a young man, and I have seen a lot in my lifetime. But Lucifer himself could not possibly have devised a worse hell. Can you imagine 3,000 corpses, recently alive, burning all at once on such an immense pyre? Looking at the faces of the dead, one can ordinarily think that they might arise momentarily and awaken from their deep slumber . . . But here, at a given signal, they set the giant torch on fire and it burned with a huge flame.[1]

Confronting a comparable sight at the end of the war, another observer wrote, "A protective veil falls over the mind, insulating one from the experience."[2] However, the author of the description of Treblinka had no such protective veil. The war was continuing, he was a witness, and still alive.

The passage is from one of the earliest written works about Treblinka. There are very few. The narration begins with direct address, "Dear Reader." The author sought to complete an act of communication to a living reader with his words; everything in the manuscript is subordinated to the task of communication. On August 2, 1943 he escaped from Treblinka. He was informing the reader about what had been, until that moment, one of the most carefully kept secrets of the world, with the tightest security. He was uniquely positioned to describe the camp. How could anyone describe Treblinka with words? It was a difficult test of verbal communication.

Treblinka had been called a "labor camp"; the crematoria there were shrouded in total secrecy, the Warsaw ghetto knew almost nothing about them.[3] Jankel Wiernik was at Treblinka for twelve months during its most intense activity. At one point the crematoria killed between 10,000 and 12,000 people each day. This included the period of the April 1943 revolt in the overcrowded Warsaw ghetto, when it held 450,000 people. A direct railway line linked Treblinka to the ghetto; spur of railway tracks led directly inside the ghetto and to the *Umschlagplaz* or boarding place.

The author's main intentions were accuracy and objectivity. To record in a "documentary" or neutral manner was probably out of the question. He wrote "I almost went insane on the day when I first saw men, women and children being led into the house of death." Insanity is a recurrent theme, and what he calls "spiritual suffering." Was it possible for anyone to write about an operation of such magnitude, carried out with such concentrated destructiveness?

The escape of one man among a million was what the author called "a true miracle." The escape was carefully planned in advance. A dozen men seized weapons from the guardhouse, killed guards in the towers, and tried to reach the woods five miles away. Just short of the trees, a pursuer caught up with Wiernik and ordered him to halt. His pistol jammed. Wiernik struck him with the hatchet he was carrying. "I ran into the woods. After penetrating a little deeper into the thicket, I sat down among the bushes. From the distance I heard a lot of shooting . . . was alone, resting."

Of the dozen who tried to escape, Wiernik was the only one to survive. He remained concealed in the woods and then made his way to Warsaw, where he went into hiding, writing the original manuscript of "A Year in Treblinka." Serious challenges of transmission and communication to others remained—these would be part of a multi-stage process, with many obstacles.

The language is plain and direct. The original manuscript was accompanied by a map of the two sections of Treblinka, with careful measurements and numbers. The author had no literary pretensions, he disavowed what he called "verbal felicity." He considered himself a vehicle for what he wrote, and the information he presented. There was no place for the imagination in his narrative: "No imagination, no matter how daring, could possibly conceive of anything like that which I have seen and lived through. Nor could any pen, no matter how facile, describe it properly. I intend to present everything accurately so that all the world may know." This was an essential assertion. Events at Treblinka surpassed the workings of the normal human imagination to such a degree that any "imagination" had to be completely set aside.

For many years the author, Yankel Wiernik, had worked as a member of the Warsaw Trades Chamber or professional guild. He was fifty years old when the war broke out. His skills as a master carpenter and construction worker helped him survive in the camp; the Germans used him to construct new buildings, were satisfied with his work, and preserved his life. Wiernik was aware he was in a unique situation, without predecessors.[4] Two years earlier the historian Simon Dubnov exhorted eye-witnesses to "Write and record!" what they saw, but this was unknown to the author, he wrote before terms like "genocide" or the "Holocaust" were in use. He believed his report was the first of its kind.

The author sensed he was in a race against time. He believed that writing his manuscript—publishing it as quickly as possible, and disseminating it—would save lives. His first sentence stresses the importance of his act of communication with the reader: "For your sake alone I continue to hang on to my miserable life, though it has lost all attraction for me." His remaining life would be devoted to writing and communicating the truth about Treblinka. No one knew the reality of Treblinka; once "the world" learned about the camp it would not permit functioning to continue. Wiernik assumed that the existence of the camp depended on secrecy, once the secrecy was broken it would be forced to close. The revelation would save lives. A postwar view might find this optimistic, but the author earnestly believed it.

What he proceeded to describe, soberly and methodically, was not "war": the war of fronts, of invasion or retreat, defense or offense. It defied taxonomy, it was outside any accepted category. This put an additional burden on the writer as unique witness. He had to describe it accurately and fully.

Wiernik was a careful observer:

> Between 450 and 500 persons were crowded into a chamber measuring 125 square feet. Parents carried their children in the vain hope that the latter would thus escape death. On the way to their doom, they were pushed and beaten with rifle butts and gas pipe. Dogs were set on them, barking, biting and tearing at them. To escape the blows and the dogs, the crowd rushed to its death, pushing into the chamber, the stronger ones shoving the weaker ones ahead. The bedlam lasted only a short while, for the doors were shut tightly with a bang. The chamber was filled, the motor turned on and connected with the in-flow pipes, and, within 25 minutes at most, all were stretched out dead or, to be more accurate, stood dead. There being no free space, they just leaned against each other."[5]

The insistence on accuracy can be seen throughout the description, and the entire narration: dimensions, the number of feet, of minutes.

A second feature of Wiernik's narrative is his stress on the frenetic activity in the camp itself, both before and after destruction in the gas chambers. It was not a mechanical "conveyor belt." Death was not enough; it was a place of constant torture, most of it done in the open air; almost every action in the camp accompanied by torture and cruelty.

Wiernik wrote about these tortures as essential features of Treblinka. He described Camp No. 2:

> The blood froze in my veins. The yard was littered with thousands of corpses, corpses of the most recent victims. Germans and Ukrainians were barking orders loudly and brutally beating the workers with rifle butts and sticks. The faces of the hapless workers were bloody, their eyes blackened and their clothes had been torn by dogs . . . Two watch towers, both two-storied, stood at the entrance of Camp No. 2. These were ascended by means of ladders, and on these ladders some victims were being tortured. Legs were placed between the rungs and the gang boss held the victim's head downward in such a way that the poor devil couldn't move while he was being beaten mercilessly, the least punishment being 25 lashes. I saw that scene for the first time in the evening. The moon and the reflector lights illuminated that appalling massacre of the living and the corpses that were strewn all over the place. The moans of the tortured combined with the swishing of the whips made an infernal sound.[5]

An important theme of the narrative is to demonstrate the close connection between the torture, accompanied by sadism, and mass killing. At one point he tries to explain this connection in general terms, describing the system of promotion in the camp, what he calls "preferment." "Good patriots can always be found who will execute every order. There are always men who are ready to destroy and kill their fellow men . . . Preferment depends on how much one has destroyed, on how many one has killed. These people . . . are being paid homage to . . . they are held aloft so the world may pay them honor." Wiernik thought the "system" abetted and accelerated sadism. Preferment required it in order to get ahead.

Wiernik had a sharp eye for details of sadistic behavior. A typical squad commander, with his inseparable dog, was named Franz:

> Agile and quick of movement, he was here, there, and everywhere. He looked us over appraisingly . . . He was the vilest of them all. Human lives meant nothing to him, and to inflict death and untold torture was a supreme delight. For the guards, seeing the suffering of prisoners was a source of pleasure; the least detail might cause

delight. In winter, while corpses were burning, the guards enjoyed the warmth of the fires: they rejoiced, each day perfecting the hell they created. It gave light and warmth . . . The Commander who devised this inferno sat by the fire, laughing, and fondling it with his eyes.[6]

Torture was not cold-blooded. It was a source of pleasure. Even at their most brutal the guards would laugh or make faces. When transports arrived from Warsaw in April 1943, the armed struggle still raging in the ghetto, they were treated with exceptional cruelty.

The women fainted from fear and the brutes dragged them to the fires. Panic-stricken, the children threw themselves in their mothers' arms. The women begged for mercy, with eyes closed so as to shut out the sight of their horrible surroundings, but their tormentors only made faces and kept their victims in agonizing suspense for minutes on end. While one batch of women and children was being killed, others stood around waiting their turn. Time and again children were dragged out of their mothers' arms, and tossed into the flames alive while their tormentors laughed, urging the mothers to jump heroically into the fire after their children, mocking them for their cowardice.

Other authors who published books about the camps also singled out sadism among Germans and the SS. Gisela Perl, who wrote a fine book about the camps at the end of the war, declared on the title page that her book was a "monument to German sadism." Eugene Weinstock wrote that in the camps, "sadism was elevated to a metaphysical principle."[7]

In the course of the author's twelve-month stay at Treblinka, a major change took place. The number of transports began to diminish. Wiernik wrote,

At that time Katyn was being much talked about by the Germans, who used the topic for propaganda purposes. Accidentally, we got hold of a newspaper from which we learned about those atrocities. According to rumors, Himmler himself had come to Treblinka because of those incidents and ordered that all the corpses of the murdered victims be burned. And there were plenty of corpses to burn.[8]

German attention had shifted to destroying evidence. The German armies advancing into the Soviet Union had discovered graves of thousands of massacred Polish officers, and they sought to score a propaganda victory by publicizing it. When an airplane flew over Treblinka, the guards quickly tried to cover the bodies with foliage. The organizers of the camp became aware that the presence of bodies, both on top of the ground and under the ground, was a liability.

The period of great pyres at Treblinka had begun. These were graphically described by Wiernik. The summer weather was extremely hot, the stench unbearable: "The bodies had had no chance to cool off. They were so densely packed that, when the graves were opened on a scorchingly hot day, steam belched forth as if from a boiler."

The need to escape increased daily. There were fewer and fewer prisoners in Treblinka. Those still alive had a single function: to assist the guards in destroying evidence of the camp's existence. The prisoners kept alive were a temporary expedient, they were needed for the tasks of unearthing and burning. The Germans were determined to leave no buried bodies behind as evidence. At the end of July 1943, in a heat wave and stench so great the workers were barely able to stand on their feet, "about 75 percent of the corpses had now been cremated. All that remained to be done was to grade down the soil, to straighten it out in such a way that not a trace could be found of the crimes committed on that spot. Ashes are silent."

As the prisoners looked on, their precarious situation was obvious. They were at the end of the list of "evidence" to be destroyed. Their time alive was measured by the decreasing number of unburned bodies. "We knew what this earth hid beneath its surface. We were the only witnesses of it. In silence we took leave of the ashes and vowed that, out of their blood, an avenger would arise."

2

"Our Language Lacks
Words . . ."

Not long after Wiernik's escape, Treblinka was liquidated by the Germans themselves. The exhumation and burning were completed. The last prisoners were killed, none were left to be witnesses. The population of the Warsaw ghetto had been reduced to a tiny fraction of what it once was, and attention turned to other camps, primarily the death camps in the south, Auschwitz and Birkenau. The terrain at Treblinka was sold to a Ukrainian farmer, all traces of the camp were hidden underneath barns and ploughed fields. The farm was burned down by its Ukrainian owner in June 1944.

After his escape, Wiernik was determined to write a description of the camp. His act of writing and communication would compel belief, it would change everything. The process of secrecy and disguise would be laid bare. What language would he use? His native language was Polish, and this was the language of his original narrative. But an independent Polish state no longer existed. The war continued. How could his narration be transmitted? Was Polish a language that could reach a larger international audience, "the world"? What organizations should be contacted?

A small "Clandestine Booklet" was published in Polish by an underground "Coordinating Committee." This was translated into Yiddish, later the Yiddish version was translated into English and published in February 1945 by the Jewish Labor Movement in New York.

But to "tell the world" proved to be a difficult process during the war itself. Before 1945 many people in the West were disinclined to believe stories about the death camps. In appearance they seemed extreme. An insuperable problem was the prevalence of propaganda, and inflated stories about the war coming from all sides. Critical distance away from the

shrill language of propaganda had to be established, but this was difficult. Western notables and political figures refused to believe accounts
they thought were exaggerated or had traces of propaganda. Jan Karski,
an officer in the Polish underground, was brought inside the camp at
Maidanek and the Warsaw ghetto, then he travelled to London and New
York to speak with Western leaders. After listening to a detailed oral report
by Karski, Lord Selbourne in London said his descriptions were "atrocity
propaganda" like that of World War I (*Greuelpropaganda*). They were not
to be believed.[9]

Wiernik thought that a written report about Treblinka would compel
the camp to cease functioning; during the years 1943-45 many other witnesses also singled out the wish to counter secrecy as their main reason for
writing. As long as secrecy was maintained, the crematoria could continue
to operate. It was a powerful drive and a torment at the same time. Many
survivors believed they had to write their testimony rapidly, at top speed.
It could save lives.

The French playwright Jean-Jacques Bernard was released from the
camp at Royallieu near Compiegne in January 1943; he wrote his book
The Camp of Slow Death "at white heat" between February and March
1943.[10] He was particularly concerned about friends who had been sent
from Compiegne to the transit camp at Drancy. He feared—correctly it
turned out—they would be sent from there to Auschwitz.

A similar sense of urgency and need for speed informs other works
about the camps. Primo Levi wrote in *If This Is a Man*:

> I recognize, and ask indulgence for, the structural defects of the
> book. Its origins go back, not indeed in practice but as an idea,
> an intention, to the days in the Lager. The need to tell our story to
> "the rest," to make 'the rest' participate in it, had taken on for us,
> before our liberation and after, the character of an immediate and
> violent impulse, to the point of competing with our other elemen-
> tary needs. Hence its fragmentary character. The chapters have
> been written not in logical succession, but in order of urgency.[11]

Levi described a boast frequently made by SS guards to their Jewish
prisoners: no matter what happened, no one would ever believe what they
said. Levi claimed that almost all survivors described a similar dream,
whether orally or in written memoirs. The details varied but the dreams

had a common content. They had returned home. They were describing to a relative, or loved one, what had happened to them. And they were not believed. They were not even listened to.[12]

During the winter of 1944–45, the destruction of the crematoria and other buildings was not cause for joy in the camps. Kitty Hart wrote: "One thought tormented us, that the world outside would never know, for we were sure that when we were of no further use to them our turn would come, and then all traces would be destroyed."[13]

Simon Wiesenthal recalled an SS guard who boasted to his prisoners:

However this war may end, we have won the war against you; none of you will be left to bear witness, or even if someone were to survive, the world will not believe him. There will perhaps be suspicions, discussions, research by historians, but there will be no certainties, because we will destroy the evidence together with you. And even if some proof should remain, and some of you survive, people will say that the events that you describe are too monstrous to be believed: they will say that they are the exaggerations of Allied propaganda and will believe us, who will deny everything, and not you. We will be the ones to dictate the history of the Lagers.[14]

Until 1945 that fear was real and constant. It seemed very likely secrecy would win. But in the middle of the dynamiting of crematoria, the huge fires and destruction of documents, in the midst of the activity of digging, exhumations and burning pyres, the use of General Bloedel's heavy bone-crushing machines and continued attempts to round up former captives on the roads—these were suddenly interrupted. They were abandoned in full view. The guards fled. What had once been most secret, most carefully hidden from the view of outsiders, became most public, open for thousands to see.

A great shift occurred. Before long the camps would become "news." The novelist Jean-Louis Curtis described how that moment came to France: "Huge posters on the walls revealed to us the existence of certain places of rest and repose called Buchenwald, Dachau, Auschwitz . . . with photographs attached. We collapsed in horror at the sight of them. Here was something so scandalous that no intelligent person could assimilate it."[15]

Before 1945 it was a near-impossibility for a prisoner to communicate with the outside world by the published word. During 1945 and just after, many superb, probing, well-written works of testimony were published and translated. Writers were able to address serious problems of words and language. Wiernik wrote that "no pen" could ever describe Treblinka. Now, writers attempting to describe other camps echoed him but at greater length, with greater resources.

Gisela Perl was one of many who claimed that no one could ever describe what she witnessed in several camps and evacuations. Which words would she use? No language was able to account for the events, or render them: "Belsen Bergen can never be described, because every language lacks the suitable words to depict its horrors. It cannot be imagined, because even the most pathological mind balks at such a picture."[16] Almost all concepts, metaphors, and historical comparisons were inadequate.

In addressing these problems many writers admitted defeat. Yet at the same time some of the finest works were produced. Primo Levi wrote: "For the first time we became aware that our language lacks words to express this offense, the demolition of a man." Eugene Kogon: "The human mind is unequal to picture these awful scenes." Odd Nansen: "The language is exhausted . . . Normal human imagination falls short." Another writer: the horrors committed by the Germans "surpassed any of the inherited notions of evil."[17]

After the war, Simon Wiesenthal attended many of the trials of accused war criminals and Nazis. He had the opportunity to listen to them, and to observe their behavior. Most of them, he wrote, regretted only one thing: that witnesses had survived to tell the truth.[18]

X
The Great Revolt

1

The Revolt against Rhetoric

*R*evolt *against the war was multifaceted and powerful, beginning during the war itself and always hindered by secrecy, disguise, and propaganda. The sense of revolt was widespread, shared by writers and nonwriters alike. The literature of this revolt created an indelible imprint on the literatures of all of the countries that took part in the war. It had a revolutionary effect on language, on every literary form, and almost every discipline.*

* * *

Interned in a prisoner-of-war camp on the Rhine in 1945, the German writer Guenter Eich wrote an "inventory" of all his belongings. These were all the things he could count as his own:

Inventory

This is my cap,
this is my coat,
here is my shaving gear
in the linen bag.

Tin cans:
my plate, my cup,
I have scratched my name
in the tin.

Scratched here with this
precious nail
which I hide
from covetous eyes.

In the knapsack are
a pair of woolen socks
and a few things that I
reveal to no one.

Thus it serves as a pillow
for my head at night.
The cardboard lies here
between me and the earth.

The pencil lead
I love most of all:
it writes verses for me by day
that I devise at night.

This is my notebook.
This is my tent,
this is my towel,
this is my twine.[1]

Eich's poem has a stark simplicity that can be found in other works written at the end the war. In appearance it is a simple catalogue. It is a list of the author's most basic, tangible belongings. His vision is restricted to what he can call his own. The objects are not described but simply named. There are few adjectives, no expressions of feeling, impressions, or subjectivity. At this stage of radical simplification, description is not yet possible. But the objects are useful, "precious." Even these few belongings are threatened by the acquisitiveness of others, their "covetous eyes."

The poem does not address a specific audience or reader. The author includes nothing that might belong to others. It seems to be a private poem. Yet one object stands out: a writing instrument, the pencil lead. It is not even a whole pencil, just a piece of lead. The poem contains two rudimentary acts of writing. The author's name, scratched on his cup with a nail, is a claim of ownership. And he is able to write words or "verses" with the pencil lead or stub. These are the beginnings of the act of writing.

"Inventory" was the first written work by Eich in six years. Throughout the war he found it impossible to write. With this poem, his "Inventory," he was trying to shake off the influence and models of the past.

Many writers felt in 1945 that the Second World War was too large, too chaotic for any person to grasp. General formulations and rhetoric were to be avoided. In a world of inflated, competing claims and no certainties, the best that an individual could do was to make an inventory of the most basic tangible things. This is what Gunter Eich did when he found himself in a prisoner-of-war camp administered by the U.S. Army.

The significance of the poem was immediately perceived by other writers and critics at the time. Hans Magnus Enzensberger, a younger writer, wrote:

After the entry of the Allies, Germany was mute, in the most precise meaning of the word, a speechless country. There is a poem in which this paralysis has itself become language. Eich's poem is as quiet as it is radical . . . The poet is taking a claim to the absolute minimum that remains; to a material, spiritual, and linguistic remnant. His manner of writing corresponds to this. It is stripped down as far as poetry can be stripped. The text sounds like a man learning to speak; it is with such elementary sentences that language courses begin. This was the position of German literature after the war: it had to learn its own language.[2]

Other writers turned to the form of the "inventory," or basic catalogue, found in Eich's poem. The intent behind the use of the form was serious: it was to perform an act of taking stock. These were quests for what was real, what was solid in a world that seemed to be in total flux.

A passage from Samuel Beckett's novel *Watt* could be called "an inventory":

Here he stood. Here he sat. Here he knelt. Here he lay. Here he moved, to and fro, from the door to the window, from the window to the door; from the door to the window; from the fire to the bed; from the bed to the fire; from the bed to the fire, from the fire to the bed; from the door to the fire, from the fire to the door; from the fire to the door, from the door to the fire; from the window to the bed . . .[3]

Watt was composed in Roussillon, in the south of France, during the last years of the war. Beckett was in hiding, and wrote about the room where he was temporarily living. His description became an inventory of the articles in the room, continuing for almost two pages. Beckett first included each item, piece of furniture and feature defining the room such as the window, door, and fireplace. Then he described the possible combinations of these items and their relations to each other, shuffling them. Beckett's catalogue is deflationary, omitting subjectivity or impressionism. But the shifting point of view is inventive.

Beckett's purpose in making this inventory in *Watt* was simple, similar to Eich's intention. It was to record everything that was tangible and amenable to the senses. Anything not solid, that could not be verified, was omitted. It was an act of stock-taking, recording what was real and at the same time rejecting what was not real, questionable, or abstract.

A biographer has written that *Watt* was composed during a period of breakdown, and writing the book became a daily therapy, what Beckett later called "only a game, a means of staying sane. a way to keep my hand in."[4] If it was a game, and mixed with humor, its purpose was serious, and the passage in *Watt* represents a trial version of the exploration in Beckett's postwar trilogy of novels *Molloy*, *Malone Dies*, and *The Unnamable*. These novels used similar concrete, modest household settings, turning them into large-scale explorations of the reality of the senses and the mind. Beckett was continuing his exploration of reality begun during the war in Roussillon in his novel *Watt*.

Many works written during the war and near its end contained visceral reactions against prewar culture. Some were against literature in general. Eich's poem implicitly expressed a reaction against prewar culture; he deliberately chose objects not associated with culture such as tin cans, socks, a knapsack, a pencil lead. A piece of cardboard separates him from the earth when he sleeps.

Hans Magnus Enzensberger thought Eich's poem "Inventory" was emblematic of a whole generation of writers emerging from the ruins of the war. It was Eich who rhymed, in another poem, the title of Goethe's famous poem "*Faust*" with the word "*verlaust,*" "covered with lice." Eich's ode to a louse and his poem "Latrine" were seen by many as a repudiation of the traditional prewar German "*Naturlyrik*" of Heine, Moericke, and others.[5] Many writers revolted against the usages and forms current before 1939. Sometimes the revolt included the entirety of what they called, in quotes, "literature." When the Catholic thinker Emmanuel Mounier wrote that he expected "the collapse of the whole wormeaten hulk," he was referring to all prewar and contemporary culture. His revolt was remarkably complete. The sense of upheaval was not confined to literature but extended to other disciplines, psychology, sociology, the social sciences.

A large number of writers who lived through the war assumed it was impossible to pick up where their lives had ended in 1939. A statement of revulsion was written by Theodor Adorno, a critic of literature, music, and member of the "Frankfurt School" of social scientists: "Neutralized and ready-made, traditional culture has become worthless today . . . Cultural criticism finds itself faced with the final stage of the dialectic of culture and barbarism."[6] In another essay he claimed that writing lyric poetry after Auschwitz had become impossible. Other writers made comparable assertions: "Next to the atrocious facts, the very idea of literature seems indecent, and one doubts whether certain zones of reality can ever be the subject of poems or novels."[7]

The revolt against prewar culture extended to the tenets of religious belief. Primo Levi singled out the popular belief in Providence: "Today I think . . . no one in our age should speak of Providence."[8] During the war itself many attacked the concept of God or a higher being.[9] Indictments of God by the poet Władysław Szlengel were especially powerful, and before his death in April 1943 he wrote two poems attacking God that were mentioned by Emanuel Ringelblum in the archive he buried in the Warsaw ghetto. In "It Is Time!" God is described in the context of an extermination camp. It is God, not humans, who is tortured and gassed:

And You will cry out, You will want to flee.
When the torture is finished, and the agony of death,
They will drag You and cast You into a hideous pit,
They will tear away Your stars—the gold teeth in Your jaw—
Then burn You.
And You will be ash.[10]

The revolt against prewar culture included most disciplines and the arts. One writer made a collective portrait of the skeptical intellectual at the end of the war:

He has been deceived so often that he does not want cheap consolation which will eventually prove all the more depressing. The

War left him suspicious and highly skilled in unmasking sham and pretense. He has rejected a great many books that he liked before the War, as well as a great many trends in painting and music, because they have not stood the test of experience. The work of human thought *should* withstand the test of brutal, naked reality. If it cannot, it is worthless.[11]

Many writers were harsh in their revolt, questioning all literature and the ethics inherited from the past:

Pink quartered ideals
hang in abattoirs.[12]

These "ideals"—hanging like animal carcasses in a slaughterhouse—were concepts that once animated society such as beauty, nobility, and transcendence. Tadeusz Rozewicz thought these had now become obsolete. He wrote:

The following are empty synonyms:
man and beast
love and hate
friend and foe
darkness and light

The way of killing men and beasts is the same
I've seen it: truckfulls of choppedup men
who will not be saved.

Ideas are mere words:
virtue and crime
truth and lies
beauty and ugliness
courage and cowardice.

In an interview he explained, "We learned language from scratch . . . One of the premises and incentives for my poetry is a disgust with poetry. What I revolted against was that it had survived the end of the world, as though nothing had happened . . . The production of 'beauty' to induce 'esthetic experiences' strikes me as a harmless but ludicrous and childish preoccupation."

Left-leaning writers often had strong, sweeping opinions of rejection. A short story titled "Shakespeare" ("Szekspir"), written at the end of the war, satirized a group of mostly communist writers: "Nothing satisfied us. We asked loudly: 'Where is literature? Perhaps there is no literature capable of nourishing us? Where are the writers? Do you call writers those old men, and halfway old men, who have wasted their lives without really writing anything?' Our severity had no limits, we were deeply convinced, we consciously believed, that literature began with us . . . Oh, our tone! Even Shakespeare could not have had a better tone."[13]

Helen of Troy and the
"Bloodthirsty Abstractions"

Three of the finest wartime writers wrote with eloquence about the manipulation of language and the use of abstractions. They focused on the everyday speech of ordinary people, also on political rhetoric. Simone Weil, Albert Camus, and George Orwell were concerned with uses of common language that frequently took unexpected, unintended, and dangerous forms. They also wrote perceptively about the words used by indoctrinated groups.

Earlier writers like Wilfred Owen had warned against abstractions and rhetoric, but the revolt during and just after the Second World War was sharper and even more intense. The abstractions they targeted came from several sources: methodical exaggeration in the media, military propaganda, stereotypes dating back to the 1930s, and ordinary human psychology that was easily manipulated, lapsing into bad habits of thought. The links of abstract words to the war were direct: these were what Simone Weil called "bloodthirsty abstractions" in whose name people went to war.

In the 1930s, Simone Weil had been astonished by the strong effect abstractions had on large groups of people. In an imaginative passage in her book *The Iliad or the Poem of Force*, written in the first year of the war, she described how abstractions can cause people to undergo a transformation, acting "on the level of blind force, which is pure momentum."[14] Abstractions were able to exert extraordinary emotional power that had little to do with rational thought or a real, valid concept. For Weil they resembled the seductive power of Helen of Troy, the original cause of the Trojan War.

Earlier, Weil wrote in her essay "Let Us Not Start the Trojan War Again": "The role of Helen is played by words with capital letters. If we grasp one of these words, all swollen with blood and tears, and squeeze it, we find it is empty. Words with content and meaning are not murderous . . . But when empty words are given capital letters, then, on the slightest pretext, men will begin shedding blood for them and piling up ruin in their name."[15]

"On the slightest pretext"—it didn't matter what pretext, and the door was open to manipulation, to any cause or word. Weil found that a classical text about an ancient war, *The Iliad*, was remarkably relevant to the contemporary world. She was fascinated by a basic imbalance she discovered in *The Iliad*: "The person of Helen was so obviously out of scale with this gigantic struggle that in the eyes of all, she was no more than the symbol of what was really at stake. But the real issue was never defined by anyone, nor could it be, because it did not exist."

Weil made a list of the "bloodthirsty abstractions" that were found in most political and social vocabularies. She noted it was difficult to qualify these words. Phrases such as "There is democracy to *the extent that* . . ." or "There is capitalism *in so far as* . . ." were almost never used, and in practice were beyond our intellectual capacity: "Each of these words seems to represent for us an absolute reality, unaffected by conditions, or an absolute objective, independent of methods of action, or an absolute evil; and at the same time we make all these words mean . . . anything whatsoever." She concluded pessimistically that in what is called "an age of technicians," the only battles we know how to fight are battles against windmills.

Weil thought that almost any word could become "swollen." The process was far from inevitable. Many of the concepts so fervently believed had an empty core, and were irrational.[16] But once a word was spelled with a capital letter, it was endowed with a life of its own, raised to a higher, more absolute and potentially murderous power. A word became like Helen, "the face that launched a thousand ships."

Weil died in 1943, but several of the main themes of her essay, "The Power of Words," were taken up by other writers. No country, no matter what its politics or ideology, was immune to the symptoms she diagnosed. Both Albert Camus and George Orwell were alarmed by ideological abstractions, which were used to hide and to disguise. Both wrote about them extensively and eloquently, focusing on their usage in practical life.

Camus observed the direct influence of abstractions on people's behavior during the war. In 1944, he had come to believe that abstractions were an essential part of what he called the collaborationist mentality. He developed his ideas in the short, trenchant essays he wrote at the time, originally published in the resistance newspaper *Combat* and later included in his collected essays.[17] An early study on the function of abstractions was Camus' article on Pierre Pucheu, that appeared in the illegal underground newspaper *Les Lettres Francaise Clandestines* in 1944. Pucheu was Minister of the Interior for the Vichy regime. He was arrested by the Free French in Algiers, accused of systematically tracking down and murdering members of the underground.

Camus wrote:

> He believed, for example, that a defeated government was a government like all the others, and that the words "minister," "power," "laws," "sentence" did not change their meaning when France itself had changed. He believed that everything could continue, that it was always the same abstract administrative system in which he had always lived . . . For this kind of person it is always the same abstraction, and I suppose that their greatest crime is never to have come close to a body who has been tortured . . . with his own eyes, and with what I could call the physical notion of justice. It must be learned throughout France (and in all the governmental ministries) that the Time of Abstraction has ended.[18]

The historian Marc Bloch also noted the penchant for abstractions in the French Army prior to the 1940 collapse. Staff officers took refuge in rigid concepts, and had a "passion for paper and general ideas" without seeing that these "remained mere verbal counters, having no connection with actuality." Camus believed the French language had been badly corrupted by the Vichy regime. There was an immense need for "a language of flesh and blood, and true images."[19]

In France the issue of abstractions and ideological beliefs was thrust onto the national stage by the first trials of collaborators in 1944–45. Camus was not only an observer, he was a central actor and maker of policy. As editor of the underground newspaper *Combat*, he held a unique position. After liberation, *Combat* was one of the few French newspapers licensed by the Allies to publish. Writing as editor, Camus articulated the need for justice after the war. He advocated formal trials of those who collaborated with the Germans, and were accused of war crimes.

During the French trials, the problem of language suddenly became important. A consistent code of justice had to be applied to the collaborators. But the Resistance had partly shared the vocabulary of its enemies.[20] For example, both the Resistance and Vichy revolted against the abuses of the Third Republic, which was nevertheless a democracy. Both were suspicious of the word "democracy," criticizing the Third Republic's parliamentary corruption, unbridled capitalism, egotism, narrowness, and individualism. Both the Resistance and Vichy admired qualities of courage, enthusiasm, and willingness to sacrifice for an ideal. Both professed faith in a "spiritual revolution" while indulging in antibourgeois rhetoric. Vichy and the Nazis both claimed to serve a "national revolution" against the liberal order. But Camus and the editors of *Combat* also sought a "national revolution." The ideals served by both groups were perilously close to each other. Could the courts distinguish between these goals, between "good" and "bad" abstractions?

In the debate about what course the trials should take, Camus found a worthy opponent in Francois Mauriac. In 1944, Camus was emerging from obscurity and had little reputation. On the other hand Mauriac, a devout Catholic and Nobel Laureate for Literature in 1936, was twenty-eight years his senior and known throughout France. Mauriac wrote for *Le Figaro,* and in mid-1944 initiated the exchange with Camus, suggesting that a spirit of charity would more become the Resistance in its hour of triumph than the strict pursuit of justice.[21] Camus replied that Mauriac's position was "appeasement at any price," and asserted that "a terrible law" compelled France to destroy "a still living part of the country"—that is, the collaborators—in order to save its soul. Mauriac promptly challenged Camus in a *Figaro* editorial, "A Reply to *Combat,*" asking him to define what this "terrible law" was. "Either I have misunderstood," Mauriac wrote, "or what I do understand is repellant."[22] The challenge struck home. Camus' "terrible law" resembled the abstractions he had previously criticized.

Camus backed down, and advocated a "middle road" between severity and leniency. In a later essay, Camus wrote magnanimously, "M. Mauriac got the better of me."[23] But if we consider Camus's position in the context of his earlier writings, it is clear that his prior agreement with Mauriac was substantial.

The debate was about general principles: how they should be applied in ethics, law, and life. It was one of the most interesting discussions at the end of the war, and the two leading protagonists were among the finest

French writers of prose in the twentieth century. What Camus modestly called his "defeat" was actually in keeping with his distrust of what he called "systems." The courts showed it was impossible to legislate justice, or create what Camus hopefully called "a new social contract." Camus agreed that some of the most important and noble concepts of the Resistance— Justice, Revolution, Loyalty—were too abstract for people to be sentenced to death in their name.

In *The Rebel* Camus presented a sustained critique of what he called "secular religions," doctrines of salvation in the last two centuries. These had taken the form of political revolution and culminated in terror, totalitarian states, and the Second World War.[24] Camus' position was succinctly summarized by Martin Esslin: "The decline of religious faith was masked until the end of the Second World War by the substitute religions of faith in progress, nationalism, and various totalitarian fallacies. All this was shattered by the war."[25]

Some critics faulted Camus, and argued that no work of analysis can avoid abstraction.[26] But Camus should not be willfully misunderstood. He did not attack all abstract propositions but criticized, above all, those that used the rhetoric of generality, and concealed disguised agendas. These were structurally necessary for the totalitarian states of the twentieth century. They denied the lives of large categories of people, using quasireligious doctrines to justify what he called "logical murder."[27]

In England, George Orwell carried out an attack against ideological abstractions as sharp and impassioned as the attack by Camus. Orwell focused on habits of thought in everyday life, on the way ordinary people expressed themselves in speech as well as writing. In his essay, "Politics and the English Language," published at the end of the war, Orwell observed that language and thought went hand in hand. "The slovenliness of our language makes it easier for us to have foolish thoughts."[28] Orwell pinpointed many thought processes or "bad habits" that produced false abstractions. He showed how words are regularly used to deceive or to manipulate variable meanings, usually dishonestly. Foremost were the words *class, totalitarian, science, progressive, reactionary, bourgeois,* and *equality.* These were similar to Weil's "words with capital letters." Orwell described many of the mental and verbal procedures that distort the meanings of these words: "dying metaphors," "verbal false limbs," pretentious diction, mixed metaphors, prefabricated phrases, and a host of other verbal tricks used in daily speech.

Throughout the war Orwell was concerned with the manipulation of language that went beyond bad habits. In *Inside the Whale* and *The Lion and the Unicorn*—published in 1940—he observed the interrelations of language and politics, and recommended a careful, deflationary use of words. *Inside the Whale* included some of Orwell's finest essays of literary criticism. Works of literature contained many of the same verbal deceptions found in everyday speech. Orwell's analysis of W. H. Auden's poem "Spain" cut through many of the poem's fashionable activist gestures. It was a measure of Orwell's perceptivity that decades later, Auden came to disapprove of his own poem and declined to republish it in his *Collected Poems.*[29]

The culmination of Orwell's interest in the misuse of language was *Nineteen Eightyfour,* and his description of the "imaginary" language "Newspeak." Written just after the end of war, the novel was based on Orwell's observations of manipulation of language during the previous decade. He took several themes from "Politics and the English Language," and cast them in novelistic form in an imagined future. The misuse of language for political purposes became codified in "Newspeak." The novel even had a special appendix on the abuse of language, "The Principles of Newspeak." What Orwell called "doublethink"—the "central secret" of the society he described, and clue to its mystique—was based on a synthesis of contemporary speech habits, the discourse of political parties, and methodical manipulation at home and abroad. What Orwell called "newspeak" and double-think were used in democratic and totalitarian societies alike. Their main function was to hide: to cast a veil over real events.

Simone Weil, Albert Camus, and George Orwell all found a close connection between wartime events and the use of language for deception and disguise. They were three of the writers who stressed, at an early date, the power of words to alter consciousness and action.

3

The Literary Movements

Many prominent artistic movements, that became well-known after 1945, began during the war itself. They reflected projects that had been kept on hold because of censorship.[30] Most of these "movements" were informal and at first did not think of themselves as movements or organized groups at all. French Existentialism, "Neo-Realism" in Italy, the German "Group 47" (*Gruppe 47*), and the "Theater of the Absurd" became well-known later. Others were less familiar but no less distinctive: the Japanese "Wasteland" *(Arechi)* and A.S.A. groups, "The Movement" in England, the "War Generation" or "Columbuses" (*Kolumbowie*) in Poland, "Modernists" in Hungary, "Pickaxe and Spade" writers in Yugoslavia.[31]

Unlike the prewar avantgarde movements—Futurism, Dada, and Surrealism— the groups were not doctrinaire, and at first did not think of themselves as "groups" at all; they avoided programs, manifestoes, and group declarations, reacting against the ideologyinspired violence of the preceding years. Writing about Italian Neo-realism, Italo Calvino insisted "it is not a school."[32] What came to be called the "Theater of the Absurd" was at first a very loose grouping of writers that included both English- and non-English-speaking playwrights such as Samuel Beckett and Vaclav Havel. Martin Esslin noted that they were individuals who usually regarded themselves as lone outsiders.[33]

Some of the movements were shortlived, lasting only a few years; others like the German "Group 47" continued to be active as late as the 1970s. Both the Japanese *Arechi* ("Wasteland") group and the Czech "Group 42" began to meet during the war itself. Probably we should not draw too sharp a line for the beginning and end of these movements, as all of their formative experiences predated 1945.

Almost all the groups were hostile to cohesive doctrines. This reflected their opposition to ideological abstractions they often identified with the causes of the war they just lived through. Some of the most original, striking movements developed in countries that were defeated in the war, and had been subjected to the most extreme abuse of language, distortions, and rhetoric. We consider here several of the informal movements: the German "Group 47," Italian "Neo-Realism," and the Japanese "Wasteland" or *Arechi* group.

Group 47, which later became one of the most influential literary groups in Europe, emerged in the ruins of a country that had caused much of the suffering in World War II. Gunter Eich became a member of Group 47,and he was the recipient of the first of a series of prizes given to contemporary writers.

One of the first concerns of German writers was language. Several wrote that people were surrounded by the "rubble" of language just as they were surrounded by the rubble of cities. They directed their revolt against the German language that had been abused, manipulated, and deformed during the past thirteen years. A metaphor repeated by writers in Germany during the years 1945–46 was *Kahlschlag*. Literally it meant "complete deforestation" or "clear-cutting." It was a graphic image for the necessary "clearing out" of language. The main task was to remove the superfluous growth that had inundated the spoken and written German word. Language had been subordinated to the party's needs, and became an instrument of control. Helmuth von Moltke, executed by the Nazis in 1942 for conspiring against the regime, wrote in his diary in 1941, "Words . . . serve the state."[34] The metaphor of "the clearing out of language" emphasized the necessity to start from zero. It was a need not just for change but complete change. The metaphor also applies to Eich's poem "Inventory" written in a camp for prisoners of war—"This is my notebook, / This is my tent"—that expressed a revolt against rhetoric and inflationary language.

1945 marked the beginning of attempts to reformulate the German language. In an inaugural issue the editors of *Die Zeit* described "Our Task" in this way: "The years that lie behind us, especially the six years of war, have shut off the German reader from the world and surrounded him with a fog of propaganda." The editors of *Frankfurter Hefte* wrote: "We—meaning the editors, staff, and readers included—wish to help all to clarify the opaque and the enigmatic, insofar as that is permitted to us as we emerge from the depths." The philosopher Karl Jaspers noted at this time: "We can speak publicly with one another once again. Let us see what we have to say."[35]

One of the most influential new newspapers was called *Der Ruf* ("The Call") that later became the nucleus of Group 47. Its two principal editors,

Alfred Andersch and Hans Werner Richter, wrote that they shared a desire to liberate German politics from "the totalitarian demands of doctrine" and "from empty abstractions." They wanted to avoid an outlook either too mechanistic or too theoretical when confronted with the reality of "the concrete." Andersch, Richter, and Eich were founding members of Group 47.

Although some readers saw in Eich's poem "Inventory" a sort of declaration, Group 47 never adopted a formal program. This is one of the most unique features of the group, if it was a "group" at all. Texts were read aloud and debated. The group supplied badly needed contact and continuity to writers dispersed in a country that had no dominant cultural center. Richter noted: "Only (the possibility of) communication within one's own circle remained—reading aloud and criticism as substitutes for a journal that we did not possess and for a literary public that did not exist."

The movement had a long life, and almost all the major German writers attended its meetings at one time or another: Heinrich Boell, Eugen Kogon, Guenter Grass, Paul Celan, and Uwe Johnson.[36] The group's membership fluctuated. Richter wrote, "There was no program, no theme, no welcoming speeches, no rules, no ceremonial dinner, no treasurer's report." Nor were there dues, officers, or memberships. Anti-authoritarian in orientation, it did not exclude writers from behind the Iron Curtain, and welcomed every kind of literary project from realism to experimentalism.

Richter summoned the group to a meeting by ringing a cowbell. They took turns reading their works, the reader sitting in what was humorously called "the electric chair." One participant recalled, "We squatted in unconventional fashion . . . on the floor, smoked tobacco that did not always smell very good, and read from our works . . . What the debaters lacked in subtlety of formulation they redeemed with their ruthless but friendly candor. No one took offense at another since we were united by a common goal: to indicate a new, realistic path for German literature, free from false emotional outpourings." Probably an important reason for the group's continued success was its lack of any narrow program.

One of the best-known artistic movements of all was Italian "Neo-Realism," that produced some of the most famous films after the war: *The Bicycle Thief,* and *Open City.* It coincided with a flowering of literature and other arts. Almost all of the chroniclers of Neo-Realism agree that it was neither a "school" nor a movement.

Italo Calvino always used the term "Neo-Realism" in quotes. He wrote categorically, "'Neo-Realism' was not a school. (We must try to state things precisely.) It was a collection of voices, largely marginal, a multiple discovery of the various Italys, even—or particularly—the Italys previously unknown to literature."[37] Calvino also spoke of an "atmosphere," and "the anonymous voice of that time." Critics have spoken of Neo-Realism as "a state of mind," and "a catchword, a slogan, at best a kind of useful orientation."[38]

Like other postwar cultural movements it was a pent-up, explosive reaction to what had preceded it. Several of the "postwar" movements were wartime movements postponed because of material obstacles and censorship. Calvino described the moment when Italy emerged from a world war that overlapped with another, civil war: "With our renewed freedom of speech, all at first felt a rage to narrate: in the trains that were beginning to run again, crammed with people and sacks of flour and drums of olive oil, every passenger told his vicissitudes to strangers, and so did every customer at the tables of the cheap restaurants, every woman waiting in line outside a shop. The grayness of daily life seemed to belong to other periods; we moved in a varicolored universe of stories."

What Calvino called "the explosive charge of freedom that animated the young writer" came from the endurance of twenty-three years of Fascism. Toward the end it coincided with the presence of one of the largest resistance movements in Europe; the *Resistenza Armata* counted more than 200,000 men and women, dwarfing the French "*Resistance.*" Italian Fascism had made a cult of abstractions. Many refused to take its pretensions seriously, calling it "exhibitionistic narcissism." As far back as 1925 Benedetto Croce had attacked Fascism for its loose inconsistent rhetoric: "(It was) an incoherent and bizarre mixture of appeals to authority and demagoguery, of proclaimed reverence for and actual violation of laws, of ultramodern concepts and moldy rubbish, of absolutist attitudes and bolshevist tendencies . . . of loathing for culture and sterile groping for culture without a basis, of mystic sentimentality and cynicism."[39] Fascism had followed another tradition dating back to the nineteenth century that was rhetorical and formal, erecting a high barrier between life and literature.[40]

This long period of deprivation explains Calvino's insistence on the multitude of diverse "voices" clamoring to be heard, also why a desire to simplify language went hand in hand with a use of dialect. There was no contradiction between the two. The desire to cleanse language of the rhetorical excesses practiced for decades was best put by Ignazio Silone in his early novel *Fontamara*: "For our old Baroque culture it would be an immense good fortune if we could start from the beginning, recommence with fresh straw and clear water, if we could pick our way gingerly, putting big words *(parolini)* through a sieve one by one."[41]

The postwar desire to cleanse language of the muddy distortions of propaganda was intense. Above all came the desire to return to honest, direct language, and communication. In Italy the abstractions were often more hollow than deadly; the antidote was a return to everyday speech with human voices. For Italian writers like Pavese and Pintor, language was the symbol of a great gap between an aristocratic and a popular culture. For generations symbolism and allegory were accepted as necessary literary tools. Now, writers sought a language that would speak to the masses and intellectuals alike, that would be inclusive and not exclusive. In a country riven by regional, political, and cultural differences, they would find a common tongue for men of good will.[42]

The emphasis on the spoken voice can be seen in the novel, the cinema, and poetry. Regional dialect was revived— dialect, voice, and sense of place merged. Calvino wrote of the discovery of "the variety of dialects": "Local characterization was intended to give the flavor of truth to a depiction in which the whole wide world could be recognized."[43] Novels by Pratolini, Vittonini, Pavese, and Cassola published at the close of the war were about the lives of ordinary men and women. This was also true of the films of the period. A scenario writer, Cesare Zavattini, wrote: "The true function of the cinema is . . . to tell a reality as though it were a story: there must be no gap between life and what is on the screen."[44] The reaction against the old rhetorical tradition, that insisted on separating life and art, could not be more complete; now the two were a seamless continuum.

Much of the art of *The Bicycle Thief* and the early Rosselini films consisted in an apparent lack of illusion. The main ingredients of the style were shooting on location, use of natural lighting, and untrained, nonprofessional actors. The footage of *Open City*—a harsh depiction of the final days of the Resistance in Rome—included scenes of German soldiers taken secretly from rooftops at the actual time of their departure. The result was that each spectator became both a spectator and an eyewitness.

Neo-Realism stressed the concrete, the specific, and the tangible; in another part of the world, in Japan, other movements—"The Wasteland" *(Arechi)* and A.S.A.—discovered entirely new genres and forms. "Concrete poetry" was widely practiced. The pictorial nature of Japanese ideograms lent itself to this highly visual genre.[45]

The Japanese group "The Wasteland" is little known in English-speaking countries, yet it was one of the most original movements to re-emerge from the war. The group took its name from a translation of Eliot's *The Wasteland* by Ayukawa as early as 1940. A small magazine was put out with that same title, which took from Eliot's poem a central image but not all Eliot's metaphysics. The magazine was suppressed, its title declared to be "dangerously negative." The friends scattered.[46] After the war the poet Tamura Ryuichi returned to Tokyo where he took a job editing children's picture books. Soon he was using the second floor of the company as a meeting place of the new "Wasteland" group, and they revived the old *Wasteland* magazine.

The group was informal, enjoyed humor and parody, and had a whimsical side. A dominant characteristic of the group was skepticism. They doubted everything, and every value. Tamura insisted that the group was not nihilistic:

> We were glad to be the living dead with nothing to lose. We wanted to question the basic Principles behind an industrial society based on the illusion of the isolation of the individual and the deification of economic growth based on war and imperialism. I tried to make my poems into holes or windows, to catch sight of the invisible spiritual waste as well as the obvious material destruction.[47]

Tamura's main effort was to discover ways to bypass the old Japanese lyric mode that was anti-critical and antiphilosophical. He embarked on a frontal attack on prewar Japanese traditions. One device he discovered was creating fictional characters or personae in his poems. It was an attempt to break away from what he called the confessional monologue, the voice of authority that had obsessed prewar Japanese poets and novelists. Tamura wanted to wring the neck of this lonely, selfabsorbed "I." He would juxtapose it against other voices that violently collided with it and limited it, achieving honesty. Tamura wrote that the old "singlevoiced" poet believed that he was a unique center of meaning: that his personal wounds were as absolute and beautiful as flowers.

Hence, Tamura claimed, the confessional and narcissistic prewar "I" was none other than the emperor himself. The emperor, whose countless imperial symbols such as the chrysanthemum and rising sun accompanied the Japanese Imperial armies and navies on their invasions abroad.

By extension, Tamura thought that the Second World War could be seen as the ultimate "lyric" poem. The war was the expression by a group—or the whole state—of the primacy of its own "me-feeling." By means of the lyric, a poet reduced himself to a single "I." Subjectivity, above all collective subjectivity, was the basis for authority. Through war, a nation could act as a single subject.

In support of Tamura's thesis we could quote a poem written by Admiral

Ugaki of the battleship *Yamato*. After a victory in which he sank four American aircraft carriers and three battleships, he promptly retired to the solitude of his cabin and wrote three *haiku* poems:

After the battle I forgot the heat
while contemplating
the sixteen-day moon.

Contemplating the moon,
I mourn
the enemy's sacrifice.

Beneath the moon
stretches a sea at whose bottom
lie many ships. [48]

The Admiral, withdrawing to his cabin where he could contemplate the moon, was indeed conjuring up a lyrical and lonely poetic mood. Many Japanese admirals and generals wrote poetry of this type. According to Tamura the "I-" or "me-feeling" acquired absolute primacy.

The lyrical feeling described by Tamura recalls the German tradition of *innerlichkeit* or "inwardness"; Thomas Mann also criticized a tradition of "powerprotected inwardness." [49] Tamura stressed that it required aggrandizement and action. Hence, expansionist war was the ultimate lyric poem.

Tamura claimed that the most powerful modern Japanese "poem" ever written was the announcement of war by the Japanese High Command on December 8, 1941:

Before dawn this morning, the 8th, the Imperial

Army and Navy entered a condition of combat with
American and British forces in the Western Pacific.

Tamura claimed that no other Japanese poem had with so few words
made so many people shudder so deeply.[50]

The identification of the "me-feeling" with expansionism and declaration of combat cut through thickets of rhetoric, euphemisms, propaganda, and mythology. It was an act of great daring. Tamura's originality was to bring the Japanese High Command into the domain of poetry. His criticism was satirical, but at the same time deeply serious.

The Italian Neo-realists had also broken through a barrier separating art forms from contemporary events, introducing documentary footage and nonprofessional actors into a film; Tamura's revolt against earlier wartime traditions was to point out the close connection between culture and war. They were not separated, there was no gap between the two, the war was a kind of "poetry." Japanese society and the training of the ordinary soldier—with highly emotional, subjective ceremonies, symbols, and rituals—were pervaded by the "lyric" emotion he described. The surge toward expansionism depended on it. It required isolation from others, both "loneliness" and collective feeling at the same time.

4

Which Tongue, Which Speech?

The variety of the many movements at the end of the war stands out, and also the completeness of their revolt. They were more united by what they found unacceptable, and wanted to avoid, than by specific solutions. Few usages and traditional practices escaped untouched. For example, a staple of narrative writing and literature in the past was the single "point of view." In a spirited assertion, Jean-Paul Sartre wrote that the language of narration in all past literature had now become obsolete. He examined past methods of narration in a book *What Is Literature?* written at the very end of the war:

> In the stable world of the prewar French novel, the author, placed at a gamma point which represented absolute rest, had fixed guide marks at his disposal to determine the actions of his characters . . . Whereas our predecessors thought they could keep themselves outside of history, and that they had soared to heights from which they could judge events as they really were, circumstances have plunged us into our time. If we wished to give an account of our age, we had to people our books with minds that were half lucid and half overcast . . . none of which would have a privileged point of view.[51]

The "gamma point" was the omniscient perspective of an author who knows the outcome of events in a narration. Sartre recommended that future literary works have no privileged subjectivity or "providence." The words in these future books "will be toboggans . . . which hurl the reader into the midst of a universe where there are no witnesses."

Sartre scornfully wrote that omniscience was obsolete and psychologically false. It was the knowledge of an outcome that H. Stuart Hughes thought was a liability both for the historian and any writer composing a narration true to the psychology of the events in the past. It was the concept of absolute historical truth that Raymond Aron claimed "must vanish along with theology."

Several writers in Western and Eastern Europe, obeying an impulse similar to Sartre's, attempted to create a completely "unprivileged" consciousness. For example, in prose it can be seen in works by the German writer Wolfgang Borchert. A passage from his story "Along the Long Long Street" reads:

Wall wall door window glass glass glass lamp old woman red
red eyes fried potato smell house house piano lesson ping pang
the whole street long[52]

The texture resembles the interior monologues of avant-garde writers such as James Joyce, but it is probably more an "exterior monologue" than an" interior monologue." It raises the question, Can an "unprivileged" consciousness even exist? During the next decade, writers would address the problem. It raises another question, What is the psychological basis for punctuation? As a character's senses and perceptions travel from one object to another, are the senses naturally "punctuated"? Do the senses pause, like a comma? Or like another punctuation mark? During the war Paul Eluard and Louis Aragon experimented with punctuation, and abandoned it entirely. Their practice influenced many other writers in both Eastern and Western Europe.[53]

In appearance many of these writings resemble avant-garde works of the 1920s and 30s, but the impulse behind them is entirely different. Authors rarely had a confident sense of "the new" and what it required. Many writings at the end of the war are characterized by deflation and doubt. One critic called it an "age of austerity"; another, Northrop Frye, wrote that it favored a "low mimetic."[54] Distrust of literary forms was international. No literary practices would remain untouched.

Even the most conventional grammar taught in elementary schools could be mocked, or discarded, or treated with humor. Samuel Beckett made fun of pronouns:

Someone says you, it's the fault of the pronouns, there is no name
for me, no pronoun for me, all the trouble comes from that . . .
Someone speaks to himself, that's it, in the singular, a single one,
the man on duty, he, I, no matter, the man on duty speaks of

257

himself, it's not that, of others, it's not that either, he doesn't know, how could he know.[55]

The "man on duty" is a narrator or speaker in any kind of discourse. In his playful way, Helmut Heissenbuettel also insisted that the artistic act should contain no illusions. This led him to praise—very much with tongue in cheek—tautologies:

the shadow that I cast is the shadow that I cast
the situation into which I have got is the situation into which
I have got[56]

After euphemisms had reigned supreme under the Nazis and other authoritarian governments, tautologies had a special appeal. Words could finally mean what they were supposed to mean. Wolfgang Borchert also wanted to restore literal, jargon-free meanings to words: "We who call a tree tree and a woman woman and say yes and say no: loud and clear . . . and without subjunctives."[57]

Another writer called for a new "contract" between a word and its meaning. Jan Skacel had been a member of the Czech wartime group "Skupina 42"; in a poem titled "Contract" he recommended a new and closer link—a "contract"—between words and the world of reality:

I do not blaspheme. All I want is for pain
Really to hurt, and a tear to be a tear.[58]

The "contract" would be new and revolutionary. The old "contract" between words and things, between words and life, had been broken, for many years it took grotesque and violent shapes.

The sense of revolt at the end of the war was intense. The memory of the misuse of language—of methodical deception, of propaganda, rhetoric, and words used for disguise—was vivid. Emmanuel Mounier wrote that he expected "the collapse of the whole worm-eaten hulk."

Further, language had been used from the very beginning to camouflage and to hide aggressive action. The events in the war were paralleled by language intended to turn them into something else. Words and euphemisms transformed lethal intentions and lethal events into something harmless or benign. Major actions far too numerous to count flowed from the secret Pacts and the Protocols of 1939. These continued to be hidden until the end, most people did not know that they existed. But they were interwoven into events as they unfolded, camouflaged by propaganda and rhetoric, hidden behind facades, *Tarnung* (disguise), and theatrical *Tufta* ("fakery").

The writer spoke for many when he recommended a new "contract." The old contract between words and things, between words and life, had been broken. A new "contract" had to be put in its place.

Language was an instrument capable of describing the real world. There was a bond between people and the real world. Words and language offered the opportunity to re-establish this bond. It would be one of the great tasks for writers in the postwar world; in 1945 it was a project for the future.

* * *

The investigation of wartime experiences and themes would last many decades after the end of the Second World War. An unusual feature of the literature about the war was that an extremely large number of works were composed long after the events of 1939–45, sometimes twenty, thirty, forty, or fifty years afterward. During the second half of the twentieth century many literary movements came and went, but cumulatively works about the Second World War would form a powerful undercurrent, continuing until the century's end. In the Soviet Union it was only during the so-called "glasnost" period—beginning in 1985, forty years after the end of the war—that writing was freed of some of the worst constraints of censorship. One of the last bastions of secrecy about the war was finally opened, the curtain of disguise lifted. Participants in the war were still alive. For the first time forbidden themes—the prohibited "white spots" that had been denied by censorship—could be explored. In the 1980s and 90s investigators with tape recorders were permitted to locate survivors of the war, deportations and camps, to interview them and record their answers.[59]

Was the Second World War a violent break in historical continuity, or was it part of a longer development that includes us? Answers vary. Some have declared we are beyond the reach of the past. The need for revolt against the past, against the events of 1939–45 and their rhetoric, once so overpowering, has diminished. Contemporary endeavors in literature, culture and the social sciences are "new." We are both "postwar" and "post-Modern" at the same time; this has prompted an author to joke that we are now all "posties."[60]

It is a temptation to deny a past as lethal as the Second World War, or to set it apart from us at a distance, even a very great distance. It is tempting, also, to reduce it to national myths or fictions, to imagine that now we are more privileged. But when we look at the forms that writers gave their experiences, we can see it is our human nature they were describing, these are also our forms. No matter how much we wish to distance ourselves, or to create legends about the war, we find our own human likeness in these works; it is ourselves we see—with a shock of recognition—as in a cracked mirror.

Notes

Preface

1. "*Inter arma silent Musae*"; the Latin phrase for "The Muses are silent in time of war" is often repeated, see Czeslaw Milosz, *A Year of the Hunter* (New York, 1994), 217–18.

2. Andre Malraux, *The Walnut Trees of Altenburg*, trans. Fielding (London, 1954), "Note of the Author"; Deming Brown, *Soviet Russian Literature since Stalin* (Cambridge, UK, 1978), 74; Alexander Solzhenitsyn, *The Gulag Archipelago*, vol. I, 136–37; Curzio Malaparte, *The Volga Rises in Europe* (London, 1961).

3. Tzvetan Todorov, "Humanly Plural" in the *Times Literary Supplement* (London), June 14, 1985.

4. Dmitri Shostakovich, quoted by Manashir Yakubov to Symphony No. 7, the USSR Ministry of Culture Orchestra, Melodiya Stereo A10 00257 006 (1987).

5. Arthur Koestler, *The Invisible Writing* (New York, 1984), 490–92.

6. One of Wilson's "Fourteen Points" at the Versailles Peace Conference was that no secret treaties would be made in the future, all treaties would be reviewed by the League of Nations. Later this was not observed; Grenville and Wasserstein, *The Major International Treaties of the Twentieth Century* (London, 2001).

7. On deception, Sun Tzu, *The Art of War*, 53, 66, 106; Raymond Aron, *Clausewitz, Philosopher of War* (Englewood Cliffs, NJ, 1985), especially "The Meeting of Two Revolutions" and "War is a Chameleon." On Stalin's "necessitarian deception," Andrzej Walicki, *Marxism and the Leap to the Kingdom of Freedom* (Stanford, 1995),430.

8. On Roosevelt's insistence on unconditional surrender and his awareness of German "atrocities" and "crimes": Churchill, "The Hinge of Fate" (vol. IV of *The Second World War*), 615–18; and Sherwood, *Roosevelt and Hopkins*, 696. Russian discoveries of German massacres of civilians in 1941–42 strongly motivated subsequent defense; the Dyess escape from Mindanao to Melbourne influenced strategies of MacArthur and Truman.

9. B. H. Liddell Hart, "National Object and Military Aim" and "Grand Strategy" in *Strategy* Second Rev. ed., 1991); and Liddell Hart, *History of the Second World War* (New York, 1971), 415.

10. Michael Howard, *The Invention of Peace* (New Haven, 2000), 72; Ronald Lewin, *Hitler's Mistakes* (London, 1984), 25, 67; Jan Patocka, *Essais heretiques sur la philosophie de l'histoire* (Paris, 1981), 141–45. John Keegan noted that war is always an expression of culture: Keegan, *A History of Warfare* (New York, 1993); Christopher Lehman-Haupt, "On the Making of War . . ." in *New York Times*, Oct. 25, 1993; Leszek Kolakowski's Jefferson address "The Idolatry of Politics," given in Washington D.C. on May 12, 1986; *Modernity on Endless Trial* (Chicago, 1990), 146–61.

11. Donald Keene, "The Barren Years. Japanese War Literature," *Monumenta Nipponica*, XXXIII, 1 (Spring,1978), 106–7.

12. Ants Oras, *Baltic Eclipse*, 33; Arved Viirlaid, *Graves without Crosses* (Toronto, 1972), 43. Possible annihilation was taken seriously, partly explaining why the war against evidence was so ferocious. See Alexander Nekrich, *Forsake Fear*, 201–2; Nikolai Tolstoy, *Stalin's Secret War*, Chapter X "Forest Murmurs"; Matthew P. Gallagher, *The Soviet History of World War II*, xiii; and Petro Grigorenko, *Memoirs* (New York, 1982), 330–33.

13. Simone Weil, *The Need for Roots* (New York, 1952), 221.

14. Robert Wistrich, "The Politics of Rescue" in *Times Literary Supplement*, Dec. 4, 1981.

15. Peter Paret, ed., *Makers of Modern Strategy. From Macchiavelli to the Modern Age* (Princeton, 1986), 8; and "Grave Guesses" in *The Economist*, May 6, 1995, 22; Paul Fussell also complained about U.S. "military romanticism" in *The Boys' Crusade.*

16. Deborah Shapley, *Promise and Power: The Life and Times of Robert McNamara* (New York, 1992); John Byrne, *The Whiz Kids* (New York, 1993); and George Ball, "The Rationalist in Power," *New York Review of Books*, April 22, 1993. The lingering bias continued into the twenty-first century, probably contributing to the misadventures of the U.S. military in Iraq; see Victor Hanson, *Carnage and Culture,* "Epilogue."

Chapter I ("Unreal War!")

1. Herbert Read, *Collected Poems* (Horizon, NY, 1966), 157–64.

2. B. H. Liddell Hart claimed "nothing may seem more strange" to future historians than the failure of Western democracies to respond to Hitler's "well-advertised warnings": *Strategy* (London, 1967), 207; even Napoleon, he wrote, did not disclose his intentions as clearly as Hitler in his many speeches and *Mein Kampf.*

3. Anthony Powell, *The Kindly Ones* (London, 1962), 172. The attack against the Incas by Pizarro in 1532 was a copy of an identical strategy by Cortez several years earlier. Jared Diamond has posed a question: If the Incas had learned of the previous Spanish

strategy and attack, what defense might they have made? *Guns, Germs and Steel* (New York, 1997), 79.

4. George Orwell, *Collected Essays, Journalism and Letters* (New York, 1968), vol. II, "My Country Right or Left 1940–1943," 56.

5. J. B. Priestley wrote a perceptive portrait of a Nazi follower in one of his *Postscripts* (June 23, 1940); and Harold Nicolson's journal gained in awareness from his prewar experience in Berlin as a diplomat. Winston Churchill was well informed about Germany in the 1930s: Ronald Lewin, *Churchill as Warlord* (New York, 1973), 15; William Manchester, *W.S. Churchill, Alone (1932–1940)*, New York, 1988), 126. Richard Hillary vividly described a trip with his King's College rowing crew to Germany in 1937; the experiences, being spat upon and harangued, strengthened his sense of purpose in aerial combat during the war. Lords Astor, Darlington, and Londonderry were enthusiasts of Hitler in the 1930s; Neville Chamberlain rented his house on Eaton Square to Ribbentrop: Kazuo Ishigura, *The Remains of the Day* (London and New York, 2000). See Noel Annan, *Our Age*, 182; "Cato" (Michael Foot and Frank Owen), *Guilty Men* (London, 1940), 29; M. F. Perutz, "What If?" *New York Review of Books*, March 8, 2001; John Lukacs, *Five Days in London, May 1940* (New Haven, 2001).

6. Constantine FitzGibbon, *The Blitz* (London, 1957), 38; Tom Harrisson, *Living through the Blitz* (New York, 1976), 50–58; and Winston Churchill, *The Gathering Storm* (Boston, 1948), 134; *Their Finest Hour* (Boston, 1949), Chapter XV.

7. H. Stuart Hughes, *History as Art and as Science* (New York, 1964), 11 (author's italics). On the historian taking a stance outside history, Berel Lang's "Introduction" to *Writing and the Holocaust* (New York, 1988).

8. J. P. Stern, *On Realism* (London, 1973), 174; Raymond Aron, *Introduction to the Philosophy of History* (London, 1961), 38, 132, 179; Leszek Kolakowski, "*Fabula Mundi* and Cleopatra's Nose" in *Modernity on Endless Trial* (Chicago, 1990), 242–48. Gerard Genette distinguishes between "real time" and "narrative time," each depending on the relative knowledge of the speaker: *Narrative Discourse* (Ithaca, 1980), 30, 33, 157–58. (See the discussion in Chapter VII below.)

9. Noel Annan, *Our Age*, 192.

10. Donald Kagan, *On the Origins of War* (New York, 1995), 412–14; and John Lukacs, *Five Days in London, May 1940* (New Haven, 2001). In the nineteenth century Alexis de Tocqueville titled a chapter in his book *Democracy in America*, "Causes which Render Democratic Armies Weaker than Other Armies at the Outset of a Campaign, and More Formidable in Prolonged Warfare".

11. Harold Nicolson, "The War Years," volume II of *Diaries and Letters* (New York, 1967), 93.

12. With typical understatement F. W. Winterbotham called it "a very close shave": *The Ultra Secret* (New York, 1974), 25, 34. An Ultra intercept alerted Churchill to the Brauschnitz Plan to encircle the British Expeditionary Force.

13. Richard Hillary, *The Enemy Within* (London, 1942), 119–25. The American title of Hillary's book, *Falling through Space* (New York, 1942), misses the self-criticism implied by the British title, see 261–63.

14. A. Price, *The Battle of Britain* (London, 1979), 109, 95.

15. Richard Hough and Denis Richards, *The Battle of Britain* (London, 2001), 211, 301.

16. Elizabeth Bowen, *The Demon Lover and Other Stories* (London, 1945), 175, 192–93.

17. Tom Harrisson, *Living through the Blitz* (New York, 1989), 307–9.

18. William Sansom, *Westminster at War* (London, 1947), 94, 78. Sansom quoted in Robert Hewison, *Under Siege* (London, 1977), 87–88.

19. Michael Howard wrote that the sense of "reality" in both peace and war is a synthetic construct, it depends heavily on concrete experience: *The Invention of Peace* (New Haven, 2000).

20. Jiri Mucha, *The Problems of Lieutenant Knapp* (London, 1945), 112.

21. John F. Kennedy used the metaphor of sleep for willful denial in his book *While England Slept*, as did Gordon Prange in his book about Pearl Harbor, *At Dawn We Slept* (New York, 1991).

22. John Keegan, *The Face of Battle* (New York, 1976).

23. Joseph Czapski, *Memories of Starobielsk (Souvenirs de Starobielsk)*, (Paris, Temoignages, 1945), 22–24; Nikolai Tolstoy, *Stalin's Secret War* (New York, 1981), chap. VII ("Digesting the Plunder").

24. Walter Laqueur, *The Terrible Secret* (New York, 1982), 99, 206.

25. *Nazi-Soviet Relations, 1939–1941*, ed. Raymond Sontag and James Beddie (Didier, NY, 1948), v. Not everything was published; German Foreign Office documents going back from von Bulow to Bismark, to the philosophy of Fichte and Hegel, were included in the packets. In 1948, the Soviet Information Bureau promptly published a rebuttal of the State Department publication in a pamphlet *Falsificators of History* (Moscow, 1948), and a collection of captured German documents, *Materials Relating to the Eve of the Second World War.* See Matthew Gallagher, *The Soviet History of World War II* (New York, 1963), 60–62; and Walter Laqueur, *Russia and Germany* (New York, 1965, 1990), 265–71. A broad view of disguise was taken by the ancient Chinese strategist, Sun Tzu, *The Art of War*, ed. Liddell Hart (London,1963), 53–54; Sun Tzu claimed all war depends on deception. See *Oxford Companion to World War II*, ed. I.C.B. Dear (New York, 1995), 283 ("deception"); Ronald Lewin, *Hitler's Mistakes* (London, 1984), *Ultra Goes to War* (London, 1978), 104; and F. W. Winterbotham, *The Ultra Secret*, 70.

26. Reuters Dispatch, "Archives Yield Soviet-German Pact" in *New York Times*, Oct. 30, 1992; *The Economist*, May 6, 1995, 22. The events prior to the signing of the Molotov-Ribbentrop Pact are well described by Timothy Snyder in *Bloodlands: Europe between Hitler and Stalin* (New York, 2010), Chapters 1–4.

27. Jan Gross, "The Paradigm of Social Control," *Revolution from Abroad* (Princeton, 1988); Nikolai Tolstoy, "Digesting the Plunder" in *Stalin's Secret War* (New York, 1981); Grigore Gafencu, *Prelude to the Russian Campaign* (London, 1945).

28. Aleksandr Nekrich, *Forsake Fear* (London, 1991), 103; Gerhard Weinberg, *A World at Arms* (Cambridge England, 1994), 894–97; John Keegan, *The Second World War* (London, 1996), 588–95, "Conclusion"; Robert Goralski, *Second World War Almanac 1931–1945* (New York, 1981), 425–29; *The Oxford Companion to World War II*, "Casualties"; Bohdan Wytwycky, *The Other Holocaust* (Washington DC, 1980), 87–92; Robert Conquest, *Harvest of Sorrow* (New York, 1986), 7; Stephane Courtois et al., *The Black Book of Communism*, (Cambridge, MA, 1999), 4.

29. *"Aktion AB"* (Allgemeine Befriedung, "General Pacification"); Simon Wiesenthal, *Justice, not Vengeance* (London, 1989), 165.

30. Czeslaw Milosz, "Meeting in Budapest" (conference of the Wheatland F o u n d a - tion), *New York Times*, June 22, 1989.

31. Anonymous, *The Dark Side of the Moon*, preface by T. S. Eliot (London, 1978), 66.

32. One historian preferred the word *Kulturkreis*, "region of cultural influence."

33. Arthur Koestler, *The Yogi and the Commissar* (New York, 1946), 89–92.

34. Walter Laqueur, *The Terrible Secret*, 91, 100, 125, 149, 154, 186, 206.

35. Odd Nansen, *From Day to Day* (New York, 1947); the Norwegian title was *Fra dag til dag*, Oslo, 1946.

36. Nansen, *From Day to Day*, 443–44.

37. Thucydides, *The Peloponnesian War*, end Chapter 1 of Book I.

38. Albert Camus, *The Plague* (New York, 1972) (*La Peste*, 1948), 36–37.

39. Laqueur, *The Terrible Secret*, 99.

40. Krystyna Zywulska, *I Came Back* (New York, 1951), 110; Margarethe Buber, *Under Two Dictators* (New York, 1950), 152.

41. Emanuel Ringelblum, *Notes from the Warsaw Ghetto*, ed. Sloan (New York, 1958), 321.

42. Michel Mazor, *La Cite englouti* (Paris, 1947); *The Vanished City* (New York, 1993), 133; Juri Becker, *Jacob the Liar* (New York, 1969).

43. Gerald Fleming, *Hitler and the Final Solution*, 22.

44. Libushe Zorin, *Soviet Prisons and Concentration Camps, an Annotated Bibliography, 1917–1980* (Newtonville, MA, 1980); Chapters VI and IX below.

45. Milovan Djilas, *Wartime* (New York, 1977), 435; Nikolai Tolstoy, *Stalin's Secret War*, 12–13.

46. Varlam Shalamov, "Lend Lease," *Kolyma Tales* (New York, 1980), 179–80. On the American program of "Lend-Lease," W. Averell Harriman, *Special Envoy to Churchill and Stalin* (New York, 1975), 150–51.

47. The question was not fanciful, and Russian demographers have made the same point: Sergei Maksudov, "Pertes subies par la population de l'URSS, 1918–1958" in *Cahiers du monde russe et sovietique*, XVIII ^{3}, juillet-septembre 1977, 223–65; Sergei

Maksudov, *Poteri Naselenia CCCP* (Chalidze, Benson VT, 1989); Robert Conquest, *The Harvest of Sorrow* (New York, 1986), 7, 299–307.

48. Louis deJong also referred to elements of nature when describing disbelief and casualties during the war, quoting La Rochefoucauld: *Le soleil ni la mort ne peuvent se regarder fixement*—"Man cannot stare at the sun or at death."

Chapter II (Carnivals)

1. Mikhail Bulgakov, *The Master and Margarita*, trans. Mirra Ginsburg (New York, 1967), 117. (*Maister i Margarita*, Moscow, 1967). The novel first appeared in Russian in the magazine *Moskva* in late 1966 and early 1967; on Bulgakov's life and career see Elendea Proffer, *Bulgakov* (Ann Arbor, MI, 1984).
2. Roy Medvedev, *Let History Judge* (New York, 1971), 367.
3. Nikolai Tolstoy, *Stalin's Secret War* (New York, 1981), 55, 382.
4. Andrei Sinyavsky, *Soviet Civilization: A Cultural History* (New York, 1990),106–13.
5. Quoted by Roy Medvedev, 289, 327; Lewis Siegelbaum and Andrei Sokolov, *Stalinism as a Way of Life* (New Haven, 2000), 29, 88, 263; and Dariusz Tolczyk, *See No Evil* (New Haven, 1999).
6. Arvids Grigulis, "An Evening in Moscow" ("Vakars Maskava," Nov. 1940) quoted in Rolfs Ekmanis, *Latvian Literature under the Soviets, 1940–1975* (Belmont, MA, 1978), 57.
7. The poem "A Letter to Stalin" appeared on March 18, 1941; Rolfs Ekmanis, *Latvian Literature under the Soviets*, 51. See Katerina Clark, *The Soviet Novel: History as Ritual* (Chicago, 1985), Chapter 6.
8. Nikolai Aseev, "*Vo ves' rost.*" See *Pravda*, September 18, 1939. Ewa Thompson has analyzed much of this material in "Soviet Russian Writers and the Soviet Invasion of Poland in September 1939," Chapter 11 of *The Search for Self-Definition in Russian Literature*, ed. Ewa Thompson (Houston, 1991), 158–66.
9. Many Soviet articles and poems published about the invasions of Russia's western neighbors contained the phrase "holy hatred" (*"sviataia nenavist'"*). It is instructive to compare "holy hatred" in two very different contexts, the offensive war of 1939–41 and the defensive war against the Germans of 1942–45. The phrase derived probably from "holy malice" used in Blok's 1918 poem "The Twelve." I am grateful to Deming Brown for pointing this out.
10. Semen Kirsanov, "Strana-Magnit" in *Pravda*, July 23, 1940; Nikolai Tolstoy, *Stalin's Secret War* (New York, 1981), Chapter VII, "Digesting the Plunder."
11. Ants Oras, *Baltic Eclipse* (London, 1948), 79; Arved Viirlaid, *Graves without Crosses* (Toronto, 1972), 34.
12. Zbigniew Herbert, "Isadora Duncan" in *Notes from the Besieged City* (New York, 1985), 60.

13.Umberto Eco, "Ur-Fascism" in *Five Moral Pieces* (San Diego and New York, 2001), 72.

14.Mabel Berezin, *Making the Fascist Self* (Ithaca, NY, 1997), 94.

15.Borden Painter, *Mussolini's Rome. Rebuilding the Eternal City* (New York, 2005), 71;

16.Paul Baxa, *Piacentini's Window, the Modernism of the Fascist Master Plan of Rome* (Cambridge, UK, 2004).

17.Umberto Eco, "Ur-Fascism," 71–73.

18.Gottfried Benn, "Answer to the Literary Emigrants" (1933) in *Primal Vision* (New York, 1971), 46–47.

19.Joachim Fest, quoted in Gordon Craig, *The Germans* (New York, 1982), 68.

20.Neville Henderson, *Failure of a Mission* (New York, 1940), 72; Albert Speer, *Inside the Third Reich* (New York, 1970), 57–59, 166; John Flower and Ray Davison, "France" in *The Second World War in Fiction* (London, 1984), 48; Alphonse de Chateaubriant, *La Gerbe des forces* (Paris, 1938), 318.

21.Ingmar Bergman, *The Magic Lantern* (New York, 1988), 120–24.

22.William Shirer, *Berlin Diary* (New York, 1941).

23.Bernt Engelmann, *In Hitler's Germany* (New York, 1986); Ilse McKee, *Tomorrow the World* (London, 1960), Chapter 1; and Marianne Mackinnon, *The Naked Years* (London, 1987), part 1.

24."To stem from": *abstammen*. Leni Riefenstahl, *The Triumph of the Will* (*Triumph Willes*, 1934), original German Language Version, Leni Riefenstahl Productions, 1935, 1975, Janus Collection. Essay on the film, Ian Buruma "A Lethal Thing of Beauty" in *Times Literary Supplement*, Oct. 9, 1992; Susan Sontag, "Leni Reifenstahl" (1965) in *Against Interpretation* (New York, 1966). Sontag's assessment was different in "Fascinating Fascism" (1974), *On Photography* (New York, 1977); Steven Bach, *Leni* (New York, 2007).

25.Kurt Karl Eberlein, "What Is German in German Art?" in *Nazi Culture*, ed. George Mosse (New York, 1966), 163; Ludwig Clauss, "Racial Soul, Landscape, and World Domination," *Nazi Culture*, 67.

26.Hugh Trevor-Roper, *The Last Days of Hitler*, 5; Hans Buchheim et al., *Anatomy of the S.S. State* (London, 1968), 199; Joachim Fest, quoted in Craig, *The Germans*, 68; Erik Erikson, "The Legend of Hitler's Childhood" in *Childhood and Society* (New York, 1950), 302–11; and Fritz Stern, *The Politics of Cultural Despair* (Berkeley, 1961), 293.

27.Gordon Craig, *The Germans* (New York, 1982), 194, 209.

28.Quoted in Craig, *The Germans,* 190. On Romanticism and totalitarianism, Tzvetan Todorov, "Avant-gardes and Totalitarianism," *Daedalus* (Cambridge, MA, winter 2007), 51.

29. Ralf Dahrendorf, *Society and Democracy in Germany* (Berkeley, CA, 1967), chapter. 22: "Humanistic Theory and Practical Inhumanity: An Excursus." On sadism in prewar German culture, Maria Tatar, *Lustmord: Sexual Murder in Weimar Germany* (New York, 1995).

30. Alexander Rossino, *Hitler Strikes Poland* (Lawrence, KA, 2003), 227. Von Brauchnitsch's order was dated April 28, 1941. A "Jurisdiction Order" recommending harshness to civilians was also written, Antony Beevor, *Stalingrad*, (New York, 1998), 14–17; Gordon Craig, "The Goblin at War," *New York Review of Books*, Dec. 4, 2003.

31. Guy Sajer, *The Forgotten Soldier* (New York, 1971), 135. Sajer was Alsatian, *Le Soldat oublie* (Paris, 1967).

32. Saul Friedlander, *Reflections of Nazism. An Essay on Kitsch and Death* (New York, 1984), 30; Matei Calinescu, *Five Faces of Modernity* (Durham, NC, 1987), 225–62.

33. Gottfried Benn, "Double Life: Block II, Room 66" in *Primal Vision*, 136, 139.

34. Ernst Juenger, *Journaux de guerre*, "Jardins et routes," 129.

35. Hans Habe, *A Thousand Shall Fall* (New York, 1941), 252, 283, 286, 329, 332.

36. Antony Beevor, *Stalingrad*, 73–76.

37. Theodor Plievier, *Moscow* (Garden City, NY, 1954), 25 (*Moskau*, 1952); and Theodor Plievier, *Stalingrad* (New York, 1984), 273, 299, 336. Most German soldiers took the myths and rituals of the Nuremberg rallies with them on their military campaigns after 1939. See the portrait of General Juergen Stroop, sentenced to be executed for war crimes, demonstrating to cell-mates in 1952 how he goose-stepped at Nuremberg; Kazimierz Moczarski, *Conversations with an Executioner* (Englewood Cliffs, NJ, 1981), 55, 66.

38. Considerations of defense were also real, the USSR had reason to fear a rearmed Germany. Averell Harriman records that in 1942, Stalin told him he was afraid Chamberlain at Munich would sign a "confidential" pact with Hitler; *Special Envoy to Churchill and Stalin* (New York, 1975), 163.

39. Milija Lasic, *Enemies on All Sides* (Washington, DC, 1976), 23.

40. "The History of a Manuscript," *Kaputt* (London, 1948), 7–10.

41. Pearl Buck, *The Promise* (New York, 1943), 240–41.

42. Norman Mailer, *The Naked and the Dead* (New York, 1948), the last ninety pages; Holger Klein, ed., *The Second World War in Fiction* (London, 1984), 177, 229.

43. Mailer is quoted that "Mount Anaka" was similar to mountains in Luzon; Louise Levita, "The *Naked* Are Fanatics and the *Dead* Don't Care," *New York Star Magazine* 22, Aug. 1948, 3; Robert Solataroff, *Down Mailer's Way* (Urbana, 1974, 18 n.

44. John Dower, *War without Mercy*, 206, 222–23, 274; Paul Johnson, *Modern Times*, 180; and William A. Owens, *Eye-Deep in Hell* (Dallas, 1989), ix.

45. Hanama Tasaki, *Long the Imperial Way* (Cambridge MA, 1949), 233–45.

46. See the title story in Masui Ibuse's collection, *Captain Lookeast*, trans. Bester (London, 1971).

47. Charles MacKay, *Extraordinary Popular Delusions and the Madness of Crowds* (London, 1841). Expansion has retained potent and nationalistic appeal in ever-new situations, see Chris Hedges, *War Is a Force That Gives Us Meaning* (New York, 1999).

Chapter III (The Firestorm)

1. Hans Habe, *A Thousand Shall Fall* (New York, 1941), 137–38.
2. Ernst Juenger, *Wartime Diaries*, 134. Other works describing the French civilian side of this front: Victor (Vladimir) Pozner, *Deuil en 24 heures* (New York, Brentano's, 1942), 21–22; Rene Benjamin's *Tragic Spring* (Le Printemps tragique, 1940), Claude Jamet's *Notes of a Defeat* (Carnet de deroute (1942). See John Flower and Ray Davison, "France" in *The Second World War in Fiction*, ed. Holger Klein (London, 1984), 52–53.
3. Yuri Bondarev, *The Hot Snow* (Moscow, 1976), 155.
4. Dan Billany, *The Trap* (London, 1950), 334–36.
5. William Manchester wrote that no man in combat is really sane: "The Bloodiest Battle of All," *New York Times Magazine*, June 14, 1987, 44.
6. Fritz Bayerlein in Eversley Belfield and Essame, *Battle for Normandy* (London, 1965), 183.
7. Antoine de St.-Exupery, *Flight to Arras* (trans. of *Vol de Nuit*), 66.
8. J. P. Stern, *On Realism* (London, 1973), 52–56; Robert Scholes and Kellogg, *The Nature of Narrative* (London, 1966), 203.
9. Harry Brown, *A Walk in the Sun* (New York, 1944), 186–87.
10. John Steinbeck, *Once There Was a War* (New York, 1958), 198.
11. Victor Nekrasov, *Front-Line Stalingrad*, trans. by Floyd of "*In the Trenches of Stalingrad*" (London, 1953), 127; Catherine Merridale, *Ivan's War* (New York, 2006), 50–51, 156–58.
12. James Jones, *The Thin Red Line* (New York, 1962), 188.
13. Ernie Pyle, quoted in *World War II*, ed. Sulzberger (New York, 1966), 530.
14. David Piper, *Trial by Battle*, preface by Frank Kermode, (New York, 1959), 176.
15. Eric Bergerud, *Touched with Fire* (New York, 1996), 312. On night fighting in Russia, Victor Nekrasov, *Front-Line Stalingrad*, 199-200; Richard Overy, *Why the Allies Won* (New York, 1995), 76.
16. Brian Horrocks, *A Full Life* (London, 1960), 122. On "Bodyguard," "FUSAG" and other deceptions, Richard Overy, *Why the Allies Won*, 151, 163.
17. Horrocks, *ibid.*, 131.
18. Richard Hillary, *Falling through Space* (English title, *The Enemy Inside*), 144–45.

19. See Chapter VIII below, "Defense," especially part 4 "Which Past, Which Future?" Pierre Clostermann, *The Big Show* (London, 1951); (*Le Grand Cirque*, 1948); a second, definitive French text was published in Paris in 2001. A cousin of Clostermann, who had the same family name but beginning with K, fought for the Wehrmacht.

20. S. L. A. Marshall, *Men against Fire* (New York, 1947), 101. John Keegan called the book "a masterpiece," but many criticisms of Marshall's methods were made, *New York Times*, Feb. 19, 1989, and *American Heritage*, Feb. 1989. The many failures described by Marshall point to bad morale and poor leadership; see Generals Gavin and Ridgway in Max Hastings, *Armageddon* (New York, 2004), 232. On the "gulf" between those directing a battle and those fighting it, Belfield and Essame, *The Battle for Normandy* (London, 1965), 132; Paul Fussell, *Wartime* (New York, 1989), and *Doing Battle* (Boston, 1996). Fine examples of the "mole's view" and talk about "the million-dollar wound" is given by Tony Hillerman in *Seldom Disappointed* (New York, 2001), 93.

21. Victor Nekrasov, *Front-Line Stalingrad*, 189–92. On N.K.V.D. and Komsomol "Blocking Detachments," see Vasily Grossman, *A Writer at War* (New York, 2005), 136, 141. On exhaustion: David Piper, *Trial by Battle*, 176; Goronwy Rees, *A Bundle of Sensations* (London, 1960); Ronald Lewin, *Churchill as Warlord* (New York, 1973), 154–60.

22. John Keegan, *The Face of Battle* (New York, 1976), 30–33.

23. Several writers of fiction attempted panoramic coverage of the war, from Norman Mailer's *Naked and the Dead* (1948) and Alexander Baron's *From the City, from the Plough* (1948), through Herman Wouk's *War and Remembrance* (1970) and *Winds of War* (1971), to Vasily Grossman's *Life and Fate* (1985). See Holger Klein, ed., *The Second World War in Fiction*, 25–37, 173–85.

24. Quoted in Philip Knightley, *The First Casualty* (New York, 1975), 333; Garry Wills, "Rule Number One: Nations at War Lie on Principle," in *New York Times*, Sept. 14, 1975; Paul Fussell, "The Real War Will Never Get in the Books" in *Wartime*, 267–97; and "Writing in Wartime: The Uses of Innocence" in *Thank God for the Atom Bomb and Other Essays* (New York, 1988), 36–61.

25. John Hersey, "War: It's Hard to Get It Right" in *New York Times*, Sept.10,1989, 44–45.

26. Philip Knightley, *The First Casualty*.

27. Alan Moorehead, *Desert War* (New York, 1943, 2001), 242.

28. Erwin Rommel, Field Marshal, ed. by B.H. Liddell Hart, *The Rommel Papers* (New York, 1953) 236. Rommel was aware of the bad morale Among Allied troops in North Africa, especially the Eighth Army, which he considered a "moral" victory for German forces.

29. Ronald Lewin, *Churchill as Warlord*, 144–45, 154–60. The morale of Allied troops was bad in other areas of combat, see remarks by General Gavin and others in Max Hastings,

Armageddon (New York, 2004), 232–33, 68, 183, 193, 346; S. L. A. Marshall, *Men against Fire, passim.* On the "million-dollar wound," Tony Hillerman, *Seldom Disappointed*, 131.

30. Gebele, quoted in Antony Beevor, *Stalingrad*, 372.

31. Catherine Merridale, *Ivan's War*, 50–51.

32. Antony Beevor, *Berlin. The Downfall, 1945* (New York, 2002), 218.

33. Horrocks, *op. cit.*, 156; Max Hastings, *Armageddon*, 295.

34. Vasily Grossman, *A Writer at War* (New York, 2005), 146.

35. Beevor, *Stalingrad*, 85; Max Hastings, *Armageddon*, 238.

36. Merridale, *Ivan's War*, 200; Matthew Gallagher, "Realistic Pages from Wartime Literature" in *The Soviet History of World War II* (New York, 1963), 104–10.

37. For extreme examples, Guy Gabaldon, *Saipan: Suicide Island* (Saipan, 1990), 74, 85, *passim.*

38. Quoted in Beevor, *Berlin*, 220.

39. On "tongues," Nekrasov, *Front-Line Stalingrad*, 213; Vasily Grossman, *A Writer at War*, 41, 220.

40. Marshal Zhukov was known for attention to detail: Georgi Zhukov, *From Moscow to Berlin* (Costa Mesa CA, 1991), 207–41; Zhukov, *Memoirs of Marshal Zhukov* (London, 1971), 427–66. An excerpt from his uncensored memoirs was published in *Pravda* (Moscow) on Jan. 20, 1989. See Richard Overy, *Why the Allies Won*, 71–72, 91–95.

41. Pierre Clostermann, *The Big Show*, 161.

42. On Allied censorship of news of the undergrounding of the Luftwaffe, and German synchronized attacks on Allied airfields by General Sperrle on January 1, 1945, see Clostermann, *Le grand cirque 2000* (Paris, 2001), 281.

43. John Keegan suggested there might be a "biorhythmic significance" in a ten-year interval of gestation prior to writing: *The Times Literary Supplement* (London), May 17, 1985.

Chapter IV (Scraps of Paper, Plaster Walls)

1. "Mitard" in Henri Pouzol, ed., *La Poesie concentrationnaire* (Paris, 1975), 33–34.

2. Michel Borwicz, *Les Ecrits des condamnes a mort sous l'occupation allemande, 1939–1945* (Paris, 1954), 5.

3. Henri Calet, *Les Murs de Fresnes* (Paris, 1945), 99.

4. Unto Parvilahti, *Beria's Gardens* (London, 1959), 12.

5. Calet, *Les Murs de Fresnes.*

6. Illustration, "Konigsgraben," Mary Costanza, *The Living Witness*, (New York, 1982), 9.

7. Adolf Rudnicki, "Note found under the Wall of Execution" (*Kartka znaleziona pod murem stracen*), in the collection of short stories *Szekspir* (Warsaw, 1946), 65–76.

8. (Anonymous), *The Dark Side of the Moon* (New York, 1947, preface by T. S. Eliot), x, 51; Simon Wiesenthal, *Justice not Vengeance* (London, 1989), 165. The German program was cynically called "pacification," "Aktion AB"; the years 1990–91 brought many revelations about the early participation of the Wehrmacht and local militias in shooting Jews: John Tagaliabue, "Nazi Archives in Moscow Detail Fate of Jews," *New York Times*, Nov. 17 1991.

9. Joseph Czapski, *Souvenirs de Starobielsk* (Paris: Temoignages, 1945), 22–23. Among the officers were many professors and scientific specialists. A writer, Pivovar, was among them, also Joseph Czapski. Nikolai Tolstoy, *Stalin's Secret War* (New York, 1981), Chapter X ("Forest Murmurs").

10. Czapski, *Souvenirs de Starobielsk*; Czapski, *The Inhuman Land* (New York, 1952), 8.

11. Michael T. Kaufman, "After 40 Years, a Soviet War Story Comes Undone," *New York Times* Feb. 19, 1989.

12. Jan Gross, *Revolution from Abroad* (Princeton, 1988), Chapter 3, "The Paradigm of Social Control"; Michael Borwicz, *Ecrits des condamnes*, and Borwicz, *Piesn ujdzie calo* (Warsaw, 1947).

13. Gustav Herling-Grudzinski, *A World Apart* (London, 1951), 9; David Dallin and Boris Nikolaevsky, *Forced Labor in Soviet Russia* (London, 1948); Nikolai Tolstoy, *Stalin's Secret War*, 12–13, 367; Libushe Zorin, *Soviet Prisons and Concentration Camps. An Annotated Bibliography 1917–1980* (Newtonville MA, 1980); Mikhail Heller, *The World of Concentration Camps and Soviet Literature* (London, 1974).

14. Czapski, *Souvenirs*, 88.

15. Unto Parvilahti, *Beria's Gardens* (London, 1959), 62, 236.

16. Stefan Knapp, *The Square Sun* (London, 1956), 50–52, 61.

17. Osvalds Freivalds, *Liela sapjzu draudze* (*Community of Suffering*) (Copenhagen, 1952), 128–29.

18. Alfreds Berzins, *The Unpunished Crime* (New York, 1963), 71, 74,120, 135; the official text of the Serov-Abakhumov plan ("Order no. 001223") is published in Arveds Svabe, *Genocide in the Baltic States* (Stockholm, 1952), Appendix 1.

19. Margarethe Buber, *Under Two Dictators* (New York, 1950) (*Als Gefangene bei Stalin und Hitler*, 1948).

20. Berzins, 109 (documents found at Valka), 120; Michal Borwicz, *Piesn ujdzie calo . . .*, 21. Contemporary communication theory was largely developed after 1945, but a few studies bear on World War II, for example, by Lev Vygotsky and Charles E. Osgood.

21. Roosevelt's insistence at Casablanca on unconditional surrender was largely motivated by an awareness of German "atrocities" and "crimes": Churchill, "The Hinge of Fate" (vol. IV of *The Second World War*), 615–18; and Sherwood, *Roosevelt and Hopkins*, 696. Russian discoveries of German

massacres in 1941–2 strongly motivated subsequent defense. The Dyess escape from Mindanao to Melbourne influenced overall strategies of MacArthur and Truman. (*In Medias Res*: People as Things)

22. Czeslaw Milosz, *Native Realm* (Berkeley CA, 1981), 204.

23. Milosz, *The Witness of Poetry* (Cambridge MA, 1983), 80.

24. Anna Swirszczynska, *Building the Barricade*, trans. Magnus Krynski and Robert Maguire (Cracow, 1977), 35, 41. On "Swir's" poetry, Czeslaw Milosz, "Anna i Wojna," *Tygodnik Powszechny*, August 6 1995; Milosz, "Jakiegoz to goscia mielismy," *Tygodnik Powszechny* 18–25 December, Cracow, 1994.

25. Swirszczynska, "A Fine Painting" in *Building the Barricade*, 157.

26. Swirszczynska, 83.

27. Erich von Manstein, *Lost Victories* (*Verlorene Siege*) (Bonn, 1955), 275–95; Ronald Lewin, *Hitler's Mistakes* (London, 1984), 25.

28. General Halder, present at the meeting on August 22, 1939, wrote that Hitler called for the "physical annihilation of the Polish population." For Hitler's 1939 *Fuehrerbefehl* to Heydrich on social policy, Alexander Rossino, *Hitler Strikes Poland*, xv, 9–15; laws passed in Berlin in 1939 literally gave Germans impunity in dealings with non-Germans; Raymond Sontag, *A Broken World* (New York, 1968), 376.

29. Swirszczynska, "The German Soldier," 83.

30. Swirszczynska, "Hair like a Waterfall," 117.

31. Tadeusz Rozewicz, "Leave Us" in *Conversations with the Prince and Other Poems* (London, 1982), 62.

32. Francis Ponge, "My Creative Method" trans. by Lane Dunlap in *Quarterly Review of Literature*, vol. XV nos. 1–2 (1967), 147–48. John and Bogdana Carpenter, "The Ordinary Material Object: Its Extraordinary Fate" in *World Literature Today* (Norman, OK), summer 1980, 372–73.

33. Natalia Ginzburg, "The Son of Man" in *The Little Virtues* (Manchester, 1983), 49–50.

34. Swirszczynska, 47, 53, 167, 189.

35. Władysław Szlengel, "New Holidays," *"Nowe Swieta"* in Michael Borwicz, *Piesn ujdzie calo*, 181.

36. Martin Gilbert, *The Holocaust* (New York, 1985); Helmut Krausnick, Martin Broszat *et al.*, *Anatomy of the S.S. State*, 66–67; Clifford Kinvig, *Death Railway* (New York, 1973), 102; Ray Parkin, *The Sword and the Blossom* (London, 1968), 3.

37. Jorge Semprun, *The Long Voyage* (*Le grand voyage*) (New York, 1964); Heinrich Boell, "The Train Was on Time" (*Der Zug war puenktlich*) in *Adam and the Train* (New York, 1970).

38. Ladislav Fuks, *Mr. Theodore Mundstock* (New York, 1968), 101; Wislawa Szymborska, "Conversation with a Stone," *Poetry Nation Review* 26 (vol. 6 no. 6), Manchester, England, 1982, 19–20; Vasko Popa, "The Quartz Pebble" (*"Belutak"*)

in *Selected Poems* (Harmondsworth, 1969), 68; Nellie Sachs, "Chorus of Stones" (*Chor der Steine*, 1959) in *O The Chimneys* (New York, 1967), 35; Agnes Gergely in *Modern Hungarian Poetry*, ed. Vajda (New York, 1977), 240.

39. Micheline Maurel, *La Passion selon Ravensbruck* (Paris, 1965), 23–24.

40. C.K. Stead, *The New Poetic. Yeats to Eliot* (Harmondsworth, 1969), ch. 4 and 5.

41. Julian Przybos, "Linia i Gwar" quoted in Bogdana Carpenter, *The Poetic Avant-garde in Poland* (Seattle, 1983), 139; see Renato Poggioli, "Agonism and Futurism" and "Technology and the Avant-garde" in *The Theory of the Avant-garde* (Cambridge, MA 1968), 68–74, 130–48.

42. T. S. Eliot, "Tradition and the Individual Talent" in *Selected Essays* (New York, 1950), 7–8.

43. See J. P. Stern's paraphrase and analysis, *Ernst Juenger* (New Haven, 1953), 29–30; 50–51.

44. Ernst Juenger, *Wartime Diaries* (*Premier Journal Parisien*), Paris, 1980.

45. Bruce Chatwin, "An Aesthete at War" in *New York Review of Books*, March 5, 1981, 23.

46. Juenger's description is an example of his constant manipulation of frame and point of view; see Bernt Engelmann, In Hitler's Germany (New York, 1986), 238–39. For a theory of culture that applies to Juenger's work, Ralf Dahrendorf, *Society and Democracy in Germany*, 329–51.

47. Michael Hamburger, *The Truth of Poetry* (New York, 1969), 123.

48. Czeslaw Milosz, *The Witness of Poetry*, 46, 52; and C. Milosz, *The Seizure of Power*, the characters Wolin and Winter.

49. Alexander Solzhenitsyn, *The Gulag Archipelago*, vol. II, 86, 104; and Solzhenitsyn, *Prussian Nights*, trans. Robert Conquest (New York, 1977), 77–79; and Conquest's commentary, 38–39, 66–67.

50. Albert Camus, "*Lettres a un ami allemand*" ("Letters to a German Friend"), trans. in *Resistance, Rebellion and Death* (New York, 1974), 21.

51. Robert Paxton, *Vichy France, Old Guard and New Order* (New York, 1972), xii, 52; Gordon Craig, "Loot" in the *New York Review of Books*, Nov. 17, 1994, 37–39; Hans Habe, *A Thousand Shall Fall*, 334, 344–51.

52. Martin Bormann quoted in Igor Golomstock, *Totalitarian Art*, 291; Hans Mommsen in Michael Marrus, *The Holocaust in History*, 47.

53. Simon Wiesenthal, *The Murderers among Us*, 245. ("Books, Toys and Everything . . .")

54. Władysław Szlengel, "Things" ("*Rzeczy*") in *Co czytalem umarlym*, ed. Irena Maciejewska, Warsaw, 1977. A translation of the whole poem can be found in *Chicago Review*, no. 3 and 4 (Chicago, 2006), trans. John and Bogdana Carpenter, with an essay "Wladyslaw Szlengel."

Chapter V (Animals)

1. Jiri Weil, "Brown and White" in *Colors,* trans. Rachel Harrel (Ann Arbor, MI, 2002), 31.

2. Jaroslav Seifert, "Song in a Mirror" (*"Pisen o zrcadle"*), trans. in *New Writing in Czechoslovakia,* ed. Theiner (Baltimore, 1969), 133.

3. Anna Swirszczynska, "Man and Centipede" (*Czlowiek i stonoga*),in *Building the Barricades* (Cracow, 1979), 189.

4. (Anonymous), *The Dark Side of the Moon,* preface by T. S. Eliot (New York, 1947), 111.

5. Pierre Gascar, *Beasts and Men* (*Les Betes*) (Boston, 1956); "The Horses" and "The Animals," 13, 66–70; Lawrence Langer comments on these stories in *The Holocaust and the Literary Imagination* (New Haven, 1975), 191–204.

6. Swirszczynska, "My Lice" (*Moje wszy*), *Building the Barricades,* 235.

7. Pelagia Lewinska, *Twenty Months at Auschwitz* (New York, 1968), 31.

8. Guenter Eich, "Spring along the Golden Mile"; James Wilkinson, *The Intellectual Resistance in Europe,* 131.

9. Varlam Shalamov, *Kolyma Tales,* 193.

10. Ernst Weichert, *The Forest of the Dead* (New York, 1947), 33; (*Der Totenwald,* 1945).

11. Elinor Lipper, *Eleven Years in Soviet Prison Camps* (Chicago, 1951), 226.

12. Shalamov, "Caligula" in *Russia's Other Writers,* ed. Scammel (New York, 1970), 157–58.

13. Sergio Malaparte, *Kaputt* (London, 1948), 338–39, 93. Malaparte's press dispatches were collected in *The Volga Rises in Europe* (London, 1957). Malaparte's real surname was Suckert, his *nom de plume* was a pun on the name "Bonaparte." He was a member of the Italian Fascist party until 1931.

14. Michael Howard, *The Invention of Peace* (New Haven, 2001), 12. Others used similar phrases ("the joy of killing brings men together"), Hermann Rauschning, *Hitler's Table Talk,* ed. Trevor-Roper (London, 1953), 51.

15. Viktor Frankl, *From Death Camp to Existentialism* (Boston, 1959), 49–50. A "realistic" version of transformation of a unit: Vaino Linna, *The Unknown Soldier* (Helsinki, 1975), 72.

16. Michel Tournier, *The Ogre* (New York, 1972); Guenther Grass, *Dog Years* (New York, 1963).

17. Eugene Ionesco, *The Rhinoceros* (New York, 1960), 70–71; (*Le rhinoceros,* 1960). Eugene Ionesco, *Present past Past present* (New York, 1968), 79. (*Present passe Passe present*).

18. Stanley Hoffman, "The Arrival of World War II: An Anticlimax" in *New York Times,* Sept. 1, 1989.

19. Charles Segal, *Tragedy and Civilization. An Interpretation of Sophocles* (Cambridge, MA, 1982); Michel de Montaigne, "Man's Presumption and Littleness"; Blaise Pascal, *Pensees*, Chapters 2 and 3; P.E. Easterling, "Between God and Beast" in the *Times Literary Supplement*, April 2, 1982, 374; David Joravski, "Is Science Beautiful?" in *New York Review of Books*, Oct. 25, 1984; Joravski, "Body, Mind and Machine" in *New York Review of Books*, Oct. 21, 1982; and John Carpenter, "Animals and Angels" in *Cross Currents 5* (1986), Ann Arbor, MI.

20. Milovan Djilas, *Conversations with Stalin* (New York, 1962), 161; Arkady Vaksberg, *The Prosecutor and the Prey* (London, 1990), 81, 83, 107, 120; Alexander Orlov, *The Secret History of Stalin's Crimes* (London, 1953), 329. Evgenia Ginsburg's *Into the Whirlwind* and *Within the Whirlwind* contain an array of descriptions of people as animals: "the Pike," "the kennel," "the Borzoi," "the two-legged Wolf," "the Snake-pit," etc. Dariusz Tolczyk analyzes the animalization of the opposition in the USSR, *See No Evil*, 80–81, 83.

21. Zbigniew Brzezinski, *Out of Control* (New York, 1993), 19, 28, 31; Brian Porter, *When Nationalism Began to Hate* (Oxford, 2000); Mircea Eliade, *The Sacred and the Profane* (New York, 1959). A few examples of purity and cleansing: the Russian *chistka* (cleaning or purge), the Japanese *misogi* (purification), the Polish *sanacja* (sanitation or purge). On secular religions, Leszek Kolakowski, "The Revenge of the Sacred in Secular Culture" in *Modernity on Endless Trial* (Chicago, 1990), 63. On "pseudo species," Erik Erikson, "Reflections on Ethos and War" in *Yale Review*, Summer 1984 (New Haven); on "false speciation," Stuart Hampshire "The Illusion of Sociobiology" in *New York Review of Books*, Oct. 12, 1978.

22. John Dower, *War without Mercy* (New York, 1986), 267; John Keene, "The Barren Years" in *Monumenta Nipponica* (Spring, 1978), 91. The five Japanese characters for pages 143–44 in text above.　米　英　于　猍　猱

23. J.-P. Sartre, "The Flies" (*Les Mouches*) in *No Exit and Other Plays*, trans. S. Gilbert (New York, 1955), 55; Andre Halimi, *Chantons sous l'occupation* (Paris, 1976); Richard Cobb, *French and Germans, Germans and French* (Boston, 1982) and *People and Places* (Oxford, 1985); James Wilkinson, *The Intellectual Resistance in Europe*, 40; Janos Pilinszky, *Selected Poems*, trans. Ted Hughes and Csokits (Manchester, 1976), 17. Miodrag Pavlovic, *The Conqueror in Constantinople*, trans. Neugroschel (New York, 1976), 12. Fernand Braudel, *Afterthoughts on Material Civilization and Capitalism* (Baltimore, 1977), 16. Pierre Gascar observed in "The Dogs": "I could talk to you for a long time about those people who have no name in history, whose life depends on a negative principle over which they have no control." Dane Zajc in *New Writing in Yugoslavia*, ed. Bernard Johnson (Harmondsworth, 1970).

24. Czeslaw Milosz, *The Witness of Poetry* (Cambridge MA, 1983), 4.

Chapter VI (Wall, Watchtower, Chimney)

1. "It is a measure . . . ." Gustav Herling, *A World Apart* (*Inny Swiat*), (New York, 1951), 175–77.
2. (Anonymous), *The Dark Side of the Moon*, 73–75.
3. Osvalds Freivalds, *Liela sapjzu draudze* (*Community of Suffering*) (Copenhagen, 1952), 128–29.
4. *The Dark Side of the Moon*, "*shag v levo, shag v pravo*," 92.
5. Ants Oras, *Baltic Eclipse* (London, 1948), 170–71.
6. Stefan Knapp, *The Square Sun*, 61.
7. *The Dark Side of the Moon*, 12.
8. Unto Parvilahti, *Beria's Gardens*, 62, 236.
9. *The Dark Side of the Moon*, 129. (June 22 1941)
10. Mikhail Heller, *The World of Concentration Camps and Soviet Literature* (London, 1974). Isaiah Berlin noted some continuity in the mobilization during earlier "command projects," the "Great Terror" of 1937–38, and the twenty-two month period of the Molotov-Ribbentrop Pact. See his "Note on the Literature and the Arts in Soviet Russia in the Closing Months of 1945, "Third Period: 1937 to the Present Day," in *New York Review of Books* Oct. 19, 2000.
11. Herling, *A World Apart*, 9.
12. Herling, *A World Apart*, 176–79.
13. Vladimir Petrov, *My Retreat from Russia* (New Haven, 1950), 3.
14. Dimitri Panin, *The Notebooks of Sologdin* (New York, 1976) (*Zapiski Sologdina*), 34.
15. Alexander Solzhenitsyn, "Prisoners" (*Plenniki*) in *Three Plays* (New York, 1986), 34; Alexander Solzhenitsyn, *The First Circle* (New York, 1968) (*V kruge pervom*).
16. Catherine Merridale, *Ivan's War* (New York, 2006), 3; Matthew Gallagher, *The Soviet History of World War II*, 8–9; Edwin Bacon, *The Gulag at War.Stalin's Forced Labor System in the Light of the Archives* (London, 1995); Robert Conquest, "Playing Down the Gulag" in the *Times Literary Supplement*, Feb. 24 1995, 8–9.
17. Anatoli Kuznetsov, *Babi Yar*, 104; Herling-Grudzinski, *A World Apart*, 174; Antoni Ekart, *Vanished without Trace*, 52, 94; Nicholas Prychodko, *One of the Fifteen Million* (Boston, 1952), 202–4. Max Hastings, an objective historian, has written "The Russian Official Histories of 1941–1945 Are Farragoes of Nonsense": "Germans Confront the Nazi Past," *New York Review of Books*, Feb. 26, 2009.
18. Ronald Lewin, *Hitler's Mistakes* (London, 1984), 115–20, 130–33; Milovan Djilas, *Wartime* (New York, 1977), 435.
19. Joseph Czapski, *The Inhuman Land* (London, 1975) (*Na nieludskie ziemi*, 1969); Czapski, *Souvenirs de Starobielsk*, 90, 106–9; Herling, *A World Apart*, 178.
20. Milovan Djilas, *Wartime* (New York, 1977), 435.

21. Holger Klein, John Flower et al., *The Second World War in Fiction* (New York, 1984), 147-150.

22. Herling, *A World Apart*, 233; by December the cruelties were popular topics of conversation.

23. Viktor Nekrasov, *Front-Line Stalingrad*, 26. The translation is not correct, see Nekrasov, *V Okopach Stalingrada*, "Sidel. Dosrochna by l osvobozhden . . ." (*Izbrannie Proizvedenia*, Moscow, 1962), 21.

24. Richard Overy, *Why the Allies Won* (New York, 1995), 19, 184–90.

25. Boris Pasternak, *Dr. Zhivago* (New York, 1958), "Epilogue." It was first published by Feltrinelli in Milan, both in Russian and Italian translation.

26. Joseph Czapski's *The Inhuman Land* remains one of the finest works about Soviet camps; also outstanding are Gustav Herling's *A World Apart,* Andrzej Kalinin's *And God Forgot Us,* Antoni Ekart's *Vanished without Trace,* Stefan Knapp's *The Square Sun,* Slawomir Rawicz's *The Long Walk.*

27. Varlam Shalamov, "The Life of Engineer Kipreev" in *Graphite* (New York, 1981), trans. John Glad, 135.

28. Vasili Grossman, *Forever Flowing* (New York, 1972) (*Vse techet*), 68–69, 229.

29. Elinor Lipper, *Eleven Years in Soviet Prison Camps* (Chicago, 1951), 111–16; 266–71; Edward Crankshaw wrote that Lipper's book was one of the finest written about Soviet camps. Michael Solomon described the prisoners massed for roll call as "a Cecil B. deMille production" in *Magadan* (Toronto, 1971), 82.

30. Owen Lattimore's article "New Road to Asia" in the *National Geographic Magazine*, December 1944 (LXXXVI), 641–76.

31. Philip Piccigallo, *The Japanese on Trial* (Austin, TX, 1979), 27.

32. Stanley Falk, *Bataan: The March of Death* (New York, 1962), 225–26.

33. James Clavell, *King Rat* (New York, 1962), 78.

34. Pierre Boule, *Le pont sur la riviere Kwai* (Paris, 1958). Boule described the first months of inactivity as "*une ere de felicite.*"

35. Gavan Daws, *Prisoners of the Japanese* (New York, 1994), 76.

36. David James, *The Rise and Fall of the Japanese Empire* (London, 1951), 178.

37. Kenneth Harrison, *The Brave Japanese* (Adelaide, 1966), 124; Melvyn McCoy and S. M. Mellnick, *Ten Escape from Tojo* (New York, 1944), 75.

38. Ronald Hastain, *White Coolie* (London, 1947), 179.

39. F. F. Liu, *A Military History of Modern China, 1924–1949* (Princeton, 1956); Hu Pu-yu, *A Brief History of the Sino-Japanese War, 1937–1945* (Taipei, 1974); and Clifford Kinvig, *Death Railway* (London-New York, 1973), 81, 86, 116.

40. John Coast, *Railroad of Death* (London, 1946), 148.

41. Ernest Gordon, *Through the Valley of the Kwai* (New York, 1962), 72.

42. Hastain, *White Coolie,* 80–81.

43. Laurens van der Post, *The Night of the New Moon* (London, 1970), 18–20, 23, 74.

44. Laurens van der Post, *A Bar of Shadow, The Seed and the Sower, The Sword and the Doll, The Night of the New Moon.*

45. Ray Parkin, *The Sword and the Blossom* (London, 1968), and *Into the Smother* (London, 1963).

46. Ian Horobin, *Collected Poems* (London, 1973), 127–42.

47. Thomas Hayes, *Bilibid Diary*, ed. A. B. Feuer (Hamden, CT, 1987), "Foreword."

48. William E. Dyess, *Bataan Death March* (New York, 1944; Lincoln, NE, 2002); E. Bartlett Kerr, *Surrender and Survival* (New York, 1985), 161–64; and Stanley Falk, *Bataan: The March of Death*, 204–9.

49. William Owens, *Eye-Deep in Hell* (Dallas, TX, 1989), 232.

50. Quoted by Barton Bernstein, "The Atomic Bombings Reconsidered," *Foreign Affairs*, Jan.-Feb. 1995, 152. President Truman explained his decision in an interview with John Toland: Toland, *The Rising Sun: The Decline and Fall of the Japanese Empire, 1936–1945* (New York, 1970), vol. 2, 946–47.

51. *Anatomy of the S.S. State*, ed. Krausnick, Broszat et al. (London,1968), 397–498; and Michal Borwicz, *Ecrits des condamnes*, 95.

52. Martin Broszat in Helmut Krausnick et al, *Anatomy of the S.S. State* (London, 1968), 483–85.

53. Gordon Craig, "The Order of the Death's Head" in the *New York Times Book Review*, March 15, 1970.

54. Michael Marrus, *The Holocaust in History* (New York, 1987), 54, 59; Christopher Browning, *Fateful Months: Essays on the Final Solution* (New York, 1985), Chapter 1.

55. Chaim Kaplan, *Scroll of Agony*, ed. A. Katsh (New York, 1965), 10; and Emmanuel Ringelblum, *Notes from the Warsaw Ghetto*, ed. Sloan (New York, 1958), ix.

56. Sebastian Haffner, *The Meaning of Hitler* (Cambridge, MA, 1983), 126–27.

57. Martin Gilbert, *The Holocaust* (New York, 1985), 229–30. The Yiddish prefix *far-*, like the German *ver-*, indicated perfective usage.

58. Yitshak Katznelson, *Vittel Diary* (Tel Aviv, 1964), 18.

59. "*Dzielnica-oboz.*"

60. Marek Edelman, *The Ghetto Fights* (New York, 1946), 31.

61. Emanuel Ringelblum, *Notes from the Warsaw Ghetto*, xxi–xxii.

62. The full title of Borwicz's anthology was: Piesn ujdzie calo. Antologia wierszy o zydach pod okupacja niemiecka (Warsaw-Lodz-Cracow, 1947).

63. Borwicz, *Ecrits des condamnes*, 208–10.

64. Borwicz, *Piesn ujdzie calo,* 31.

65. On Vrba and Wetzlar, Walter Laqueur *The Terrible Secret*, 98, 145.

66. Gusta Draenger, *Memoirs of Justyna* (*Pamietnik Justyny*), in *A Holocaust Reader*, ed. Lucy Dawidowicz, 340–47. David Roskies, *Against the Apocalypse* (Cambridge, MA, 1984), 221.

67. Wladyslaw Szlengel, *Co czytalem umarlym*, ed. Maciejewska (Warsaw, 1977), 57.

68. The text of the complete "Counterattack" in English translation can be found in the *Chicago Review*, Summer 2006, trans. with introduction by John Carpenter; "Call in the Night" (*Wolanie w nocy*). Polish text in Szlengel, *Co czytalem umarlym*, 138.

69. John Carpenter, "Communication across Time: The Boxes at 68 Nowolipki Street" in *Cross Currents 9* (Ann Arbor, MI, 1990). On Jodl, Gerald Fleming, *Hitler and the Final Solution*, 22; and Heinz Guderian, *Panzer Leader* (New York, 1952).

70. Abraham Suckever, "Grains of Wheat" (*Kerndlekh Veyts*, 1943) in *Lider fun geto*; "Secret Town": (*Geheymshtot*, 1947). For other versions see Suckever, *Selected Poetry and Prose*, trans. Harshav (Berkeley, CA, 1991), 156–58.

71. *Ziemia bez boga*, 1947; Michal Borwicz, *Ecrits des condamnes*, 91, 92.

72. "Song of the Murdered Jewish Nation" and "Vittel Diary": *Dos Lied fun Oisgehargetn Yiddishn Folk*, and *Pinkas Vittel*; Anita Shapira, *Berl: The Biography of a Socialist Zionist* (Cambridge, 1984), 320.

73. *The Book of Alfred Kantor*, pref. Wykert (New York, 1968).

74. Mary Costanza, *The Living Witness* (New York, 1982), 61, 137.

75. Kitty Hart, *I am Alive*, 118.

76. Michael Hanusiak, *Lest We Forget* (New York, 1975), 64.

77. Filip Mueller, *Auschwitz Inferno* (London, 1979), 143.

78. Miklos Nyiszli, *Auschwitz* (New York, 1960), 156.

79. Many narratives singled out this date, for example Olga Lengyel, Five Chimneys, 80; Sebastian Haffner, The Meaning of Hitler, 126.

80. Borwicz, Piesn ujdzie calo, 41–43 ("Archiwum pod gruzami"). John Hersey fictionalized some of these events in *The Wall* (New York, 1950).

81. Czeslaw Milosz, The Witness of Poetry (Cambridge MA, 1983), 67–68; Borwicz, Ecrits des condamnes, 87–88, 262, 266-7. See Sidra Ezrahi, Not by Words Alone, 24–48; James E. Young, Writing and Rewriting the Holocaust (Bloomington, 1988), 15–39, 68; and Berel Lang,

82. M. Gebirtig and Stanislaw Lec in *Ecrits des condamnes*, 169.

83. Robert Desnos, "Dernier Poeme" in Henri Pouzol, ed., La Poesie concentrationnaire, 134. 96.

84. Mieczyslaw Jastrun, "Pogrzeb" in Piesn ujdzie calo, 98; Jan Holuj in *Ecrits*, 177.

Chapter VII (The End of Time)

1. Alexander Bek, Volokolamsk Highway (Volokolamsko shosse, 1944; 1956) (edition in English, Moscow, 1956), 141, 193. General Chuikov used a more direct formulation: "Time is blood," quoted by Vasily Grossman, A Writer at War, 147.

2. Francis Clifford, A Battle Is *Fought to be Won* (New York, 1963), 13.

3. John Steinbeck, *Once There Was a War* (Harmondsworth, 1971), "The Five Men" (Dec. 8, 1943), 166.

4. James Jones, *The Thin Red Line*, 184.

5. Grigory Baklanov, *South of the Main Offensive* (Philadelphia, 1963), 61; and Grigory Baklanov, *Forever Nineteen* (New York, 1989), 32.

6. Cecil Day Lewis, The Pathfinders (London, 1943), 157.

7. Pierre Colstermann, *The Big Show*, 18

8. St.- Exupery, *Flight to Arras*, 75.

9. Kurt Vonnegut, *Slaughterhouse Five*, 18.

10. Odd Nansen, *From Day to Day*, 188; Victor Frankl, *From Death Camp to Existentialism*, 70.

11. Christopher Burney, *Solitary Confinement*, 23.

12. Alexander Baron, *From the City from the Plough* (New York, 1948), 197–98.

13. Antoine de St.-Exupery, *Flight to Arras*, 51.

14. Close analysis of many works by civilians written between 1939 and 1945 shows the strong influence of the war even when not explicitly mentioned. In 1943, in German-occupied Greece, Yannis Ritsos was moved to write "Old Mazurka to the Rhythm of Rain" about his childhood (in Chrysa Prokopaki, *Yannis Ritsos*, 77–92). In German occupied Warsaw in 1943 Czeslaw Milosz wrote a series of Twenty poems about his childhood called "The World." ("The World," "Swiat") in *The Separate Notebooks* (New York, 1984). Dylan Thomas' poem "Fern Hill" was clearly influenced by the experience of bombardment in London: Paul Ferris, *Dylan Thomas: A Biography* (New York, 1977), 192–98; Constantine FitzGibbon, *The Life of Dylan Thomas* (Boston, 1965), 255, 277. Some of these poems have a precision and loving concreteness not found in comparable works written before 1939 or after 1945. See Bruno Bettelheim *The Informed Heart* (New York, 1971), 162, 192.

15. Frank Kermode, *The Sense of an Ending*, 160. Some have pointed out that both myth and religion rely heavily upon narrative: R. G. Collingwood, *The Idea of History* (Oxford, 1946).

16. David Holbrook, *Flesh Wounds* (London, 1966), 15.

17. Vance Bourjailly, *The End of My Life* (New York, 1984), 137.

18. Holger Klein, "Britain" in *The Second World War in Fiction*, 25–35; John T. Frederick, "Fiction in the Second World War," *College English* 17, no. 4 (Jan. 1956), 197–204.

19. Cecil Day Lewis, *The Pathfinders* (London, 1943).

20. Rex Warner, *Why Was I Killed?* (London, 1943), 28, 30.

21. H. G. Wells, "Mind at the End of Its Tether" in *A Short History of the World*, new edition (Harmondsworth, 1946), 288–99; and C. Milosz, "On the Agony of the West," *Dissent*, winter 1973, 23.

22. Tzvetan Todorov, "Les categories du recit litteraire" in *Communications 8* (Paris, 1966). Gerard Genette describes how there must be an "export" of posterior after-the-event knowledge onto the events themselves; these can be shared with the reader

in different ways, operating on different levels when the past is described: *Narrative Discourse*, 25–33, and *Figures III* (Paris 1972). H. Stuart Hughes, *History as Art and Science*, 70–73; and Leszek Kolakowski, "*Fabula Mundi* and Cleopatra's Nose," *Modernity on Endless Trial*, 242–45. See J.P. Stern, *On Realism*, 56; and Wayne Booth, *The Rhetoric of Fiction* (Chicago, 1961), 155–63.

23. One novelist commented of a character, "He remembered only that once (but what did 'once' mean?)" Aleksandar Tisma,*The Uses of Man* (San Diego, 1988), 15.

24. Harold Nicolson *The War Years, 1939–1945*. (June 5, 1940)

25. Winston Churchill, *Their Finest Hour* (Boston, 1949), 124; Ronald Lewin, *Churchill as Warlord* (New York, 1982), 81.

26. Spengler quoted in Fritz Stern, *The Politics of Cultural Despair*, 254.

27. Carol Gluck, "The Idea of Showa," *Daedalus* (Summer, 1990), 3; and John Toland, *The Rising Sun,* vol. I, 324.

28. William A. Owens, *Eye-Deep in Hell. A Memoir of the Liberation of the Philippines, 1944-45* (Dallas, 1989), 221–22.

29. Roy Medvedev, *Let History Judge*, 377; Catherine Merridale describes the period before Barbarossa as one of constant "armed struggle," *Ivan's War*, 45, 48.

30. Raymond Aron, *Introduction to the Philosophy of History* (London, 1961), 319–20.

31. Marc Bloch, *Strange Defeat* (London, 1949), 37.

32. Elinor Lipper, *Eleven Years in Soviet Prison Camps*, 272–74.

33. Arnulf Overland, "Jul i Sachsenhausen" and "Fjerde jul i fangenskap" in *Samlede Dikt, 1945–1965*, 75-82; and Odd Nansen, *From Day to Day*, 333.

34. S. B. Unsdorfer, *The Yellow Star*, 112, 174–75.

35. Władysław Szpilman, *The Pianist* (London, 1999), 54.

36. Andre Malraux, *The Walnut Trees of Altenburg*, 23 (*Les noyers de l'Altenbourg*). The book, part novel and part autobiography, was written in 1940. The manuscript, partly destroyed by the Gestapo and never rewritten by the author, was published in 1948.

37. Eugen Kogon, *The Theory and Practice of Hell*, 300. (Der SS Staat, 1948.)

38. Quoted in Jan Gross, *Revolution from Abroad*, 154. Alexander Wat, *Moj Wiek*, vol. I, 341.

39. Vasily Grossman, *Forever Flowing*, 240.

40. John Coast, *Railway of Death*, 96; Ray Parkin, *Into the Smother*, 80.

41. Yannis Ritsos in Chrysa Prokopaki, *Yannis Ritsos* (Paris, 1972), 22–23.

42. Tadeusz Borowski, "Auschwitz, Our Home (A Letter)" in *This Way to the Gas, Ladies and Gentlemen*, 131.

43. Simone Weil, *The Need for Roots* (*L'Enracinement*, 1949) (New York, 1971), 221–25; "The Great Beast" in *Selected Essays, 1934–1943*, ed. R. Rees (London, 1962), 378.

44. Goronwy Rees, *A Bundle of Sensations*, 170–71.

45. Ronald Lewin, *Churchill as Warlord*, 74–75, 154; Harold Nicolson, "The War Years" (vol. II of *Diaries and Letters*), entries of Feb. 12, 1942 ("There is something deeply wrong with the whole morale of our army . . .") and Feb. 24, 1942 ("Our army has not fought well . . ."); Brian Horrocks, *A Full Life*, 110–11; Max Hastings, *Armageddon*, 232–33, 346.

46. B. H. Liddell Hart, *History of the Second World War* (New York, 1971), 277, 283.

47. Theodore Plievier, *Stalingrad*, 100.

48. A Nobel-Prize winning biologist has speculated that future-oriented myths have existed so long, and in so many different societies, they might be genetically coded: Jacques Monod, *Le Hasard et la Necessite* (Paris, 1970), 182–92. Stephen Jay Gould, *Time's Arrow, Time's Cycle: Myth and Metaphor in the Discovery of Geological Time* (Cambridge, MA, 1987); Frank Kermode, *The Sense of an Ending*, 160. Some have pointed out that myth and religion rely heavily upon narrative: R. G. Collingwood, *The Idea of History* (Oxford, 1946).

49. Yoshida Mitsuru, *Requiem for Battleship Yamato*, trans. Richard Minear (Seattle, 1985), 105.

Chapter VIII (Defense)

1. Yrjo Jylha, "The Ghost Patrol," trans. by Taina Luhtala from *Kiirastuli* (Helsinki, 1951), 14–16.

2. Michael Howard, *The Mediterranean Strategy in the Second World War*, 15. The report on the poor condition of the Red Army probably contributed to Hitler's decision to attack the USSR in June 1941; see Nikolai Tolstoy, *Stalin's Secret War*, 118–25, 149, 157.

3. On the distinction between "nationalism" and defense: Isaiah Berlin's essay "The Bent Twig: On the Rise of Nationalism " in *The Crooked Timber of Humanity* (New York 1959), and "Nationalism: Past Neglect and Present Power" in *Against the Current* (London, 1979). Attempts have been made to construct a "model" or "ideal type" of defensive war; Martin Ceadel, *Thinking about Peace and War* (Oxford, 1987), "Militarism." For a view that wars are decided by fixed battles see Victor Hansen, *Carnage and Culture* (New York, 2001).

4. Krzysztof Kamil Baczynski, "The dark city breathes . . ." ("*Oddycha miasto ciemne*) in *Utwory wybrane* (Cracow, 1976), 120; see Madeline Levine, *Contemporary Polish Poetry 1925–1975* (Boston, 1981), 68.

5. Władysław Szlengel, "Counterattack" (*Kontratak)* in *Co czytalem umarlym* (Warsaw, 1977), 134–39. Ceadel, *Thinking about Peace and War* (Oxford-New York, 1987), 72–100, 166, 189. (Ties that Bind: City City)

6. Milada Souckova, *A Literature in Crisis: Czech Literature 1938–1950* (New York, 1954), 60.

7. Marc Bloch, *Strange Defeat*, 131; Robert Paxton, *Vichy France, Old Guard and New Order, 1940–1944*, 8-9.

8. Paul Eluard, "To Kill" (*Tuer*) in *Uninterrupted Poetry. Selected Writings of Paul Eluard* (New York, 1975), 97.

9. Marcel Ayme, "*Le Passe-muraille.*" See John Flower and Ray Davison, "France" in *The Second World War in Fiction*, 57.

10. Walter Citrine, *My Finnish Diary* (New York, 1940), 78–96; and Eino Luukkanen, *Fighter over Finland* (London, 1963), 98–99.

11. Anna Swir, "A Truck" in *Happy as a Dog's Tail*, trans. by Milosz and L. Nathan (San Diego, 1985), 105.

12. Tadeusz Gajcy, "To My Descendant" ("*Do Potomnego*") in *Wybor Poezji* (Wroclaw, 1992), 213; Madeline Levine, *Contemporary Polish Poetry*, 64.

13. Tadeusz Gajcy, "Song of the Walls" ("*Spiew Murow*") in *Wybor Poezji*, 1992; and Edward Dusza, *Poets of Warsaw Aflame* (Stevens Point, WI, 1977), 36.

14. Miron Bialoszewski, *Memoir of the Warsaw Uprising*, 178.

15. Czeslaw Milosz, "In Warsaw" ("*W Warszawie*"), *The Collected Poems* (Hopewell, NJ, 1988), 76–77; and Norman Davies, *God's Playground*, vol. II, 477.

16. Dylan Thomas, *Deaths and Entrances* (London, 1946), 39.

17. Evelyn Waugh, *Officers and Gentlemen* (London, 1955), 1.

18. Nikolai Tolstoy, *Stalin's Secret War*, 241.

19. Don Piper in *The Second World War in Fiction*, 154.

20. Ales Adamovich, *A Book of the Blockade* (*Blokadnaya kniga*, written with Daniil Granin); Elena Skrjabina's *Siege and Survival* (*V blokade*), and poems by Olga Berggolts such as "The Third Zone," "Leningrad Autumn" and "The Swallow." Translations of Berggolts can be found in *Russian Poetry: The Modern Period*, ed. John Glad and Weissbort (Iowa City, 1978), 183–88.

21. A. Chakovski, *It Was in Leningrad* (*Eto Bylo v Leningrade*), Moscow, 1949, 46.

22. Don Piper in *The Second World War* in Fiction, 156.

23. Konstantin Simonov, *Days and Nights* (New York, 1945), 245. On Simonov, see Orlando Figes *The Whisperers* (New York, 2007).

24. Grossman, *For a Righteous Cause* (*Za pravoe delo*, 1952); Victor Nekrasov, 104.

25. Vasily Grossman, *Life and Fate*, 231–32; (*Zhizn' i Sud'ba*, 1980).

26. Grigori Svirski, *A History of Post-war Soviet Writing* (Ann Arbor, MI, 1981), 46–47, 207–13; Rosette Lamont, "Vasili Grossman's Zhizn i Sud'ba" in *World Literature Today*, vol. 59 no. 1 (Winter 1985), 47; see also Pursglove, "Vasili Grossman" in *The Modern Encyclopedia of Russian and Soviet Literature*, ed. G. Gutsche, vol. 9, 109–13.

27. Mao Tse-tung, "The Turning Point in World War II" in *Selected Works of Mao Tse-tung*, vol. 4, 1941–45 (New York, 1956), 99.

28. Andre Malraux, *The Walnut Trees of Altenburg* (London, 1952), 221. The same passage can be found in Malraux's *Anti-Memoirs* (New York, 1968), 217.

29. Pentti Haanpaa, *War in the Wilds* (*Guerre dans le desert blanc*), Paris, 1942, 188.

30. Kai Laitinen, "The Finnish War Novel" in *World Literature Today*, vol. 58 no. 1 (winter, 1984), 31.

31. Vasil Bykov, *Sign of Misfortune* (New York, 1991), 154; (*Znak bedy*, 1983). Bykov, or Bykaw, was Belorussian.

32. A selection of Kai Munk's poems translated into English can be found in *A Second Book of Danish Verse*, trans. Charles Stork (Princeton, 1947), 117–20.

33. *Scandinavian Plays of the Twentieth Century*. Second Series (Princeton, 1944), 173.

34. Kai Munk, *"Niels Ebbesen"* in *Scandinavian Plays*, 205.

35. Yannis Ritsos, *The Lady of the Vineyards*, Part XIX, trans. Athanassakis (New York, 1978).

36. Yannis Ritsos, *Riomiossini*, Part VII , trans. O. Laos (Paradise, CA, 1969); *Yannis Ritsos* by Chrysa Prokopaki (Paris, 1972), 22–25.

37. Hanama Tasaki, *Long the Imperial Way*, 339–40.

38. Italo Calvino, "Preface" to *The Path to the Nest of Spiders*, ix.

39. "Cornflowers" by P. Mustapaa in *Modern Scandinavian Poetry*, ed. Allwood (New York, 1982), 365.

40. Tarjei Vesaas, "Snow and Spruce Woods" in *30 Poems* (Oslo, 1971), 13. On landscape, Simon Schama, *Landscape and Memory* (New York, 1995), "Wood," "Water."

41. Milada Souckova, "Village Speech" in *A Literature in Crisis*, ix.

42. Roman Jacobson's "Preface" to *A Literature in Crisis*, vii–ix.

43. Pentti Haanpaa, *War in the Wilds* (Guerre dans le desert blanc), trans. Sauvageot (Paris, 1942), 188.

44. Clostermann, *The Big Show*, 252.

45. Stalin's statement to Averell Harriman, September 1941: Nikolai Tolstoy, *Stalin's Secret War*, 257; Arthur Koestler, *The Yogi and the Commissar*, 187–92; Alexander Werth, *Russia at War*, *1941-1945* (London, 1964), 415, 738–44.

46. On Stalin's conversation with Elena Stasova, Nikolai Tolstoy, *Stalin's Secret War*, 256–58, 427; and Roy Medvedev, *On Stalin and Stalinism* (Oxford, 1979), 124. Catherine Merridale, in *Ivan's War*, stressed Communist motivation.

47. Yuri Bondarev, *The Hot Snow*, 110–11.

48. Ivor Brown, quoted in Eric White, *The Arts Council of Great Britain*.

49. Anna Akhmatova, "To the Londoners" in *Poems of Akhmatova*, trans. Kunitz (Boston, 1973), 121.

50. Lucy Dawidowicz, *The War against the Jews*, 255, 313.

51. Alexandra Kurosheva, untitled poem in Piper, "Soviet Union," *The Second World War in Fiction*, 143.

52. Milovan Djilas, *Wartime*, 115–16, 175–79.

53. Vera Panova, *The Train* (Moscow, 1976), 114.

54. Isaiah Berlin, "The Bent Twig: A Note on Nationalism" in *Foreign Affairs* 51, (1972,), 11-30; and "Two Concepts of Nationalism: An Interview with Isaiah Berlin" in *New York Review of Books*, Nov. 21, 1991, 19-22.

55. Joseph Brodsky in "Literature and War—A Symposium" in *The Times Literary Supplement*, May 17, 1985; Semyon Lipkin in Serge Schmemann, "At Moscow Book Party," *New York Times*, March 6, 1992.

56. Alexander Solzhenitsyn, *Gulag III*, 28.

57. Harold Nicolson, *The War Years, 1939–1945*, vol. II of *Diaries and Letters* (New York, 1967), 117.

58. Alexander Dovzhenko, *The Poet as Filmmaker: Selected Writings* (Cambridge MA, 1973), 46.

59. See the "Holy Hatred" on September 26, 1939 in *Literaturnaia Gazeta*. On the Soviet writings supporting the invasions of 1939–41, see Ewa Thompson, *The Search for Self-Definition in Russian Literature* (Houston TX, 1991), 158–66.

60. Works by Antokholsky ("Son"), Sel'vinsky, Kazakevich, Surkov: Don Piper, "Soviet Union" in *The Second World War in Fiction*, 146–55.

61. Albert Camus, *Resistance, Rebellion and Death*, 39, 43–45.

62. Harry Summers, "The Men in Company E" in *New York Times Book Review*, Sept. 6, 1992; and J. Glenn Gray, *The Warriors*, Chapter 2.

63. Milovan Djilas, *Wartime*, Chapter 5 "The New Regime"; Harry Benda, *The World of Southeast Asia* (New York, 1967), 224–54: and Ba Maw, *Breakthrough in Burma*, 218–31.

64. Joseph Kessel, *Army of Shadows* (New York, 1944), 51; (*Armee des ombres*, 1942).

65. Petro Vershigora, *Men with a Clear Conscience* (Moscow, 1949), 43.

66. Kitty Hart, *I Am Alive*; Pelagia Lewinska, *Twenty Months at Auschwitz*; Halina Birenbaum, *Hope Is the Last to Die*; and "Justina's Diary" in Dawidowicz, ed., *A Holocaust Reader*, 340–41.

67. Pierre Clostermann, *The Big Show*; and Romain Gary, *The Promise of Dawn* (*La Promesse de l'aube*) (New York, 1961).

68. B. H. Liddell Hart: "All conditions are more calculable, all obstacles more surmountable, than those of human resistance," *The Strategy of Indirect Approach* (London, 1945). In the 1930s, Heinz Guderian closely followed Liddell Hart's writings; he kept a tutor to translate Liddell Hart's articles the moment they were printed in England: Alistair Horne, *To Lose a Battle* (Harmondsworth, 1969), 78.

Chapter IX (Write and Record!)

1. Yankel Wiernik, *A Year in Treblinka* (New York, Jan. 1945), 29. It was first published in Polish in 1944 as a small Clandestine Booklet by the "Coordinating Committee" of Jewish survivors. It was translated into Yiddish, then from Yiddish into English and published in New York in 1945, by the "American Representation of the

General Jewish Workers' Union of Poland," 175 East Broadway, New York. Bi-lingual Polish and English translation: *Rok w Treblince—A Year in Treblinka* (Warsaw, 2003). A website is devoted to Wiernik: www.zchor.org/treblink.wiernik.htm

2. Margaret Bourke-White, *Portrait of Myself* (New York, 1963). On the transformation of the "labor camp" at Treblinka, Martin Gilbert, *The Holocaust* (New York, 1985), 320–21. Wladyslaw Szlengel probably wrote his poem *"The Little Station at Treblinka"* in late 1942: *What I Read to the Dead (Co czytalem umarlym,* Warsaw, 1977), 74.

3. Rumors about Treblinka existed in the ghetto. Szlengel wrote "The Little Station"; Katznelson described two men who escaped before Wiernik.

4. See the discussion of Chaim Kaplan and Emanuel Ringelblum in Chapter VI.

5. Wiernik, *A Year*, 15.

6. Wiernik, *A Year*, 32, 39.

7. Sadism: Eugene Weinstock, *Beyond the Last Path* (New York, 1947), 225; Kitty Hart, *I am Alive*, 42; Rudolf Vrba and Bestic, *I Cannot Forgive* (London, 1963), 174; Sim Kessel, *Hanged at Auschwitz*, 12, 72; Odd Nansen, *From Day to Day*, 417; Donat, *Holocaust Kingdom*, 185 and *passim;* Kogon, *Theory and Practice of Hell*, 177–78; Reska Weiss, *Journey through Hell*, 208; Gisela Perl, *I Was a Doctor in Auschwitz*, 62; Olga Lengyel, *Five Chimneys*, 155; Illustration by Nansen in *From Day to Day*, 422.

8. Wiernik, *A Year*, 28.

9. Walter Laqueur, *The Terrible Secret*, 32n., 94–95.

10. Jean-Jacques Bernard, *The Camp of Slow Death.*

11. The original title of Levi's first book is *If This Is a Man (Si questo e un uomo).* The title of the English translation was *Survival in Auschwitz*, trans. Stuart Woolf (New York, 1961).

12. Primo Levi, *The Drowned and the Saved* (New York, 1988), 11–12.

13. Kitty Hart, *I Am Alive* (London, 1962), 107, 118.

14. Simon Wiesenthal, *The Murderers among Us* (New York, 1967); S.S. Merz on pp. 334–35.

15. Jean-Louis Curtis, *Les Justes Causes (Paris, 1954); The Second World War in Fiction*, ed. H. Klein, "France," 73.

16. Gisela Perl, *I Was a Doctor in Auschwitz* (New York, 1948), 62, 166–67.

17. Olga Lengyel, *Five Chimneys* (London, 1947), 31, 44; Alexander Donat (Michael Berg), *Holocaust Kingdom* (New York, 1963), 312; Leon Szalet, *Experiment "E"* (New York, 1945), 137; Reska Weiss, *Journey through Hell* (London, 1960), 78, 83, 94; Eugen Kogon, *Theory and Practice of Hell* (New York, 1950), 47; Levi, *Survival in Auschwitz*, 22–23; Halina Birenbaum, *Hope Is the Last to Die* (New York, 1967), 174; Czeslaw Milosz, *The Witness of Poetry* (Cambridge MA, 1983), 67.

18. Simon Wiesenthal, *The Sunflower* (New York, 1969), 90, 94, 97.

Chapter X (The Great Revolt)

1. "Inventory" (*Inventur*) by Guenter Eich, trans. by James Wilkinson in *The Intellectual Resistance in Europe* (Cambridge, MA, 1981), 302–3.

2. Hans Magnus Enzensberger, quoted in preface to Guenter Eich, *Selected Poems: Valuable Nail* (Oberlin, OH, 1981), 10

3. Samuel Beckett, *Watt* (New York, 1959, Evergreen ed.), 203.

4. Dierdre Bair, *Samuel Beckett* (New York, 1978), 327–29.

5. James Wilkinson, 131; Emmanuel Mounier, *Oeuvres* (Paris, 1961).

6. Theodor Adorno, "Cultural Criticism and Society" in *Prisms,* 34; Theodor Adorno, "Commitment" in *The Essential Frankfurt Reader* (New York, 1978), 312. Criticisms of Adorno can be found in the *Hannah Arendt Karl Jaspers Correspondence, 1926–1969* (New York, 1992); and Paul Connerton, *The Tragedy of Enlightenment* (London and New York, 1980), 10, 113–14.

7. Milosz, *The Witness of Poetry,* 80; George Steiner, "The Long Life of Metaphor" in *Encounter,* February 1987; Lewis Feuer, "Confronting Evil and its Unreason" in *Encounter,* May 1988.

8. Primo Levi, *Survival in Auschwitz,* 143.

9. In Michel Borwicz, *Ecrits des condamnes,* 177.

10. Two poems by Wladyslaw Szlengel singled out by Emanuel Ringelblum as strong denunciations of religion: "It Is Time!" (*Juz czas!*) and "Settling Accounts with God" (*Obrachunek z Bogiem*): Wladyslaw Szlengel, *Co czytalem umarlym,* 8, 129. Ringelblum in *Kesovim fun geto,* v. 2, 1943–42 (Tel Aviv, 1985), 189; Ringelblum, *Kronika getta warszawskiego* (Warsaw, 1983), 580.

11. Czeslaw Milosz, *The Captive Mind* (New York, 1951), 40–41.

12. Tadeusz Rozewicz, "Abattoirs" in *Selected Poems,* trans. Czerniawski Harmondsworth, 1976), 31, 20. Rozewicz interview quoted in Walter Hoellerer, *Ein Gedicht und sein Autor* (Berlin, 1967), 123–24; Walter Hoellerer in *Akzente,* Munich, 1966; Michael Hamburger, *The Truth of Poetry* (New York, 1969), 247–49.

13. Adolf Rudnicki, "Szekspir" in *Szekspir* (Warsaw, 1948), 225–26.(Helen of Troy and the Bloodthirsty Abstractions).

14. Simone Weil, "The *Iliad* or the Poem of Force" *(L'Iliade ou le poeme de la force)* in *Simone Weil: An Anthology,* ed. Sian Miles (London, 1986), 204–5.

15. Simone Weil, "Let Us Not Start the Trojan War Again. The Power of Words" (*Ne recommencons pas la guerre de Troie,* 1937) in *Selected Essays, 1934–1943,* 155–56.

16. Hamburger, *The Truth of Poetry,* 153.

17. Albert Camus, *Actuelles, Chroniques 1944–1948* (Paris, 1950); *Actuelles II, Chroniques 1948–1953* (Paris, 1953).

18. *Les Lettres Francaises Clandestines,* XVI, May, 1944.

19. Marc Bloch, *Strange Defeat,* 34, 58, 113; *"Langage plein de chair et d'images varies"* in Camus, "Tout ne s'arrange pas" in *Les Lettres Francaises clandestines.*

20. Wilkinson, *The Intellectual Resistance*, 52.

21. Francois Mauriac in *Le Figaro*, 17 octobre, 1944; reprinted in *Le Baillon Denoue*.

22. *Le Figaro*, Oct. 22, 1944.

23. Albert Camus, "The Unbeliever and Christians" in *Resistance, Rebellion and Death*, trans. O'Brien, 70.

24. Albert Camus, *The Rebel* (New York, 1956), "Metaphysical Rebellion" and "Thought at the Meridian," 293–94.

25. Martin Esslin, *Theater of the Absurd*.

26. Emmanuel Mounier and A. J. Ayer; see Roy Harvey Pierce, *French Political Thought*, 11–12.

27. Albert Camus, *The Rebel*, 3, 286.

28. George Orwell, "Politics and the English Language in *Collected Essays*, vol. IV ("In Front of Your Nose"), 130.

29. Orwell, "Inside the Whale" in *Collected Essays*, vol. I ("An Age Like This"), 516; W. H. Auden, "Foreword" to *Collected Shorter Poems, 1927–1957*, 15.

30. H. Stuart Hughes, *Contemporary Europe* (Englewood Cliffs, NJ, 1981, 5th edition), 371.

31. On the movements see Wilkinson, *The Intellectual Resistance in Europe*. The movements in Eastern Europe had fluid names, and official terms were often misnomers; see George Gomori, *Polish and Hungarian Poetry*, 83, 102–8, and Gertrud Champe, "The Poetry of Postwar Yugoslavia" in *Contemporary Yugoslav Poetry*, ed. Vasa Mihailovich (Iowa City, 1977), xi–xli.

32. Italo Calvino, "Preface" to *The Path to the Nest of Spiders*, vii–viii.

33. Martin Esslin, *The Theater of the Absurd* (London, 1974), 4.

34. Helmuth von Moltke, quoted in Wilkinson, *The Intellectual Resistance in Europe*, 178; Richter, "Wie entstand und was war die Gruppe 47?"

35. Karl Jaspers, quoted in Wilkinson, *Intellectual Resistance in Europe*, 178.

36. Henry Hatfield, *Modern German Literature* (London, 1966), 143.

37. Calvino, "Preface" to *The Path to the Nest of Spiders*, vii.

38. Sergio Pacifici, *A Guide to Contemporary Italian Literature*, 227, 241; Sergio Pacifici, *Verismo*, 246.

39. Croce, "Contromanifesto" quoted in Wilkinson, *Intellectual Resistance*, 199. See Umberto Eco, "Ur-Fascism" in *New York Review*, June 22, 1995; and Tim Parks, "The Illusionist," *New York Review*, Apr. 7, 2005.

40. The tradition of rhetoric and self-imitation has been called "a parochialism of pride"; Pacifici, *A Guide to Contemporary Italian Literature*, 229.

41. Ignazio Silone, *Fontamara* (1930), 27.

42. Wilkinson, 207.

43. Calvino, "Preface" to *The Path to the Nest of Spiders*, vi.

44. Quoted by Pacifici in *A Guide*, 238.

45. Niikuni Seiichi, "Prisoner" in *Postwar Japanese Poetry* (Harmondsworth, 1972), 97.

46. Christopher Drake, Introduction to Tamura Ryuichi, *Dead Languages* (Rochester, MI, 1984), xvi.

47. Drake, Introduction to *Dead Languages*, xix.

48. Quoted in John Toland, *The Rising Sun*, vol. I, 510.

49. Michael Hamburger, *The Truth of Poetry*, 255.

50. Drake, Introduction, xiii; Tamura, 105–6.

51. Jean-Paul Sartre, *What Is Literature?* (New York, 1949), 224 (*Qu'est-ce que la lit-terature?* 1948).

52. Wolfgang Borchert, "Along the Long Long Road" ("*Die lange lange Strasse lange*," 1946) in *The Man Outside*, 222.

53. Paul Eluard, *Poesie ininterrompue*, 1946; *Uninterrupted Poetry: Selected Writings* (New York, 1975), 204; *Uninterrupted Poetry: Selected Writings* (New York, 1975), 204; see Arthur Koestler, "The French Flu" in *The Yogi and the Commissar*, 15–21. In Poland, Tadeusz Rozewicz and Zbigniew Herbert.

54. Northrop Frye, *Anatomy of Criticism*, 34; Michael Hamburger, *The Truth of Poetry*, 231–35; "New English Poets" in the *Times Literary Supplement*, June 7, 1963, 407; Robert Hewison, *Under Siege*, 184–86, and Hewison, *In Anger*, Chapter 1.

55. Samuel Beckett, "The Unnamable" in *Trilogy*, 404. On parts of speech: Gane Todor-ovsky in *Contemporary Yugoslav Poetry*, 59–60; Zbigniew Herbert, *Selected Poems* (Harmondsworth, 1968), 64, 136.

56. Helmut Heissenbuettel, *Texts*, trans. Hamburger (London, 1977), 30.

57. Wolfgang Borchert, "This Is Our Manifesto" in *The Man Outside*, 260.

58. Jan Skacel, "Contract" (Smlouva) in *New Writing in Czechoslovakia* (Harmond-sworth, 1968), 170.

59. See works by Viacheslav Kondratev and Georgii Kumanyov, thanks to Greg Car-leton for personal communication. Mart Laar, *War in the Woods* (Washington D.C., 1992); David Remnick, "The General Line" in *Lenin's Tomb*, 398–411; on General Volkogonov's multi-volume history of the war, *Nezavisimaya Gazeta*, June 18, 1991.

60. Richard Rorty, "Posties" in *London Review of Books*, Sept. 3, 1987; Tzvetan Todorov, "Postmodernism, a Primer," *The New Republic*, May 21, 1990; Leszek Kolakowski, *Modernity on Endless Trial*, 3–13; Matei Calinescu, *Five Faces of Modernity* (Durham NC, 1987), 265–312; Juergen Habermas, *The Philosophical Discourse of Modernity*.